Common Truths

New Perspectives on
Natural Law

Edited by Edward B. McLean

ISI Books
Wilmington, Delaware
2000

Cataloging-in-Publication Data

Common Truths : new perspectives on natural
     law / edited by Edward B. McLean —1st ed.
     —Wilmington, DE : ISI Books, 2000.
     Printed in Canada.
          p. cm.
     ISBN 1-882926-35-8
      1. Natural law. I. McLean, Edward B.

K460 .C66 2000   00-64352
340/.112--dc21   CIP

Published in the United States by:

ISI Books
P. O. Box 4431
Wilmington, DE 19807-0431
www.isi.org

Common Truths

Goodrich Lecture Series
Edited by Edward B. McLean

Derailing the Constitution
The Undermining of American Federalism

An Uncertain Legacy
Essays on the Pursuit of Liberty

Common Truths
New Perspectives on Natural Law

Contents

Preface

Common Truths comprises lectures delivered as part of the distinguished Goodrich Lecture Series at Wabash College and reflects the growing interest in natural law. Each chapter is predicated on the desirability of replacing the dominant school of positive law and its majoritarian legitimating principle with a commitment to natural law doctrines, which alone are capable of providing the informing principles necessary for a vital, free, and virtuous society. The contributors make cogent arguments for the necessity of restoring natural law as the basis for our social and legal order but are realistic about such a prospect. The essayists agree that if any hope remains of refurbishing our civil social order, it lies in reasserting the unassailably valid natural law standards of right conduct as a guide to all human action and choice.

Natural law doctrines reject standards of conduct that come from human will only, that bear no imprimatur other than the desires of the individuals who promulgate the rules of behavior. Such positivist standards foster individual arrogance and, indeed, operate to dissolve society's capacities for functioning and sustaining itself. But a society does not intentionally set itself on a course of destruction. To shore up the legitimacy of its system of law, a positivist society must therefore establish a "new religion." Given its secular premises, however, such a religion, and hence any state based upon it, will have no legitimacy; adherence will be achieved by coercive power only.

There are three major parts to the present collection. Part one discusses certain historical dimensions in the history of natural law philosophy. Part two deals with thematic topics related to natural law. Part three focuses on the applications and importance of natural law to certain areas of legal practice. The collection is preceded by an introductory essay and closes with a prospective view of natural law's role in the twenty-first century.

Some of today's most distinguished public intellectuals and legal scholars have contributed to this unique and timely work—a fact, one hopes, that will make this collection a significant contribution to the dialogue that must occur regarding the current state of law in our society.

Edward B. McLean
Wabash College

Chapter 1

Are There Moral Truths That Everyone Knows?

RALPH MCINERNY

In this paper I intend to approach natural law, as I find the idea presented in the works of St. Thomas Aquinas, in a somewhat unusual way. It is insufficiently appreciated that natural law is not a theory we are asked to adopt, but rather is the claim that there are certain judgments we have already made and could not help making. Natural law—the theory—maintains that there is a common fund of knowledge, truths we can assume that everyone—anyone—already knows. My approach is suggested by the constant procedure of Thomas Aquinas in these matters, namely, to see the practical order in terms of an analogy with the theoretical or speculative.

It has become fashionable to criticize modernity and to assert that we have entered a postmodern age. Most versions of postmodernity I have seen make modernity almost attractive. Leszek Kolakowski,[1] makes an observation that suggests that the direction to go from modernity is not "post-" but rather "pre-." We have come to see and to say with some sophistication that a culture from which God has been driven will find it impossible to hang onto moral values. But, Kolakowski observes, that is precisely what simple priests and ministers have been saying from their pulpits in less complicated language for the past three centuries. Not all of those religious speakers have been simple priests, however. Leo XIII, on August 4, 1879, issued a famous encyclical called *Aeterni Patris*, in which he argued that we can find in St. Thomas Aquinas, and thinkers like him, the remedy for the ills of modern society and culture.

If there is any characteristic of modernity that stands athwart the path I wish to tread in this paper, it is the quite central claim that, prior to the ministrations of philosophy, prior to the application of a validating method, we can make no justified claim to know anything or to possess any truths. This elitist aspect of modernity is obscured when Rene Descartes, the father of modern philosophy, begins Part One of his *Discourse on Method* with the observation that common sense is something that everyone thinks he has a sufficient amount of.[2] This may seem to say that there is a fund of beliefs or truths held in common by human beings. Of course, Descartes thought no such thing. The turn into modernity is taken precisely when it is denied that common sense claims can count as knowledge.

Consider what a burden Descartes put upon philosophy. Of course, he is charmingly autobiographical and often suggests that he is not legislating for others so much as recounting his own experience. You recall that experience. Finding himself in the army, in winter quarters in Germany, with time on his hands, Descartes, in a well heated room, recalls his college days and all the things he learned. Certainly his head is chock full of information, facts, opinions—a vast inventory. Reflecting on this, Descartes asks himself, but what do I know for sure? What do I really know? And he tells us what he means by really knowing something. I really know something if I cannot even imagine it to be false, if doubting it is impossible.

Thus does the drama of modern philosophy begin, and it is a drama as Descartes recounts it, exhibiting the features of story as set forth in Aristotle's *Poetics*. An attractive protagonist confronts an important problem. In seeking to overcome the obstacles to his objective, he gets deeper and deeper into trouble, until a point is reached when all seems lost: the dark moment, just before the peripeteia, the swing in the hero's fortunes. That comes when, by his own efforts and plausibly, our hero wins through to victory. So it is with Descartes's quest for certain knowledge. In looking for some knowledge claim that can successfully resist even the possibility of doubt, Descartes first considers all judgments based on sense experience and, because his senses sometimes deceive him, dismisses all supposed truths about the physical, sensible world. He goes on to reject all mathematical truths, on two bases. Thus he arrives at the dark moment. He seems to have run out of candidates for real knowledge. No matter what he thinks to be true, he may be deceived so to think. And then, surprisingly, the light shines through. Even if he is deceived about everything he thinks he knows, he cannot be deceived that he who is deceived exists. *Cogito ergo sum.*[3]

Given this first indubitable truth, Descartes goes on to prove the existence of God and then, on the basis of God's veracity, he recovers the physical world as well.[4] Everything is as it *was*, apparently, yet nothing will be the same again. Philosophy has become the indispensable condition *for* having true knowledge. Prior to the study of philosophy, you know nothing for sure. Knowledge claims must be processed through a sophisticated method in order to receive endorsement.

What this means, of course, is that there can be no appeal to common sense, to any presumed common fund of knowledge. Only philosophers really know. Now, even on the most depressing estimate, philosophers make up a minuscule subset of human beings. The vast, vast majority of human beings will have neither the leisure nor the time to undertake philosophy. Presumably they must rely on experts, trust the cognoscenti, believe that what the philosophers say is true.

There is irony here. The movement begun by Descartes blossoms into the Enlightenment, which promises to deliver men from the oppression of priests and princes. This epistemological turn, as we may call it, at least as a practical matter, puts 99 percent of the race in the position of having to take the word of the 1 percent as to basic truths.

The alternative to the Cartesian view can be sought, of course, in the situation he sought to replace. As Descartes saw it, his predecessors had spent centuries addressing more or less the same questions, and they had come up with a bewildering variety of answers. Call this the "Scandal of Philosophy." How is it possible that so many brilliant thinkers failed to achieve agreement on even the most basic things? Descartes's answer was that they did not have the appropriate method that would enable them to achieve true knowledge. This was what he sought to repair.

There is nothing libelous about Descartes's claim that his predecessors present a veritable Babel of opinions. Of course things have been pretty much the same since Descartes, so that if his method were judged in terms of what it sought to achieve, it would have to be accounted a failure.

It is easy to find predecessors of Descartes who, like him, dismissed the knowledge claims of the unwashed. Think of Parmenides. Think of Socrates. We could name quite a few. Nonetheless, what I suggest is that, on the point I have stressed in the Cartesian project, there are a significant number of philosophers in the premodern period who assumed that there are certain substantive truths about the world and ourselves that are in the common domain, truths everybody knows. In other words, there are truths we know by ourselves, without the help of others. These are not the products of any sophisticated pursuit, but of the ordinary use of our natural equipment. Far from *conferring* such truths on us, the study of philosophy presupposes them. They are that to which appeal is made in the student by the teacher.

Thomas Aquinas devoted a disputed question to the topic of teaching in his *De magistro,* with his title deliberately evoking memories of St. Augustine's famous dialogue with his son Adeodatus. For St. Thomas, the human mind is a capacity that cannot fail to grasp certain truths, the starting points or principles of thinking. St. Thomas calls this use of our mind *invention* as opposed to *discipline,* learning or being taught.[5] These are not pure alternatives, of course; the latter presupposes the former. That is, someone can teach us something new only if we already know something. We can be helped to new knowledge by someone else only if we are first capable of knowing something on our own.

Because this capacity to know things by oneself is not taken to be unevenly distributed, as if some have it and others do not, but is understood as what every human being as human has by nature, there is something democratic, even egalitarian, in this classical alternative to Descartes.

This is not of course to say that there is no such thing as the "Scandal of Philosophy," but that it can be regarded simply as a special case of the fact that human beings often disagree with one another for reasons good and bad. The difference between the modern and the premodern approaches (i.e., classical) turns on how such disagreements can be settled.

The differences between these two positions could be developed, emphasized, and underlined, but enough has been written to show that they are indeed pretty radically different views. It may seem a little unfair, merely a kind of rhetorical flourish on my part, to call the one elitist and the other democratic, since this looks like a cringing, craven appeal to the prejudices of the day. In any case, it is not by such labeling that the choice between the two can be made. Nevertheless there must be a choice.

As between the view that there are certain truths that every human being can be expected already to know and the view that until there has been the application of sophisticated method, no one can claim to know anything, there is no common ground. They present us with an either/or. If the one is true, the other is false; and one or the other must be true. Which?

One way, an Aristotelian way, to settle the issue is by appeal to language, to discourse, to conversation. Consider how Aristotle deals with those who seek to deny or doubt what Aristotle holds to be the most fundamental truth of human discourse, of language, of thought. It is a truth that cannot be doubted and that no one can fail to know. What is the presumed principle or starting point of human knowledge? *It is impossible for a thing to be and not to be at the same time and in the same respect.*[6]

Imagine someone wishing to contest this. Of course, it will always be possible to find someone to contest any assertion, and that is good. Being able to hold to a belief in the face of relevant criticism is a *sign* that we know it. It is not, however, the *cause* of our knowing it. So, Aristotle says, imagine someone saying, "It is possible for something to be and not to be at the same time and in the same respect." Aristotle will take an instance, a subcase, of this to be: "It is possible for (some statement) to be (true) and not to be (true) at the same time and in the same respect." But then it is possible for the denial of the first principle to be true and not true at the same time.

Aristotle makes the point even more basically, linguistically. The words in the sentence expressing the denial of the first principle must abide by the denied first principle in order for the denial to be a denial. That is, unless words mean what they mean and not also the opposite of what they mean, language, communication, and society are impossible.[7]

The formal expression of this principle is -(p.-p). As a principle of logic, one cannot do logic without it. But perhaps someone might ask, "Who wants to do logic?" Furthermore, it might be said—it has been said—that principles like that of contradiction (Aristotelian first common principles) are, if true, not true of anything. Rather, they are formal truths, i.e., the form all truths must express or abide by. Thus they tell us something about our thinking or our language, but nothing about the world.

One way of responding to this, a way already suggested, is to take the logical or linguistic forms of the principle to be just that, special cases of "It is impossible for something to be and not to be at the same time and in the same respect."

Of the principle so stated, it cannot be said that it tells us nothing of the things that are. That is precisely what it does. It tells us something true of anything whatsoever that exists or can exist. Of course it is true that the principle does not tell us anything peculiar to this kind of thing as opposed to that, but that scarcely provides a basis for saying that it tells us nothing about the things that are.

Is this, as a critic might suppose, an appeal to innate ideas? Are we suggesting that our minds come equipped with a basic fund of concepts and judgments that are regulative of acquired knowledge? Not if our first principles are about the world of our experience. These are truths we naturally, without fail, grasp about the things of our experience. Prior to experience, prior to thinking, our minds are, in Aristotle's phrase, a blank slate on which nothing has been written. What is innate is our capacity, the power to think, not completed instances or products of the activity.

If Aristotle is right, the principles we are considering are what make human intercourse possible. Thus, they are not sophisticated judgments, the fruit of taking Philosophy 101, or even Philosophy 666. They must, then, show up in the most modest of contexts since they must show up everywhere.

Children know that it is impossible for a thing to be and not to be at the same time and in the same respect. If it is true that the bike is now in the garage, it cannot be true that it is not in the garage. If it is true that you promised something, it cannot be true that you did not. Think of children arguing.

"You did."

"I didn't!"

"You did."

"I didn't."

Or:

"It is."

"It isn't."

"It is."

"It isn't."

Such arguments take place, we can assume, because one party is of the opinion that some thing is and the other of the opinion that that same thing is not. Suppose that neither is lying. They are at loggerheads. But their disagreement presupposes a fundamental agreement. Indeed, their disagreement is possible only if it is true that a thing cannot both be and not be at the same time. At a rock-bottom level, it is not a question of one participant accepting the view of the other, as if he did not already hold it and must be persuaded to hold it on the basis of what he already thinks. Rather, we are pointing to what everyone can be presumed already to know: "It is impossible for something to be and not to be at the same time and in the same respect."

The principle we have been discussing is surely the most basic and fundamental of all. There are others. "The whole is greater than its part." "Equals taken from equals leave equals." And so on. As soon as we know what a whole is and what a part is, we immediately know that the whole is greater than one of its parts. Also, once we know what equal quantities are, we know the truth of the second statement.

There are those who suggest that these so-called truths are simply truths about the definitions we assign to the words 'whole' and 'part'. And so too with 'equals'. Of this it may be said that only a philosopher could suggest it. Wholes are not words any more than parts are; their names, namely, 'whole' and 'part' relate to one another in the way they do because of the relation between the things we name.

In the crucial text in which St. Thomas Aquinas discusses the most basic practical principles, he begins by reminding us of the theoretical order (in the way in which I have been doing).[8] I think St. Thomas is right in suggesting that we can understand the claim about the practical principles only if we are clear about theoretical principles, or principles that range over both the theoretical and practical orders but that are usually identified with the theoretical order.

What controls the theoretical order is being, that which is. The grasp of being is presupposed by the realization that a thing cannot be and not be at the same time and in the same respect. What is controlling in the practical order is the good, that which is desired or sought as fulfilling and/or perfective of the one desiring. I want something not just because I want it. When it is said that the good is that-which-is-desired, the assumption is that we desire things because having them fills some want or need.

Food is good not because it is desired but because it is desirable—that is, it relates to the one desiring as fulfilling of him. Given the nature of good, and the meaning of 'good' (that which all things seek), the principle in the practical order analogous to "It is impossible for a thing to be and not to be at the same time and in the same respect" is "Good ought to be done and pursued, and evil avoided." Evil is the negation of the good, so that if the good is to be desired, evil is not to be desired, is to be avoided.

The most frequent negative comment about this principle is that it tells us nothing. "Do good and avoid evil" does not sound like a course of action I could undertake nor the kind of answer we would expect if we wondered what we ought to do in the circumstances in which we find ourselves. If the advice applies, it applies to every conceivable situation in which anyone could find himself.

This objection is not without merit. If I find myself in circumstances in which I wonder what I should do, and you tell me, "Do good and avoid evil," I am unlikely to deny the truth of that so much as question whether it provides me with any guidance.

The analogy with this in the theoretical order, as we have already seen, is that the truth "A thing cannot be and not be at the same time and in the same respect" tells us nothing in particular; it does not express a truth that distinguishes between this kind of being and that. This, of course, is true. The principle is not the last truth about anything but the first truth about everything. To recognize it as first is to see explicitly that it is not exhausted by such special instances as "it cannot be in, and not be in, the garage at the same time and in the same respect"; and, "Miriam cannot be forty, and not be forty, at the same time and in the same respect." Of course we do not go around saying things like that. We say, "The car is in the garage," and everyone knows that if it is in the garage, it cannot not be in the garage, and so too with Miriam's age. If we disagree about where the car is or how old Miriam is, we do not disagree with either the special case of the principle or its generalized form. The principle is an expression of the underlying agreement presupposed by any disagreement.

If we are told that something is tasty, that something else is pretty, and that another thing is melodious, we would understand that the things in question are being recommended to us as pleasant to taste or see or hear. The pleasant can be taken as a special case of the good—good for the senses (i.e., for taste, sight, and hearing). But insofar as such judgments are meant to express what is good for me (that is, good for a human being), they could not be the final word unless what is good for me and what is pleasant are the same. In other words, if "Do good and avoid evil" is addressed to human agents, we could not argue simply: "Good ought to be pursued; the sweet is pleasant to taste; the pleasant is an instance of the good; therefore, sweets ought to be pursued and non-sweets avoided." The good we recognize as the object of the most fundamental practical principle is our comprehensive good, that which is fulfilling of us as human beings, and the human good is a complex thing with many components.

Disagreement about the kinds of things that should be done by us, that is, the kinds of actions performance of which is fulfilling of the kind of agent we are, is possible only against the background that we agree that it is our good we pursue and ought to pursue when we act. Recognizing this does not provide us with a principle from which we can deduce what we should do here and now, or even the kinds of things human agents ought and ought not do.

Our good is first of all articulated in terms of components of our complete good, e.g., that I should preserve myself in existence, avoiding dangers to life and fending off attacks, and that I should eat and drink to preserve my life. Recognition of these comes easily enough and is the basis on which we can disagree as to what constitutes a danger to my life, what fending off an attack amounts to, and what is an appropriate response, as well as disagree as to how much food and drink and what kinds are best for me.

Since we are products of families, we easily recognize that our good is a common, not merely a private, good. One cannot be an isolated human being. One is born into a family, raised over many years, taught, trained, etc. This means that what we are is a member of a community, and that no account of what is good for the kind of being we are can ignore our membership in society.

These departmental goods, as we might call constituents of our comprehensive good, are the basis on which we recognize our comprehensive good.

Are first principles known first or are they products of, abstractions from, the knowledge we actually have first? The general confused knowledge of being and of good is present in any and every particular instance of knowledge. The articulated, formulated principles obviously come last. But what is formulated is recognized as what we all already knew.

Just as in human knowledge generally, and in human intercommunication, there are certain truths we can expect everyone implicitly to know, so in the practical order, there are some principles implicitly known by everyone. All practical disputes and disagreements presuppose underlying and implicit agreements between the disputants. Absent these, the quest for a resolution of the dispute makes no sense. When we seek agreement from someone, we appeal to what he already knows. If we commend a position to another, we do so by linking it to what we presume he already recognizes as true. Human language, taken in its entirety, reposes on the assumption that there are common truths, theoretical and practical, implicitly known by all.

ENDNOTES

1. See *Modernity in Constant Question.* Chicago, University of Chicago Press, 1990, p. 7.

2. *Descartes: Oeuvres et Lettres,* textes présentés par André Bridoux, Bibliothèque de la Pléiade, Gallimard, Paris, 1958, p. 126.

3. Ibid., p. 147.

4. Ibid., p. 153 ff.

5. *Quaestio disputata de veritate*, q. 11. See *Thomas Aquinas Selected Writings*. Penguin Classics, London, 1998, edited and translated with an introduction by Ralph McInerny, pp. 193–216.

6. *Metaphysics*, Book Four, chapters 3 and 4. See *The Basic Works of Aristotle*, edited by Richard McKeon. Random House, New York, 1941.

7. *Metaphysics*, Book Four, chapter 4, "Let it be assumed then, as was said at the beginning, that the name has a meaning and has one meaning . . . ."

8. See *Thomas Aquinas Selected Writings*, op. cit., pp. 642–3.

Part I

Natural Law and History

Chapter 2

Natural Law: The Legacy of Greece and Rome

J. RUFUS FEARS

Elsewhere I have examined the contribution of Rome to the ideas and institutions of liberty.[1] I concluded my treatment with an evocation of the Declaration of Independence and its proclamation of the inalienable right of liberty. This conception of liberty as the universal right of all mankind was the legacy of imperial Rome to the founders of our country.

I write now of another legacy of Rome, no less seminal and no less enduring: the legacy of natural law.[2]

The Declaration of Independence established the new nation on the foundation of natural law, justifying its very independence by an appeal to the "Laws of Nature and of Nature's God." Thomas Jefferson would later claim no originality for the language and ideas of the Declaration of Independence. Indeed, he would state quite rightly that its authority rested in the fact that the Declaration of

Independence was "an expression of the American mind, . . . the harmonizing sentiments of the day, whether expressed in conversation, in letters, printed essays, or the elementary books of public right, as Aristotle, Cicero, Locke, Sidney, etc."[3] The authors cited by Jefferson were not chosen haphazardly. They reflect the twin sources of the Declaration of Independence and, later, the Constitution: the unique legacy of English liberty, stretching back to Magna Carta and beyond, and the common European heritage of Greece and Rome.[4]

No part of that common heritage has been more influential than the idea of natural law. Our exploration of this heritage will take us over the course of a millennium, from the intellectual revolution of Athens in the fifth century B.C. to the codification of Roman law by the emperor Justinian in the sixth century A.D. Natural law was conceived in Greece; but its historical influence is the result of the Roman achievement in assimilating Greek ideas and in transmuting those ideas into the concrete realities of law and empire.

Thus it is that the Roman lawyer, statesman, and patriot Cicero, so admired by the Founders, gives us what is still the best definition of natural law. In his work *On the Republic,* composed between 55–51 B.C., Cicero writes:

> True law is right reason in agreement with nature, universal, consistent, everlasting, whose nature is to advocate duty by prescription and to deter wrongdoing by prohibition. Its prescriptions and prohibitions are obeyed by good men, but evil men disobey them. It is forbidden by God to alter this law, nor is it permissible to repeal any part of it, and it is impossible to abolish the whole of it. Neither

the Senate nor the People can absolve us from obeying this law, and we do not need to look outside ourselves for an expounder or interpreter of this law. There will not be one law at Rome and another at Athens or different laws now and in the future. There is now and will be forever one law, valid for all peoples and all times. And there will be one master and ruler for all of us in common—God, who is the author of this law, its promulgator, and its enforcing judge. Whoever does not obey this law is trying to escape himself and to deny his nature as a human being. By this very fact, he will suffer the greatest penalties, even if he should somehow escape conventional punishments.[5]

Thus, for Cicero, natural law is divine law. Natural law is rooted in a belief in God and in absolute right and wrong. It is our responsibility to obey this law, and there are the most grievous consequences for breaking the law of nature. This law is truly universal; it reflects the very divine harmony of God's universe and of nature. Because of this, natural law is the law of reason and common sense. Nothing that contradicts man's natural reason and common sense can be a true law. Reason is our most human quality; it is what separates us from animals. Through our reason, we perceive natural law; and the informed conscience of the individual is the means by which we understand the law of nature. The law of nature, God's law, is higher than any laws made by men; and no human institution can absolve us from our obligation to obey natural law.

Cicero's definition of natural law is drawn from Stoic philosophy.[6] Founded by Zeno at Athens, Stoicism was one of the most significant intellectual forces in the Greek world following the death of Alexander the Great. Brought to Rome, it became a vigorous source of ideas and actions for educated Romans in the late republic and imperial periods. The idea of natural law has been seen as an invention of Stoic thinkers.[7] However, at most, the Stoics wove together separate strands of ideas that had long been developing in the Greek world. It is in the development and relation of these ideas that the origins of the concept of natural law are to be sought.

These separate strands include the concept of a divine law, universal in its application and higher than the laws of man; the notion that this divine law is inherent in nature and perceived by reason; the obligation to obey this law over and above the laws of men; the belief that the individual conscience serves as our guide in fulfilling the duty to obey this natural law; and the conviction that there are consequences for those who break the law of God.

These ideas were born out of the political freedom and the accompanying intellectual excitement of the Greek city-state, especially the democracy of Athens. The Greeks invented the idea of political liberty; and no nation untouched by the genius of the Greeks has ever developed viable institutions of political liberty. Despite the grandeur of their civilization, the Egyptians were subjects of the absolute rule of the pharaohs, lacking even a word for "liberty." In Mesopotamia, the idea of freedom existed only in the sense of "liberties," grants made by the god-chosen ruler to his subjects. Indeed, in the Persian Empire, everyone, from the lowliest servant to the grand-vizir, regarded himself as a slave of the Great King.

By contrast, from its inception, the Greek polis, the city-state, rested upon the concept of collective political authority. In Athens of the fifth century B.C., democracy was born. It was a democracy of the most radical kind. Meeting in an assembly of the whole, the citizens of Athens were the absolute and unchallenged sovereign. The majority vote of the citizens decided all matters of domestic and foreign policy, all issues of war and peace, all questions of law and justice. There was no appeal from the decision of a randomly chosen jury of Athenian citizens. The Athenian democracy was truly "government of the People, by the People, and for the People." With the notable exception of ten annually elected generals, almost all offices were filled by random allotment. The ideal, achieved to a remarkable degree, was to involve every citizen as fully and actively as possible in every function of government; and it was believed that every citizen was capable of handling any governmental task.[8] As Pericles, the founding statesman of the radical democracy, said in celebrating the achievements and values of the Athenian democracy, "We do not consider the man uninterested in politics as one who minds his own business. We think he has no business here at all."[9]

The Athenian democracy was an open society, resting upon a flourishing free-market economy. Immigrants, merchandise, and ideas from the entire Greek world flowed into Athens. The result of this political and economic freedom was an intellectual revolution surpassing the Italian Renaissance and equaled only by the explosion of science and technology in our own democratic age. In democratic Athens arose the scientific study of medicine. The critical appreciation of the Athenian democracy created an art and architecture that would forever define for us the meaning of the word "classical." The citizens of the Athenian democracy patronized the first true work of historical writing, the *Histories* of Herodotus, and invented the dramatic form of tragedy in an effort to educate themselves for the awesome responsibilities of self-government.

It was an intellectual ferment that seemed to challenge every traditional value, including the very laws and customs that bound men into a political society. At the forefront of this challenge were the first professional academics, the Sophists or "learned men." They were Greeks, but many of them were from city-states other than Athens. They were attracted to Athens by the intellectual climate of the democracy and by the opportunity to earn handsome fees by teaching. Above all, the Sophists taught rhetoric, the art of speaking well, a skill fundamental to those who would succeed in the political life of the Athenian democracy. To their critics, the Sophists seemed to specialize in making good arguments seem bad, and bad arguments seem good. However, from their intellectual gymnastics arose fundamental elements in the developed idea of natural law.

Even earlier, at the beginning of the fifth century B.C., the philosopher Heraclitus of Ephesus had declared that "all the laws of men are nourished by one Law, the divine Law; for it has as much power as it wishes and is sufficient for all and is still left over."[10] Heraclitus's conception of a common divine source for all human laws is closely connected with his idea of Logos or Reason as the underlying unity of the universe.[11] Although notoriously obscure and existing for us only in disjointed fragments, Heraclitus is important for his influence on the Stoics, who adopted him as an authority and applauded his idea of living in accord with nature.[12]

The relationship between nature and law was central to the philosophical discussions of the Sophists and to the intellectual and political life of fifth-century Athens. For some, law and nature were antithetical. Nothing is by nature just or unjust. Laws are mere conventions, which differ radically from society to society. The true law of nature is expressed in the formula "might makes right"; and justice is defined by those with the power to enforce their will upon the weak. As for the gods, they either do not exist or else abide by the same code of naked self-interest as do men.[13] This is the view attributed to the Athenians with unabashed frankness by Thucydides in his Melian Dialogue[14] and to Callicles by Plato in the *Gorgias*.[15] It is in the latter that we find what in our extant sources is the first occurrence of the term "law of nature" *(nomos tes physeos)*.[16] But it is used in a sense very different from its later meaning. For Callicles, the law of nature is the simple fact that the strong rule the weak. By this law of nature Xerxes marched against Greece. We will have true natural justice, Callicles continues, under the rule of a man whose nature is strong enough to trample underfoot the conventions of man-made justice.

Herodotus and the great tragedians, Aeschylus and Sophocles, offered strong correctives to this view. Herodotus continues to be underestimated. He is no naive storyteller. His history is the product of a profound mind; and its numerous stories are not digressions but rather links in a tightly woven chain, each relating to the central theme. The theme of Herodotus is divine law, his history a search for what is permanent behind the seemingly random and ephemeral events of history. There is for Herodotus a divine law, universal in its application. His very focus on the astounding variety of human customs and laws is meant to highlight the fact that regardless of these customs, Lydians, Persians, Babylonians, Egyptians, and Greeks are all subject to an unchanging and universal law of god. Those who violate this divine law will be punished. Ruin is the inevitable end of those who commit the sin of *hybris*—who, swollen with pride, abuse their power and outrage the innocent. Thus the gods punished Xerxes for his *hybris,* expressed in his arrogant crossing of the Hellespont, in his destruction of the shrines of the gods, and in his determination to enslave the Greeks. In the words of the ancient oracle, divine Justice quenched Excess, the child of *Hybris* and all-seeing Zeus brought to Greece the day of freedom.[17]

This is also the theme of Aeschylus' great celebration of the deliverance of Greece from the *hybris* of Xerxes. *The Persians* is our only extant tragedy set in the present. It warns the Athenian audience that they, like the Persians, are subject to the law of god. Zeus is a most grievous chastiser of those who sin against his law; and the prudent man will follow the dictates of reason and moderation.[18]

Along with the idea of divine justice, universal in its application, Athenian tragedy also taught the closely related lesson that the written laws of men are subordinate to the unwritten and unchanging laws of god. In his Funeral Oration, Pericles refers to this distinction between the written laws and those unwritten laws, which bring upon the transgressor a shame that all men recognize.[19]

The conflict between the laws of god and the laws of men is at the heart of the tragedy of Creon and Antigone in Sophocles' play. Creon demands that Antigone obey his decree that her brother Polynices remain unburied. " "Your law," she tells the dictator, "was not made by Zeus. Such is not the justice of the gods. Nor did I think that your decrees had such force that a mortal could override the unwritten and unchanging statutes of heaven. For their authority is not of today nor yesterday, but from all time, and no man knows when they were first put into force."[20]

Here then is expressed with dramatic clarity the idea that no human law or agency can absolve us from our duty to obey the unwritten and timeless laws of the gods. Antigone has interpreted the law of the gods for herself. No earthly court can pass judgment on her. It will be for the gods to judge both her and Creon.

The *Antigone* is a fundamental document in the development of the idea of conscience. Antigone proclaims the duty of the individual to follow her own conscience, regardless of the dictates of the leader, the state, or the laws of men. God speaks directly to the individual conscience, and the divine law is the supreme law. It is important to recognize that in the *Antigone*, Sophocles is speaking about the duty—not the right—of conscience; and Antigone willing accepts the consequences of following this divine obligation: her execution.

The determination of the individual to follow the dictates of god were the cause for the tragic confrontation between Socrates and the Athenian democracy. The

Stoics saw in Socrates their spiritual founder; and the teachings and influence of Socrates were seminal in the development of the idea of natural law. In fact, his pupil Xenophon attributes to Socrates a view of the relationship of justice and law very much like the developed idea of natural law as we find it in the Stoics and Cicero.[21]

Socrates was tried legally by an Athenian jury, convicted, and executed on charges of impiety and corrupting the young. Xenophon is writing to show that this verdict was wrong and unjust. Socrates, for Xenophon, was the most just man of his day and by his discussion and actions Socrates sought to encourage justice in his friends and students. In a conversation with Hippias, Socrates insists that legality and justice are and must be one and the same thing. The gods themselves have ordained that what is lawful must also be just. Such is true of the unwritten laws, which are defined as those laws which are uniformly observed in every country. These laws were made by the gods. They include paying reverence to the gods and honoring our parents. Those who transgress these divinely ordained unwritten laws pay a penalty that no man can escape, even though men do on occasion avoid the consequences for breaking man-made laws. In showing Hippias how transgressors of divine law are punished, Socrates implies that recognition of these divine laws is inherent in human nature. The laws bear in themselves punishment for their violation. So those who commit incest beget children badly and those who repay good with evil find themselves friendless and at the mercy of those who hate them.[22]

Thus, for Socrates, the unwritten laws are made by god and are universal in their application. They are in accordance with human nature; they rest upon a belief in absolute justice; and those who transgress them are punished.

In the *Laws,* Plato established the basis of all justice and laws in the belief that the gods exist, that they care for justice, and have ordained laws to ensure it. Law exists through nature and is the product of reason through thought.[23]

Aristotle develops more fully the Socratic legacy of natural law. In his work *Rhetoric,* Aristotle cites Sophocles' *Antigone* as evidence that a century earlier the idea of natural law existed.

Justice and injustice have been defined in reference to laws and persons in two ways. Now, there are two kinds of laws, particular and general. By particular laws, I mean those established by each people in reference to itself, which are again divided into written and unwritten. By general laws, I mean those based upon nature. In fact, there is a general idea of just and unjust in accordance with nature, as all men in a manner understand, even if there is neither communication nor agreement between them.

This is what Antigone in Sophocles' play evidently means when she declares that it is just, although forbidden, to bury Polynices, being just by nature: "For neither today nor yesterday, but from all eternity came these statues live and no man knows whence they came."[24]

In the *Nicomachean Ethics,* Aristotle develops still more fully his ideas on natural law.

> Political justice [i.e., justice between citizens] is of two kinds, one natural, the other conventional. A rule of justice is natural that has the same validity

everywhere, and does not depend upon our accepting it or not. A rule is conventional that in the first instance may be settled one way or the other indifferently, though having once been settled it is not indifferent: for example, that the ransom of a prisoner shall be a mina, that a sacrifice shall consist of a goat and not two sheep; and any regulations enacted for particular cases, for instance the sacrifices in honor of Brasidas, and ordinances in the nature of special decrees. Some people think that all rules of justice are merely conventional, because whereas a law of nature is immutable and has the same validity everywhere, as fire burns both here and in Persia, rules of justice are seen to vary. That rules of justice vary is not absolutely true, but only with qualifications. Among the gods indeed it is perhaps not true at all; but in our world, although there is such a thing as natural justice, all rules of justice are variable. But nevertheless there is such a thing as natural justice as well as justice not ordained by nature; and it is easy to see which rules of justice, though not absolute, are natural, and which are not natural, but legal and conventional, both sorts alike being somewhat variable.[25]

Aristotle is quite explicit in his recognition of the existence of natural law and its contrast with the laws made by men.[26] Such man-made laws, or conventional laws, are of two kinds. There is written legislation, and there is a body of accepted customs and traditions, which are accepted by all citizens of a particular city but which will vary from city to city. Thus written and unwritten conventional laws are distinguished by Aristotle from general laws, which are laws by nature and accepted by all men, regardless of their country.

With his practical, descriptive genius, Aristotle recognizes that there will be variations in the application of these laws of nature. To extrapolate from Aristotle, we might take one of Socrates' examples. Incest is a violation of the laws of nature; but different nations recognize different degrees of relationship in their estimate of what constitutes incest.

Taken together, Socrates, Plato, and Aristotle show that a fully developed concept of natural law existed in Greece well before the Stoics. Nor did this idea of natural law remain a philosophical abstraction. In a fourth century B.C. Athenian courtroom, appeal could be made to the "common law of humanity," which permits self-defense.[27]

The idea of natural law developed in the political and intellectual world of the Greek city-state. It was the achievement of Alexander the Great and the Stoics to give a universal arena to the conception of universal law. Zeno, the founder of Stoicism, taught that "all inhabitants of this world of ours should not live differentiated by their respective rules of justice into separate cities and communities, but we should consider all men to be of one community and one polity, and that we should have a common life and an order common to us all, even as a herd that feeds together and shares the pasturage of a common field."

According to Plutarch, Alexander the Great took this "shadowy picture of a well-ordered and philosophic commonwealth" and made it real. Alexander "brought together into one body all men everywhere, uniting and mixing in one great loving-cup, as it were, men's lives, their characters, their marriages, their very habits of life. He bade them all consider as their common fatherland the whole inhabited earth. . . . They should regard their clothing and food, marriage and manner of life as common to all and themselves as blended into one by ties of blood and children." For Alexander, any man of virtue was a fellow countryman; only the unjust man should be considered a foreigner.[28]

Plutarch was writing in the second century A.D. with the aim of showing that the Romans emperors were the heirs of Alexander. However, our sources suggest that Plutarch's vision actually reflects the policies and aims of Alexander in the last years of his life.[29] Certainly, the career of Alexander the Great and the spread of Greek civilization to the lands of the former Persian Empire gave an immediate reality to the idea of one world and the wise man as a "cosmopolitan," a citizen of the world.

For the influential Stoic thinker Chrysippus, law was part of this universe.

> Living virtuously is equivalent to living in accordance with the experience of the actual course of nature. For our individual natures are parts of the nature of the whole universe. And this is why the end may be defined as life in accordance with nature, or in other words, in accordance with our own human nature as well as that of the universe, a life in which we refrain from every action forbidden by the law common to all things, that is to say, the right reason which pervades all things and is identical with Zeus, lord and ruler of all that is.[30]

Chrysippus began his book *On Law* by proclaiming the sovereignty of law: "Law is the king of all things human and divine. Law must preside over what is honorable and base, as ruler and as guide, and thus be the standard of right and wrong, prescribing to animals whose nature is political what they should do, and prohibiting them from what they should not do."[31]

In these brief fragments, Chrysippus presents all elements of the idea of natural law. It is the law of Zeus, a law common to gods and men and in accordance with the nature of man and the nature of the universe. It is the standard of right and wrong, prescribing our actions.

Chrysippus was head of the Stoic school from about 230–206 B.C. His successor a century later, Panaetius, would play the critical role in conveying this idea of natural law to Rome. From 144–142 B.C. Panaetius lived in Rome, where he associated closely with the historian Polybius and with such leading Roman statesmen as Scipio Africanus the Younger and his friend Gaius Laelius. He was part of an intellectual circle that also included jurists like Manius Manilius, who was considered one of the founders of the study of Roman civil law.[32]

Panaetius wrote lucidly and eloquently, and he did much to make the main ideas of Stoicism accessible to intellectually minded Romans like Scipio and Laelius. Panaetius revitalized Stoicism by drawing extensively on the ethical and political writings of Plato and Aristotle. He admired the Roman constitution, and his influence led practical Roman politicians and jurists to place their constitutional and legal institutions into a broader philosophical framework.[33]

Cicero was profoundly influenced by Panaetius; and his definition of natural law may very well be derived from this Greek thinker.[34] However, it was the Roman

Cicero who gave the idea of natural law its central place in the philosophical legacy of Rome to the Middle Ages.[35] For Cicero, natural law is the very foundation of justice, government, and morality. Natural law is the thread that binds together his three great treatises *On the Republic (De Re Publica), On the Laws (De Legibus),* and *On Moral Duties (De Officiis).*[36]

For Cicero, a true commonwealth must be founded on justice in its highest sense. The very definition of a commonwealth expresses its intimate connection with justice. "A commonwealth is the property of a people. But a people is not any collection of human beings brought together in any sort of way, but an assemblage of people in large numbers associated in an agreement with respect to justice and a partnership for the common good."[37]

Cicero rejects the vulgar notion that some injustice is necessarily involved in the administration of government. Indeed, the state cannot exist at all unless it is founded in the highest form of justice. That justice is the law of nature. "It is right reason in agreement with nature." As God has ordained the law of nature, so God has given a divine sanction to states, which were founded so that men may live in justice.[38]

> The nature of justice must be sought for in the nature of man. . . . Law is the highest reason, implanted in nature, which commands what ought to be done, and forbids the opposite. This reason, when firmly fixed and fully developed in the human mind, is law. . . . Law is intelligence, whose natural function it is to command right conduct and to forbid wrongdoing. . . . The origin of justice is to be found in the law, for law is a natural force; it is the mind

and reason of the intelligent man, the standard by which justice and injustice are measured. . . . In determining what justice is, let us begin with the supreme law which had its existence ages before any laws were written or any states existed.[39]

As natural law is the foundation of states, so it is also for Cicero the basis of our moral code. Man is distinguished by his possession of reason. By the gift of reason, "Man comprehends the chain of consequences, perceives the causes of things, understands the relation of cause to effect and of effects to cause, draws analogies, and connects and associates the present and the future—easily surveys the course of his whole life and makes the necessary preparations for its conduct."[40]

It is a manifestation of reason and nature that man has a sense of harmony and proportion. It is from nature and reason that man's moral goodness arises. The supreme moral virtues, wisdom, justice, courage, and moderation, are all part of God's order for the universe. They are part of nature, and they are founded in reason.[41] Of these virtues, it is justice that binds men together in common society, and for that reason justice is the "crowning glory of the virtues."[42] We are all subject to the same law of nature, and that law requires that we act with justice and ensures that no unjust act can ever be advantageous to us.

For Cicero, true law and true justice are one and the same.

Nature has so constituted men that all humans share a common sense of justice. Bad habits have corrupted this natural sense of justice among many;

but if all men acted in accordance with nature all would observe the same standards of justice. For we have received from nature the gift of right reason and thus the gift of law, which is right reason applied to command and prohibition. And if we have received true law from nature, then we have also received true justice. In this gift of reason and the moral standards it conveys, all men are equal.[43]

The developed idea of natural law thus carried with it the doctrine of the natural equality of men, the idea that all men are by nature free and equal. This was indeed a revolution in thought. By his policies, Alexander the Great rejected Aristotle's view that some men are by nature free, such as the Greeks, and others are by nature slaves. For the Stoics, it was not a man's nature but his circumstances that reduced him to slavery. What was important was moral equality. Cicero gives the Stoic view that there is no race of men that, if properly taught, cannot attain virtue.[44]

The idea of the natural equality of all humans is carried further by Seneca, a century after Cicero. Like Cicero, Seneca was a major political figure.[45] He no longer served a free republic, however, but rather the whims of his pupil, the emperor Nero. Like Cicero, Seneca would die a martyr to Socrates' dictum that no honest man can survive in politics.[46]

Seneca was much more closely identified with the Stoic school than Cicero. However, he lacked Cicero's concrete attachment to the law and the legal profession. Thus there is little discussion of natural law in Seneca but a very great interest in nature itself and how to live in accord with nature, which is the path reason has revealed to man. Reason shows us that master and slave have the same nature. Virtue can be attained by all.[47] For Seneca, we are all citizens of a universal commonwealth. Indeed, we have a dual citizenship. Each of us has a particular citizenship, the accident of birth in Athens, Rome, or Carthage. The other and infinitely higher citizenship is in the universal city of humankind and of the gods.[48]

Thus, for Seneca, liberty and equality are innate faculties, belonging to all men. Because they share the same creator, master and slave share the same nature. It is fortune, not nature, that makes a man a slave. Slavery is external; it only affects the body. The mind can never be given over to slavery.[49]

With Seneca, a Stoic thinker was for a time the second most powerful man in the Roman Empire. With Marcus Aurelius, a Stoic philosopher-king ruled over the immense majesty of the Roman empire.[50] Love of our fellow man, truthfulness, and moderation, these are qualities of the rational soul, and they are equally, Marcus writes, the qualities of the law. "Thus right reason and justice are one and the same."[51] Marcus believed himself to be by nature a man of reason and a man of civic duty. As Marcus Aurelius, his city was Rome; as a man, his city was the world.[52] As emperor of Rome, he believed in a government that had one law for all, a government based on individual equality and freedom of speech, and a sovereignty that sought to ensure above all else the liberty of the individual. Like Cicero, the emperor Marcus Aurelius believed liberty to be the greatest good.[53]

This vision of good government was achieved to a remarkable degree in the Roman Empire of the second century A.D. This was the age that Edward Gibbon would call "the period in the history of the world during which the condition of the human race was most happy and prosperous.[54] Here Gibbon is but reflecting the sentiments of such contemporary writers of the second century A.D. as the Greek intellectual Aelius Aristides. In his *Panegyric on Rome*, Aristides praised the Roman achievement:

> Neither sea nor intervening continents are bars to citizenship, or are Asia and Europe divided in their treatment here. In your [Rome's] empire all paths are open to all. No one worthy of rule or trust remains an alien, but a civil community of the world has been established, as a democracy under one man, the best man, ruler and teacher of order; and all are come together as into a common civic center, in order each man to receive his due.[55]

The Pantheon in Rome, designed by the emperor Hadrian, was the architectural statement of this vision of one universal city.[56] The imagery of imperial power celebrated the emperor as the elect of the gods, chosen by the supreme lawgiver of the universe to rule the earth with justice as the vice-regent of the gods.

This was translated into legal reality in A.D. 212 when by a decree of the emperor Caracalla, all free-born inhabitants of the Roman empire became Roman citizens.[57] Now, in fact, one law—Roman law—ensured the privileges and obligations of citizenship throughout the civilized world, the *oikoumene* as the Romans called their universal city.

The idea of natural law was a formative influence in developing the legal structures to support this universal empire. For the Romans, it was their divine mission to serve as lawgiver to the world. As the poet Virgil wrote, "Remember, O Roman, that you will rule the world with just power. These will be your special gifts: to crown peace with law, to save the weak, and war down the haughty."[58]

In the Roman imperial age, lawyers and jurists occupied positions of great prestige and influence. The advisory council of the emperor included distinguished jurists; and some of these, such as Papinian, Ulpian, and Paul, held the second most powerful position in the empire, that of praetorian prefect in the third century A.D. The training of lawyers was almost as much an academic industry as it is today. In the late empire, the law school at Beirut was famous, with a fixed curriculum and state-appointed professors.[59]

In shaping this legal curriculum, one of the most influential jurists was Gaius, a contemporary of Marcus Aurelius.[60] His textbook, the *Institutes*, would be chosen by the emperor Justinian as the basis for the official imperial textbook for first-year law students in the later Roman Empire. Gaius began his textbook by distinguishing between *ius gentium* and *ius civile:*

> The laws of every people governed by statutes and customs are partly peculiar to itself, partly common to all mankind. The rules established by a given state for its own members are peculiar to itself, and are called *ius civile;* the rules constituted by natural reason for all are observed by all nations alike, and are called *ius gentium.* So the laws of the People of Rome are partly peculiar to itself, partly common to all nations.[61]

Thus the study of law, for Gaius, begins in the recognition that some laws are common to all mankind and these are the product of natural reason. This distinction had already been made by Aristotle. Its force at Rome was the product of two mutually complementary developments, one practical, one philosophical.

The legal category of *ius gentium* arose out of the practical necessities of legal transactions. Like the Greek city-states, Roman courts throughout the history of the republic had to deal with litigation between Roman citizens and citizens of other states. In both Greece and Rome, a practical body of law arose to meet this need. However, certainly by the time of Cicero, this practical application was informed and deepened by the philosophical concept of a universal law in accordance with nature and reason.[62]

Gaius does not distinguish *ius gentium*, the common law of mankind, from *ius naturale*, the law of nature. However, a generation later, this distinction is made very explicit by the great jurist Ulpian, who served the emperor Alexander Severus as praetorian prefect from A.D. 222–228.[63] Ulpian divides private law into three parts: natural law *(ius naturale)*, the common law of mankind *(ius gentium)*, and particular civil codes of individual states *(ius civile)*. *Ius naturale*, Ulpian continues, is drawn from the precepts of nature. It is the law that humans have in common with animals. From this law springs the union of male and female and the begetting and nurturing of the young of the species. *Ius gentium* differs from *ius naturale*, in the view of Ulpian, in that it is peculiar to humans. *Ius gentium* is thus those laws which all men as men have in common.[64]

The division between the law of nature and the common law of mankind may spring in part from the Stoic idea of an original state of nature. Drawing upon a stock of mythological and philosophical sources, Seneca describes an age of innocence, when mankind was newly sprung from the gods and lived in peace, happiness, and a state of ignorant bliss. Avarice and greed rent that natural society asunder and created our own present age. One result of that loss of innocence was the creation of man-made laws, since the greed and ambition of rulers required laws to keep them in check.[65]

When Stoic writers refer to the natural equality and liberty of men, it may be this earlier state of nature they mean. Certainly, this tripartite distinction between *ius naturale, ius gentium,* and *ius civile* enabled Ulpian to explain the institution of slavery, while still believing that all men are by nature free and equal. Thus Ulpian states that according to *ius civile,* slaves are held as *pro nullis,* that is, they lack a legal persona. For its part, *ius gentium* provides for manumission. Each state has its own peculiar regulations for freeing slaves; but the act of manumission itself is part of the common law of mankind. However, in this regard both *ius civile* and *ius gentium* are contrary to the law of nature, for by nature all men are free and equal.[66]

Ulpian's identification of *ius naturale* with law common to humans and animals has long puzzled students of Roman law. Thus when Isidore of Seville in the seventh century A.D. adopted Ulpian's tripartite division of law, he specified that *ius naturale* was the universal law of all nations of men, omitting any suggestion of a union in law between humans and animals.[67] More recently, in his

Historical Introduction to the Study of Roman Law, H. F. Jolowicz notes almost with irritation that "an identification, ascribed to Ulpian, of the law of Nature with the instincts which men share with animals is unfortunately given prominence by appearing in Justinian's *Institutes,* but it is an isolated opinion in legal literature and was never made the basis of any consistent theory."[68]

In fact, Ulpian's attribution of a common law of nature to humans and animals appears in Justinian's code, the *Digest,* as well as in the *Institutes,* the textbook the emperor had prepared for law students. Moreover, it represents a very early strain in the Greek idea of natural law. According to Cicero, Pythagoras and Empedocles argued "that the same principles of justice apply to all living creatures and insisted that everlasting penalties threaten those who injure an animal. It is a crime therefore to harm a brute beast." This passage in Cicero's *Republic* is introduced within the context of the obligations of a just man to his fellow creatures. The passage is fragmentary, and we can be by no means certain that it represents Cicero's own opinion. However, it is noteworthy that Cicero himself begins his discussion of morality by pointing to qualities that both humans and animals have in common and that both possess by nature: a sense of self-preservation, of providing for themselves, of begetting young, and of caring for their young.[69]

Ulpian's idea of a common law of nature for humans and animals may be an anomaly in Roman legal theory. By contrast, his view that slavery was contrary to the law of nature is representative of the best legal thought of the age. Thus Florentinus, author of an influential legal textbook, and Tryphoninus, a member of the imperial council under Septimius Severus, both supported the opinion that slavery is a violation of natural law. This meant that the institution of slavery was contrary to reason and to human nature. Slavery thus violated the law of god and there would be consequences for such a violation.[70]

This did not remain an abstract legal idea. The view of slavery as a violation of natural law informed legislation and was the primary motive behind imperial edicts humanizing the treatment of slaves. Thus, already in the first century A.D., the emperor Claudius ruled that if a slave were deserted by his master for suffering a severe illness, that slave was to be freed. By a decree of the emperor Vespasian, slave women whose masters prostituted them were to be freed. In the second century, the emperor Antoninus ruled that slaves should be taken away from a master who treated them with undue severity.[71]

The view that slavery was a violation of natural law and that all men are by nature free and equal was adopted in the emperor Justinian's legal code. Justinian saw the codification of the enormous body of Roman law as a major element in his vision of restoring the greatness of the Roman Empire. The *Digest* of Roman law was published in A.D. 533. Along with the Ten Commandments, it is arguably the most influential and most enduring law code ever published.[72]

In its first section, the *Digest* defines *ius* as *ars boni et aequi*. Law is thus the knowledge of what is good and fair. It is Cicero's ideal that no law is a true law unless it is just. The *Digest* insists that it is the duty of the lawyer to study and understand the nature of justice and thus to distinguish the unjust from just, rather than merely the legal from the illegal. It is the obligation of a lawyer to lead men to do what is good and just. The lawyer must understand that the law is not merely a set of legal regulations. The law is the reflection of the eternal and God-given principles of justice and goodness. The law thus rests ultimately upon a belief in God and in absolute right and wrong.[73]

The *Digest* testifies to the long tradition in Greece and Rome of the idea that God is the ultimate source of all law. Thus the jurist Marcianus quotes a passage from Demosthenes, written a thousand years before the publication of the *Digest:* "The law is that which all men ought to obey for many reasons, but above all because every law is an invention and gift of the gods, a tenet of wise men, a corrective of errors voluntary and involuntary, and a general covenant of the whole State, in accordance with which all men in that State ought to regulate their lives." To this passage from Demosthenes, Marcianus adds the passage of Chrysippus that declares law to be the king of all things, human and divine.[74]

The *Digest* distinguishes private from public law and then defines private law as composed of *ius naturale, ius gentium* and *ius civile*. *Ius naturale* is defined in Ulpian's terms as that law which men and animals have in common and which is drawn from the precepts of nature. *Ius gentium* is then defined as those laws which are unique to humans and are common to all mankind.[75] *Ius civile* can be defined in the most practical fashion "as the law which emanates from statutes, plebiscites, decrees of the Senate, enactments of the emperor, and from the authority of the jurists."[76] But even the particular law of Rome or of any nation is "organically related to the ultimate law of reason and justice."[77]

The *Digest* is the law code of the Christian Roman Empire. Justinian introduces his great legal reform by an invocation to God, who has granted imperial power to Justinian and is the source of all that the emperor has achieved in war and peace.[78] The *Digest* is part of the workings of the Divine Providence of the Holy Trinity. In Christian doctrine of the age of Justinian, natural law was seen as the reflection of that same Divine Providence.[79]

Almost from its inception, Christianity adopted the teaching of natural law.[80] St. Paul was trained in Stoic philosophy; and Tarsus, his native city, was a notable center of Stoic teaching.[81] In Romans, Paul refers to a common law of mankind, which men have in their conscience. He is discussing the relationship between God and the Gentiles from the perspective that the Gentiles, unlike the Jews, have no divinely revealed law code. "

> For as many as have sinned without law shall also have perished without law; and as many as have sinned under the law shall be judged by law.; for not the hearers of a law but the doers of a law shall be justified; for when the Gentiles which have no law do by nature the things of the law, these, having no law, are a law unto themselves; in that they show the work of the law written in their hearts, their conscience bearing witness therewith.[82]

Thus for Paul, there is a law common to mankind. This law is inherent in human nature; it is justified by God; and the individual's conscience is his guide to knowing and obeying this law. This is the natural law of Panaetius and Cicero, and it is difficult not to agree with the early church fathers and to believe that this represents the direct influence of Stoic thought on Paul.

Certainly, this passage in Paul was determinative for the acceptance of the idea of natural law in the fathers of the early church. In refuting the arguments of Celsus, Origen considers the maxim of the poet Pindar that "Law is king of all things." Origen points out that we had better use the plural and say that "Laws are kings of all things," for in every nation some laws are king. Origen goes on to draw the distinction between these man-made laws, which vary from state to state, and true law, the law of God. This true law Origen defines in terms of *ius naturale*. "Law in the true sense is by nature king of all things. We Christians then, who have come to the knowledge of the law that is by nature "king of all things," and that is the same as the law of God, endeavor to regulate our lives by its prescriptions." Christians are thus enjoined to follow the true law of nature and of nature's God. In the course of this discussion, Origen makes the point that men who deny the validity of natural law are like outlaws and robbers, and they do violence to their nature as humans.[83]

For Tertullian, the Christian God is the God of nature.

> If you seek a law of God, you have that common law which prevails all over the world, engraven on the natural tablets, the law to which the Apostle referred when he says in respect to a women's veil, "does not even nature teach you,"—as when to the Romans, affirming that the Gentiles do by nature those things which the law requires, Paul suggests both a natural law and a nature which reveals law.[84]

The church fathers certainly did not uncritically take over the idea of natural law as they found it in pagan writers. Lactantius offers a detailed refutation of Zeno's concept of living in accord with nature.[85] However, largely through St. Paul, the central tenets of the concept of natural law were assimilated into Christianity and became a living legacy of classical thought to the new faith. So St. Ambrose writes that it is St. Paul who teaches us that the natural law is written in our hearts.[86] Ambrose also believes that God gave the commandments to Moses because mankind had ceased to obey natural law.[87] Thus, for Ambrose, there are two kinds of law: the written law of the tablets and the natural law. It is this natural law that is in the heart of the just man and that guides his actions.[88]

In the same way, St. Jerome writes of the natural law that is in our hearts and admonishes us to do good and avoid evil. God, Jerome says, gave the natural law to the whole human race. The law of Moses was sent by God only because men neglected the natural law. Thus natural law reflects an earlier state of grace; the written law of Moses is the result of human inability to maintain this God-given *ius naturale.*[89] Indeed, Christian thought came to distinguish two levels of natural law. The first was an absolute natural law that existed before man's fall from grace. Under such absolute natural law, there was no government and no private property. After the fall, a relative natural law arose, adjusted to man's depraved state and in which government, private property, and even slavery all found their place.[90]

Thus Christianity became the bearer of the great tradition of natural law. Aristotle and Cicero were formative for St. Thomas Aquinas and his conception that "behind the positive law of the human community there was the natural law discovered by man's divine faculty of reason, as it sought to apprehend the purpose of God's will and the rule of His reason."[91]

No less seminal was the church's role in bearing the legal legacy of the Roman concept of natural law to later centuries. As the Roman Empire collapsed, as Visigoths ruled what had once been the Roman province of Spain, and as the lamp of classical learning flickered low, the Christian theologian and archbishop of Seville, Isidore, compiled an encyclopedia. It was among the most influential works of the early Middle Ages. Isidore divides law into three types. First of all is natural law. *Ius naturale,* for Isidore, is the law common to all nations and the result of nature rather than any human conventions. Whatever is done in accord with natural law is just and good. In contrast to *ius naturale* stand *ius gentium* and *ius civile. Ius gentium* is the common law of mankind, followed by almost all nations and which all nations have in common. It covers such matters as war, truces, prisoners of war, treaties, rights of recovery, and slavery. *Ius civile* is, for Isidore, the laws by which a particular people or nation regulate their own specific divine and human institutions. Isidore thus follows Ulpian in a tripartite division of the law, but his individual definitions of these three divisions are drawn from other authorities in the *Digest* and *Institutes* of Justinian.[92]

It was due to the church that Roman law remained a living law, a *lex animata.* So in 1140, when the canon lawyer Gratian published his codification of canon law, the *Decretum,* he would refer back to Isidore of Seville and his definition of natural law. With the revival of the study of Roman law and its application in both the ecclesiastical and secular courts of Europe, natural law became a potent force shaping not only the legal but the political history of Europe and, ultimately, the New World.[93]

So it was that an idea born in the intellectual ferment of democratic Athens and shaped by the demands of Rome's imperial power would light the fires of revolution in a world the Greeks and Romans never knew existed and lead Thomas Jefferson to invoke "the laws of Nature and of Nature's God" to justify the independence of a new nation conceived in liberty.

The founders of our country took as their model Rome of the free republic, with its balanced constitution and its citizen body possessed of civic virtue. Painfully and regrettably, that is no longer our model. Our model today is imperial Rome, Rome of the Caesars. Imperial Rome was a vast and disparate nation ruled by a benevolent despotism. It was a government that gave peace and prosperity to its subjects and allowed a large degree of individual freedom. It was a society that defined liberty as freedom to live as you chose and to pursue your own career and make money, relieved from the burdens of political responsibility and military service. It was an affluent society, whose prosperity was made possible by a free-market economy, which supported a large and public-spirited middle class. The empire had a superb infrastructure, an extremely efficient army, and yet kept taxes at a minimal level. The boundaries of the empire of the Caesars stretched from the moors of Scotland to the rivers of Iraq, from the forests of Germany to the sands of the Sahara. As do we, the Romans could consider themselves the only superpower in their world. Like contemporary America, Rome of the Caesars was a diverse empire, a multicultural nation, to use the language of today. Within limits, the emperors tolerated and even fostered the various cultural and religious traditions of the peoples of their empire.[94]

Yet the best of these emperors, men like Trajan, Hadrian, and Marcus Aurelius, understood that no society can survive without a set of shared political, cultural, and religious values. For them, the idea of natural law was the foundation of such a set of shared values. Natural law teaches that there is an absolute right and wrong and that God is the ultimate source of law. It insists that this knowledge of right and wrong is part of our very nature as human beings and that evil is punished and good rewarded. Above all, to a highly legalistic society, it conveys the message that no law, no legal trick, is ultimately successful if it violates the God-given code of what is good, just, and fair. This is the legacy that natural law offers to us today.

ENDNOTES

1. J. Rufus Fears, "Antiquity: The Example of Rome," in Edward B. McLean, *An Uncertain Legacy: Essays on the Pursuit of Liberty* (Wilmington 1997) pp. 1–38.

2. This essay is intended to provide the kind of general survey of the idea of natural law in Greco-Roman antiquity for which I have felt the need in teaching my courses on the history of liberty. The lack of such a general survey is evidenced by the article on "Law of Nature" by Barry Nicholas in the third edition of *The Oxford Classical Dictionary* (Oxford 1996) p. 835. The article is brief, uninformative, and marked by a clear bias against the idea of natural law. Whether out of pedantry or necessity, Nicholas lists only two works in his bibliography, both of which would almost certainly be inaccessible to undergraduates and the general reader: E. Levy, *Gesammelte Schriften* (1963) and C. A. Maschi, *La concezione naturalistica del diritto e degli istituti giuridici romani* (1937).

The diligent undergraduate who searched out Levy's article would find it only tangentially related to the topic.

Longer and better encyclopedia articles on natural law include Paul Foriers and Chaim Perelman, "Natural Law and Natural Rights," *Dictionary of the History of Ideas*, ed. Philip Wiener (New York 1973) III pp. 13–27; and R. Brandt, "Naturrecht," *Historische Worterbuch der Philosophie*, eds. J. Ritter and K. Grunder (Basel/Stuttgart 1984) VI pp. 564–71.

Of older studies, James Bryce, "The Law of Nature," *Studies in Law and Jurisprudence* (New York/London 1901) pp. 556–606 is still very much worth reading.

3. Paul Ford, *The Writings of Thomas Jefferson* (New York 1892–99) X p. 343.

4. On Jefferson's sources, I continue to find Carl Becker, *The Declaration of Independence* (New York 1922) more convincing than Garry Wills, *Inventing America: Jefferson's Declaration of Independence* (New York 1978). For a more general discussion, see Andrew J. Reck, "The Enlightenment in American Law I: The Declaration of Independence," *The Review of Metaphysics* 44 (1990–91) pp. 549–73.

A detailed study of the influence of classical ideas of natural law upon the founding fathers remains a desideratum. Susan Wiltshire, *Greece, Rome, and the Bill of Rights* (Norman/London 1992) pp. 9–50 is superficial and derivative. A better treatment is Carl Richard, *The Founders and the Classics* (Cambridge, MA 1994) pp. 169–83.

5. Cicero, *On the Republic* 3.22.33. The Greek and Latin authors cited in the following notes are most conveniently consulted, in translation, in the Loeb Classical Library (London/Cambridge, MA). For the convenience of the general reader, translations in this essay are generally drawn, with some adaptation, from the Loeb volumes. For this specific passage from Cicero *On the Republic* 3.22.33, see also the translation in A. A. Long and D. N. Sedley, *The Hellenistic Philosophers: Translations of the Principal Sources with Philosophical Commentary* (Cambridge 1987) I pp. 432–33.

For the view of Cicero held by the founding fathers, see Paul MacKendrick, *The Philosophical Books of Cicero* (New York 1989) pp. 294–304.

6. Gerard Watson, "Natural Law and Stoicism," in A. A. Long, ed., *Problems in Stoicism* (London 1971) p. 225.

7. See Gisela Striker, "Origins of the Concept of Natural Law," and the comments on Striker's article by Brad Inwood in *Proceedings of the Boston Area Colloquium in Ancient Philosophy* 2 (1987) pp. 79–101; and Andrew Erskine, *The Hellenistic Stoa* (Ithaca 1990) p. 16 n. 13.

8. Recent books on the Athenian democracy include David Stockton, *The Classical Athenian Democracy* (Oxford/New York 1990); Moge Hansen, *The Athenian Democracy in the Age of Demosthenes*, trans J. A. Crook (Oxford 1991);

Jennifer Roberts, *Athens on Trial: The Antidemocratic Tradition in Western Thought* (Princeton 1994); J. Peter Euben, John Wallach, and Josiah Ober, eds., *Athenian Political Thought and the Reconstruction of American Democracy* (Ithaca 1994); Josiah Ober and Charles Hedrick, eds., *Demokratia: A Conversation on Democracies, Ancient and Modern* (Princeton 1996).

Less politically correct but more literate and better informed than any of these more recent books are two older books, Alfred Zimmern, *The Greek Commonwealth* (Oxford 1911 and subsequent editions) and Victor Ehrenberg, *From Solon to Socrates* (London 1968).

9. Thucydides, 2.40.

10. G. S. Kirk and J. E. Raven, *The Presocratic Philosophers* (Cambridge 1962) p. 213, frg. 253.

11. Kirk and Raven, (above n. 10) p. 214.

12. Kirk and Raven, (above n. 10) p. 186. See also A. A. Long, *Stoic Studies* (Cambridge 1996) pp. 35–57.

13. For the debate on the relationship between *nomos* and *physis* in the thought of fifth-century Greece, see W. K. C. Guthrie, *A History of Greek Philosophy* III (Cambridge 1969) pp. 55–104 and A. W. H. Adkins, *Moral Values and Political Behaviour in Ancient Greece* (New York 1972) pp. 99–112.

14. Thucydides, 5. 84–114.

15. Plato, *Gorgias* 482C–486C.

16. Striker, (above n. 7) pp. 81–83.

17. Herodotus, 8.77.

18. Aeschylus, *Persians* 800–42.

19. Thucydides, 2.37.

20. Sophocles, *Antigone* 450–70.

21. For the influence of Xenophon's portrait of Socrates on Zeno, the founder of the Stoic school, see Diogenes Laertius 7.2.

22. Xenophon, *Memorabilia* 4. 4. 1–25.

23. Plato, *Laws* 890D.

24. Aristotle, *Rhetoric* 1.13.

25. Aristotle, *Nichomachean Ethics* 5.7.

26. For the question of natural law in Aristotle, see W. von Leyden, *Aristotle on Equality and Justice* (New York 1985) pp. 71–90. For natural rights in Aristotle, see Fred Miller, *Nature, Justice, and Rights in Aristotle's Politics* (Oxford 1995) and the essays discussing Miller's book in *The Review of Metaphysics* 49 (1996) pp. 731–907.

27. Demosthenes, *Against Aristocrates* 61.

28. For Zeno, Alexander, and the idea of the brotherhood of mankind, see Plutarch *On the Fortune and the Virtue of Alexander* 6.

29. For the historicity of Plutarch's account, see Fears (above n. 1) p. 36. n. 87.

30. Diogenes Laertius 7.87–88. For the idea of "living in accord with nature" in Stoic thought, see Brad Inwood, *Ethics and Human Action in Early Stoicism* (Oxford 1985) pp. 194–205; and Long (above n. 12) pp. 189–95.

31. Long and Sedley, (above n. 5) p. 432.

32. For the lives and influence of Chrysippus and Panaetius, see the remarks by G. H. Sabine and S. B. Smith in the introduction to their translation of Cicero *On the Commonwealth* (Columbus, Ohio 1929) pp. 18–38; Erskine (n. 7) pp. 5–6, 211–14; and Long and Sedley (above n. 5) pp. 3, 503, 506. A good introduction to the Stoics and their thought is A. A. Long, *Hellenistic Philosophy* (Berkeley/Los Angeles 1986).

33. For the debate on the influence of Panaetius on Cicero's *On the Republic*, see Watson (above n. 6) p. 225; Erskine (above n. 7) p. 194 n. 27; and James Zetzel, ed., *Cicero De Re Publica: Selections* (Cambridge 1995) p. 112. For Panaetius and Cicero's *On Moral Duties*, see Andrew Dyck, *A Commentary on Cicero, De Officiis* (Ann Arbor 1996) pp. 17–29.

34. Sabine and Smith, (above n. 32) p. 215 n. 67, however, call the definition "a Stoic commonplace"; and Long and Sedley (above n. 5) p. 432 do not attribute Cicero's definition of natural law to Panaetius.

35. On natural law in Roman political thought and in early Christianity, the best single treatment and one to which I am much indebted remains R. W. and A. J. Carlyle, *A History of Mediaeval Political Theory in the West* I (Edinburgh/London 1903) pp. 1–193. Broader in its coverage and equally valuable is F. Dvornik, *Early Christian and Byzantine Political Philosophy: Origins and Background* (Washington, D.C. 1966).

36. For a bibliography and brief discussion of these three philosophical works of Cicero, see MacKendrick (above n. 5) pp. 45–79, 232–57. Zetzel and Dyck (above n. 33) provide commentaries for *On the Republic* and *On Moral Duties*. However, Zetzel omits precisely those passages which are of most interest for the role of natural law in Cicero.

37. Cicero, *On the Republic* 1.25.39.

38. Cicero, *On the Republic* 3.13.23; *On the Laws* 2.4.8; 2.6.16.

39. Cicero, *On the Laws* 1.6.17–19.

40. Cicero, *On Moral Duties* 1.4.11.

41. Cicero, *On Moral Duties* 1.4.11–1.45.161.

42. Cicero, *On Moral Duties* 1.7.20.

43. Cicero, *On the Laws* 1.12.33.

44. Cicero, *On the Laws* 1.7.22–12.34. For slavery in the thought of Aristotle and the Stoics, see Peter Garnsey, *Ideas of Slavery from Aristotle to Augustine* (Cambridge 1996) pp. 105–52. For Alexander and the equality of mankind, see Plutarch *On the Fortune and the Virtue of Alexander* 6 and Fears (above n. 1) p. 36 n. 87.

45. For natural law in the thought of Seneca, see Carlyle (above n. 35) I pp. 19–32. A general study of Seneca, his career and thought, is Miriam Griffin, *Seneca: A Philosopher in Politics* (Oxford 1976).

46. Plato, *Apology* 32E.

47. Seneca, *On Benefits* 3.18.

48. Seneca, *On Leisure* 4.

49. Seneca, *On Benefits* 3.20.

50. For the life of Marcus Aurelius, see Antony Birley, *Marcus Aurelius: A Biography* (New Haven 1987).

On Stoicism in the Roman Empire, Edward Arnold, *Roman Stoicism* (Cambridge 1911) and Samuel Dill, *Roman Society from Nero to Marcus Aurelius* (London 1928) pp. 289–528, are older but very readable and valuable studies. Lack of historical and philosophical insight mar P. A. Brunt, "Stoicism and the Principate," *Papers of the British School at Rome* 30 (1975) pp. 7–35. In general, see R. B. Rutherford, *The Meditations of Marcus Aurelius: A Study* (Oxford 1989)

51. Marcus Aurelius, *Meditations* 11.1–2.

52. Marcus Aurelius, *Meditations* 6.44.

53. Marcus Aurelius, *Meditations* 1.14.

54. Edward Gibbon, *The History of the Decline and Fall of the Roman Empire* (London 1776) chapter III. The best edition of Gibbon is that of J. B. Bury (London 1909). In Bury's edition, the quote is found in volume I pp. 85–86.

55. Aelius Aristides, *Panegyric to Rome* 60. See James Oliver, "The Ruling Power: A Study of the Roman Empire in the Second Century After Christ Through the Roman Oration of Aelius Aristides," *Transactions of the American Philosophical Society*, new series 43 (1953) pp. 871–1003.

56. William MacDonald, *The Pantheon* (Cambridge, MA 1976).

57. A. N. Sherwin-White, *The Roman Citizenship* (2nd edition, Oxford 1973) pp. 279–87, 380–93.

58. Vergil, *Aeneid* 6.850–53.

59. For legal education, the role of lawyers in the Roman Empire, and individual jurists, see H. F. Jolowicz and Barry Nicholas, *Historical Introduction to the Study of Roman Law* (3rd edition, Oxford 1972) pp. 321–515, esp. 374–94, 454, 498–500. For definitions of terms and brief biographies of individual jurists,

Adolf Berger, "Encyclopedic Dictionary of Roman Law," *Transactions of the American Philosophical Society,* new series 43 (1953) pp. 333–808 is invaluable. Introductions to Roman law include J. A. Crook, *Law and Life of Rome* (Ithaca 1967); and Barry Nicholas, *An Introduction to Roman Law* (Oxford 1962). More detailed is W. W. Buckland, *A Textbook of Roman Law from Augustus to Justinian,* 3rd edition, revised by Peter Stein (Cambridge 1963).

60. A. M. Honore, *Gaius: A Biography* (Oxford 1962).

61. Gaius, *Institutes* 1.1. See Gaius *Institutes of Roman Law* with translation and commentary by E. Poste, 4th and enlarged edition by E. A. Whittuck, with a historical introduction by A. H. J. Greenidge (London 1925) pp. 2–5.

62. Jolowicz and Nicholas, (above n. 59) pp. 102–107.

63. On Ulpian, see T. Honore, *Ulpian* (Oxford 1982).

64. *Digest* 1.1.1.

65. Seneca, *Moral Epistles* 90.36–46.

66. *Digest* 50.17.32; 1.1.4.

67. Isidore of Seville, *Etymologiae* 5.4.

68. H. F. Jolowicz, *Historical Introduction to the Study of Roman Law* (1st edition, Cambridge 1932) p. 105. By the third edition of this standard work (above n. 59), p. 107, the irritation has been toned down.

69. Cicero, *On the Republic* 3.11.19.

70. *Digest* 1.5.4; 12.6.64.

71. *Digest* 40.8.2; 37.14.7; 1.6.2. See Carlyle (above n. 35) pp. 49–50.

72. For the achievement and influence of Justinian's codification of the law, see Jolowicz and Nicholas (above n. 59) pp. 478–515.

73. *Digest* 1.1.1.

74. *Digest* 1.3.2.

75. *Digest* 1.1.1.

76. *Digest* 1.1.7. The citation is from Papinian.

77. Carlyle, (above n. 35) p. 61.

78. *Codex Iustinianus* 1.17.2.

79. Dvornik, (above n. 35) II pp. 611–850 offers an excellent discussion of the idea of kingship in the Code of Justinian.

80. Carlyle, (above n. 35) pp. 81–131.

81. Strabo, 14.5.13–14 comments on the love of learning and philosophy that characterized the citizens of Tarsus and on Stoic philosophers born in that city. For Paul's educational background, Arthur Darby Nock, *St. Paul* (London

1938) pp. 21–34 is still the best treatment for the general reader. Garnsey (above n. 44) p. 155 minimizes the influence of Greek philosophy on Paul.

82. Romans, 2.12–14.

83. Origen, *Against Celsus* 5.40. Origen, Tertullian, and Lactantius can be read in translation in Alexander Roberts and James Donaldson, eds., *The Ante-Nicene Fathers* (Buffalo 1885–86).

84. Tertullian, *De Corona [On the Chaplet]* 5–6.

85. Lactantius, *Divine Institutes* 3.8.

86. Ambrose, *Epistles* 73.2, 10.

87. Ambrose, *De Fuga Saeculi* 3.

88. Jerome, *Commentary on Isaiah* 24.6 and *Commentary on Galatians* 3.2.

89. Ernest Barker in the introduction to his translation of Otto Gierke, *Natural Law and the Theory of Society* 1500–1800 (Cambridge 1950) pp. xxxvii–iii.

90. Barker, (above n. 89) p. xxxviii.

91. Isidore of Seville, *Etymologiae* 5.4–6.

92. Barker, (above n. 89) pp. xxxvii–l.

93. See my comments on the Roman Empire and its lessons for our own day in David L. Boren and Edward Perkins, eds., *Preparing America's Foreign Policy for the 21st Century* (Norman: University of Oklahoma Press, forthcoming).

Chapter 3

Aquinas, Natural Law, and the Challenges of Diversity

THE REV. JOHN JENKINS, C. S. C.

Although my subject is Aquinas, natural law, and diversity, let me begin by recalling an event of a very different kind. In the autumn of 1989, as many of us sat down for a relaxing and entertaining evening watching the third game of the "Bay Bridge" World Series between the Oakland A's and the San Francisco Giants, a startling thing happened. The picture began to shake; panicked expressions came over faces; people began running; and eventually the screen went blank. If we continued to watch, what we saw was not a baseball game, but a report on the tremendous, and in many ways tragic, California earthquake of 1989.

It seemed so startling and unexpected. We were all set to revel in our national pastime, and this terrible natural disaster befell us. Yet geologists tell us that earthquakes like this one are not an arbitrary and freakish occurrence, but the result of steady, dynamic processes in our planet whose progress is measured in millennia. The surface of the earth, most geologists now agree, consists of several large plates that move constantly, but so slowly as to be imperceptible to unaided observation. As they move, they bump and grind against one another; and over many years, pressure and stress build along the boundaries of these plates. Eventually, when the tension becomes great enough, something gives, earth and rock snap and resettle, and the result is the violent shaking we call an earthquake. In addition, the collision of plates often causes fissures in the earth's crust, which give way to volcanic eruptions of the planet's molten inner core.

Earthquakes and volcanoes, then, are not really quirky acts of nature, but the result of centuries of shifting earth and growing structural tensions. Indeed, the same can be said for all the geographical features of our earth. As we move east from the California coast through the deserts of Nevada, over the majestic mountains of Utah and Colorado, across the plains and rolling hills of the Midwest, we are struck by the diversity, and indeed the beauty. All this, we are told, was not just here ready-made, but the result of thousands of years of geological processes.

What do these geological reflections have to do with Aquinas and natural law theory? I want to suggest that just as events and processes far back in our geological past have shaped the present geological landscape, so something far back in our intellectual history has shaped our society, its structure, and its debates. Every day you and I observe the moral and political landscape of our society as we read the newspaper or watch the news on television. Generally, we just take the lay of the land for granted, but sometimes we are surprised and our attention is focused by a particularly violent or vehement controversy (such as that over abortion, euthanasia, or the use of military force in foreign countries). These shake our society as an earthquake or volcano shakes the earth. Generally we just adopt one or another position on these debates and settle there. I want to suggest, however, that just as we do not understand the geographical landscape without understanding the long processes that produced it, so we cannot understand the moral and political landscape of our day without understanding the centuries of development that shaped it. Although medieval scholastic thinkers seem to have inhabited a world wholly different from our own, nevertheless, I want to suggest that a consideration of their views can help us gain a useful perspective on our own situation.

In this essay I will not attempt to thoroughly review medieval natural law theory. For this I would recommend *The Changing Profile of Natural Law* by Michael Bertram Crowe.[1] Although I will concentrate on St. Thomas Aquinas, I will not even attempt to give a thorough review of his account of natural law. A good summary of a Thomistic account of natural law is given by Robert George in his essay in this book: "Natural Law and Positive Law."[2] What I will do is focus on certain aspects of the views of this Dominican friar, Thomas of Aquino, who later was canonized as a saint in the Catholic Church, and whom we now refer to simply as Aquinas. Aquinas was clearly the greatest medieval proponent of natural law, and his writings have had an enormous impact on all subsequent thinking on natural law. I will focus on certain factors that led to the development of his views, and discuss interesting ways in which Aquinas's account is similar to, though different from, certain contemporary views. More precisely, I will be concerned with his views on the challenges of a society in which diverse views are represented. Once we understand the similarities and differences between Aquinas's position and contemporary ones, we may gain a better understanding of both Aquinas's views and contemporary views, and may have a better perspective on current debates.

The dominant view in political philosophy today—one might even say the reigning orthodoxy—is liberalism, in one or another of its forms. The spirit of liberalism is to hold a strong view of limited individual rights while allowing for diversity in views about morality, the nature and ultimate end of the human person, religion, and other matters as well. You may think the ultimate fulfillment for humans can only be found in sex, drugs, and rock and roll; I may think we must find it in creative self-expression; and another person may think it should be sought in Christian heaven. A liberal system claims to prescind from any particular answer to this question. The answer is a matter for individual decision. A liberal political system of laws is based not on some particular conception of the human person and his ultimate end, but on certain fundamental rights we each have that all must respect.

There is a tension between delegating to individual choice views about morality, the nature of the human person, and the end of human life, while affirming a set of fundamental and inviolable rights. What I want to argue is that Aquinas, in his account of natural law, shared some of the concerns of liberalism. What he shared was a concern that he and his society did not become narrow or sectarian, but could understand and appreciate views of the world and human life that were fundamentally different from their own. Aquinas hoped that he and others could learn from a diversity of views and could find the truth contained in each of them. Needless to say, however, Aquinas's approach was much different from that of contemporary liberalism.

There is irony in my claim that Aquinas shares some of the concerns of liberalism. Aquinas, the story goes, was a priest and a spokesman for the medieval church, a defender of the Inquisition, the advocate of religious faith over free rational inquiry, the enemy of individual freedoms and individual conscience. He did not seek tolerance of diverse views, but a rigid and close-minded conformity to Christian orthodoxy. It is precisely people like him that modern liberalism, by rejecting any commitment to a substantive account of a human person and his end, is meant to counter. The genius of liberalism, it is argued, is that it can tolerate great diversity among the members of a society; and it accomplishes this by leaving decisions about the best way of living a human life to the individual, while communal agreement is required only on a set of basic rights. Since Aquinas presented and argued for a certain account of human life and the human good that was to be the basis of society and government, he was an obstacle to and not an advocate of the appreciation of diversity.

This picture of Aquinas, though dramatic, is inaccurate. Aquinas was acutely interested in appreciating and helping others of his culture to appreciate views that differed fundamentally from his own and in bringing diverse views into fruitful dialogue. The way in which he strove to accomplish this, however, does contrast sharply with contemporary liberalism. To understand how this is so, we must understand something of the context in which Aquinas wrote and just what he achieved.

Intellectual life in thirteenth-century Europe was vibrant, but in crisis. Medieval universities, the ancestors and models for modern universities, were springing up. A great blossoming of learning and scholarship was under way. Perhaps the most important stimulus to new learning was the translation of many works of the ancient Greek philosopher Aristotle into Latin and their introduction into Western Christendom. Since the time of Boethius, who died in A.D. 524, certain logical works of Aristotle were available in the West, and, until the thirteenth century, Aristotle was known only as a logician. However, in the twelfth century there was an influx of his works, coming both through the Muslims who were then in Spain and from Greek sources in the East. Now scholars in Western Christendom had Aristotle's works on metaphysics, on the natural sciences, on the human soul or psychology, and on ethics. Also, there were available the works of the great Islamic commentators on Aristotle: Avicenna and Averroës. The medievals were certainly smart enough to recognize the genius to be found in their works. But Aristotle was a pagan, and in many places his writings were in conflict with Christian doctrine. Certainly the writings of Muslims were suspect. Thus at the University of Paris, the intellectual center of Europe during Aquinas's lifetime, a 1215 decree forbade lectures to students on Aristotle's works in metaphysics and natural philosophy.

Such was the century into which Aquinas was born. From his earliest days, however, Aquinas fell under the influence not of the dominant anti-Aristotelian group, but of those thoroughly committed to the value of Aristotle's thought. Aquinas's formal studies began at Naples, which was a center for translations of Aristotle. His teacher there was Peter of Ireland, who seems to have been strongly Aristotelian. After he entered the Dominican Order he was sent to Cologne to study under his most important teacher, Albert the Great, who wrote commentaries on most of Aristotle's works and adamantly defended their value for Christians. "They are ignorant men," wrote Albert, "who in all ways want to combat the use of philosophy. . . . Like beasts, they blaspheme against what they do not understand."[3]

From his youth, then, Aquinas thoroughly imbibed the thought of Aristotle from some of its greatest proponents. He later wrote commentaries on many of Aristotle's works and was perhaps the best expositor of Aristotle in his day. In his own works, Aquinas came to refer to Aristotle simply as "the Philosopher," with a capital "P."

In spite of what was, at the time, this suspect Aristotelian influence, Aquinas remained a thoroughly orthodox Christian. He was a member of an upstart religious band that we now call the Dominicans, but whose official title is the "Order of Preachers." This group was founded to combat, by their preaching, the spread of heresies and work for the good of the souls of their neighbors. Moreover, Aquinas's title as a professor at the University of Paris was "Master of the Sacred Page," a teacher and expert in the Bible. There were at the time instructors in philosophy, the masters of the Faculty of Arts. Aquinas, however, was not one of these; he was a Christian theologian. Furthermore, his magnum opus was called the *Summa Theologiae*, the summation of Christian theology. Finally, he was a deeply devout man who was eventually recognized as a saint in the Catholic Church.

How did Aquinas reconcile his interest in and advocacy of Aristotelian philosophy with his profoundly religious commitments and studies? How could he do this at a time when Christian theology was focused on the Bible and explicitly Christian writers? He did it by developing a systematic account of the human person and his ultimate end, of human thought and action, and of Christian theology, thus bringing together these disparate traditions in a way that made sense.

Fundamental to Aquinas's thought was the claim that grace builds on or perfects human nature. In order to understand this principle and its significance we must review, albeit in a somewhat superficial way, certain key notions in Christian theology. Our nature is best understood in terms of the fundamental powers or capacities we possess simply by virtue of being human—the power to think, act, laugh, love, etc. According to a traditional Christian view, human sin—particularly the original sin of Adam—has damaged or corrupted the goodness of this human nature with which God created us. Because of this, our lower appetites are not readily subordinated to our reason, and our reason is not properly subordinated to God. However, in spite of this diminishment of our inclination to do good, our natural capacities are intact, as is our fundamental orientation to the good.

Grace, which comes from the Latin word *gratia*, which means gift, is a key theological notion for Aquinas and for Christian theology generally. In Christian theology, grace is something God gives to us which is, in some way, over and above what He gives by creating us with a human nature. The notion is as interesting and important as it is difficult and complex, and we cannot discuss it at length. Suffice it to say that we can distinguish between two sorts of grace. Healing grace is that gift by which we are healed of the diminishments or damage to our nature that are due to original sin. Sanctifying grace is that by which we acquire virtues beyond what we are capable of by our natural powers alone. Aquinas calls these further virtues "theological virtues". They are the virtues of faith, hope, and charity. By sanctifying grace we can, for example, come to love God with our whole heart and soul.

There is, then, a distinction between what we are capable of by mere human nature, even a nature rectified by healing grace, and what we are capable of with the help of sanctifying grace. Consequently, there is an end of mere human nature, unaided by sanctifying grace, and of humans as recipients of such grace. The first is called natural or imperfect beatitude. It consists of having the cardinal moral virtues of prudence, justice, courage, and temperance, and the intellectual virtues as well. It is quite close to the life of Aristotle's virtuous person. There is also supernatural or perfect beatitude, which consists in perfect friendship with God in heaven.

When Aquinas says grace builds on or perfects but does not destroy nature, he is saying that Christian life builds on and perfects natural virtue. We cannot attain Christian charity, for example, if we do not have the natural virtue of justice.

On Aquinas's account of human nature and Christian theology, then, natural virtues have a clearly defined role and a value. They are not something contrary to a life transformed by faith in Christ, but something that is still valuable and even necessary for the Christian. Aquinas affirms not only Christian revelation, but also human nature and all it involves. Indeed, since awareness of and appreciation for natural virtues does not depend on Christian revelation but on God's creation, the realm of natural virtue has a certain autonomy, a certain independence from Christian revelation.

Aquinas's affirmation of the value of human nature and natural virtue also allowed him to affirm and value Aristotle, who elucidated this nature and these virtues. Ordinary courage, for example, is something to be studied and practiced for a Christian, and Aristotle can be read profitably because he elucidates this and other virtues. Moreover, the intellectual virtues of science and understanding are valuable, and hence rational inquiry into mundane realities, as well as into eternal divine realities, is valuable. Aristotle, above all, practices such inquiry and can teach us such truths. Therefore Aristotle is to be studied and, in an important way, imitated.

This affirmation of human nature and natural virtues is apparent in the *Summa Theologiae*. The work is clearly and explicitly a work of Christian theology. It begins with God; it moves to discuss creation and particularly human beings and human action; and it ends by considering our means to salvation, Jesus Christ and the Church. But embedded in this theological treatise, in the first volume and particularly in each volume of the second part of the work, is a discussion of human nature, human thought and action, and human virtue—a discussion that draws heavily on Aristotle. Within his theological framework, Aquinas presents a discussion of human nature and virtues that is heavily indebted to Aristotle. This second part of the *Summa* is, in many ways, the most original and interesting part of the work. It expresses what scholars have called Aquinas's "Christian humanism," his affirmation of the goodness and value of things human which are not explicitly dependent on their place in Christian salvation. It is here that the thought of the pagan Aristotle is most strongly affirmed.

One of Aquinas's most important and original contributions to the medieval debate, then, was to argue for and define the value of human nature and natural virtues as in some way independent of Christian faith and distinctively Christian virtues. No one before Aquinas had done this so clearly and comprehensively. In this respect, Aquinas was a secularist in the original sense of this term. Today when we call someone a secularist or an advocate of secularism, we mean they seek the elimination of religion from the public (or perhaps even private) sphere. Charles Taylor has pointed out that the term in its contemporary sense is a bit odd, for 'secular' concerns originally contrasted with but presupposed religious or eternal concerns.[4] That is, in its original sense a concern was secular insofar as it dealt with matters of this passing world, as opposed to a concern with our eternal destiny with, or separate from, God. Now it means a concern with the temporal to the exclusion of the eternal.

Aquinas certainly was not a secularist in the modern sense, but he can be called a secularist in the original sense. Although Aquinas held that our eternal destiny with God should be our goal and that Christian virtues are the highest and most important, he affirmed the value of temporal goals of good government, scientific inquiry, and other earthly achievements, and emphasized the importance of natural virtues. He argued that a fully virtuous Christian must attend to these matters as well.

Aquinas helped the medieval world see why Christians should study Aristotle and, indeed, all great non-Christian writers. He helped move the medievals from a strictly intramural Christian discussion and debate to one that embraced thinkers and views that were not Christian. I have focused on Aristotle for he was the biggest challenge to the thirteenth century. One could also consider how Aquinas studied and employed the writings of the great Jewish scholar, Moses Maimonides, and the Islamic writers Averroës and Avicenna. Aquinas admired and was influenced by the thinking of these writers as well.

Aquinas, then, was an advocate of diversity in public debate, of introducing a wide variety of views for rational inquiry and lively debate. It is in this respect, I suggest, we find an affinity between Aquinas and modern liberals who want to allow for diversity in the public realm. Aquinas strove and succeeded in moving away from a sectarian, exclusionist Christianity to one that could consider and engage thinkers of many different views. Of course Aquinas thought the ideal political system on earth was one in which Christian orthodoxy dominated—and this is anathema to modern liberals. However, we can see how, given Aquinas's view of natural law, we can construct a system in which no particular religion dominated. Robert George, in his essay, explains how we can make sense of this on Aquinas's view of the natural law.[5]

In spite of this affinity between Aquinas and modern liberals, there are extremely important differences. Aquinas attempted to show the value of non-Christian thinkers and writings by formulating an account of human nature and natural virtues and of their relationship to Christian faith and theological virtues, in terms of which he could make sense of the value of both the non-Christian Aristotle, on one hand, and the Bible and other Christian writings, on the other. Because Aquinas was a Christian, this account reflected his own Christian commitment and asserted that human nature was fulfilled perfectly only through Christian mysteries. Nevertheless, Aquinas's Christian understanding was one according to which he could value and enter into dialogue with non-Christians such as Aristotle. Thus, while standing firmly within his Christian understanding, he could appreciate and engage in dialogue with those with radically different understandings.

The contemporary liberal, insofar as he has a strategy for engaging thinkers with fundamentally different views, takes a different approach. Such a person does not attempt to formulate any overarching view in terms of which diverse views can be appreciated and valued. He simply stipulates that diversity is to be accepted. Any decision about why and how these diverse views are valuable, or what the criteria are for evaluating them, is left to the individual.

I want to suggest to you that Aquinas's approach, though more difficult, has important advantages. It is more difficult for it must strive for some deeper unified view through which diverse views are to be appreciated and valued. It has the advantage, however, of being better able to bring these diverse views into dialogue, for it offers common terms in light of which the dialogue can be fruitful. The liberal's strategy, on the other hand, gives us diversity but no common vision in virtue of which dialogue may be carried on. Thus, in liberal societies like our own, we find very diverse views, but little fruitful dialogue. People with fundamentally different views merely talk (or shout) past one another, or do not talk at all.

Returning to the metaphor with which I began, broad views of the world and human beings are, I suggested, like huge plates of earth that move gradually, bump against and jostle one another, and form new landscapes. In this paper I have tried to review the way in which Aquinas resolved the collision between the Christian view and the Aristotelian view. This gave rise to his 'secularist' Christianity, which allowed him to embrace both Aristotle and Christianity. Aquinas's views contribute to our present understanding, though a great deal would have to be said to understand how we arrived at the contemporary landscape. I have simply tried to portray a single shift in our cultural history.

In concluding, let me point out that my geological metaphor breaks down in at least one important respect. The geological processes I have described are inexorable and impersonal. They do not depend on us and we can, at least now, do nothing to alter them. This is not entirely true of the processes of development in our culture. We can understand these processes, take a certain position on them, and attempt to contribute to further development. That is the responsibility of each one of us. I believe a better understanding of our common past can help us shape our future. In this paper, I have argued for one way in which careful attention to Aquinas may give us a better perspective on the contemporary debate.

ENDNOTES

1. Michael Bertram Crowe, *The Changing Profile of Natural Law* (: 19).

2. Robert George, "Natural Law and Positive Law," 151.

3. *In epistoas beati Dionysii Aeropogite,* Borgnet (ed.), XIV edition, 910.

4. Charles Taylor, *Multiculturalism and "The Politics of Recognition,"* ed. Amy Gutman (Princeton: Princeton University Press, 1992), 62.

5. See Robert George, "Natural Law and Positive Law," 151.

Chapter 4

John Locke's Reflections on Natural Law and the Character of the Modern World

TIMOTHY FULLER

We live in an age fiercely committed to both universals and particulars. We speak of a new world order, of history ending in the reign of liberal democracy, but also of cultural diversity, multiculturalism, subjectivity, and individualism. Is there universal truth or only subjective opinion? Is justice in the eye of the beholder? How can we treat everyone impartially according to procedural rules, and yet at the same time treat everyone as unique, with special characteristics, and entitled to special recognition? The essays in this volume focus on natural law. The subject is appropriate to our age because the effort to articulate the idea of natural law is motivated by the desire to relate unity to diversity, to find the one in the midst of the many. I am going to consider this topic principally in reference to issues of moral and practical judgment.

This philosophical perplexity about unity and diversity is ancient. Aristotle, for instance, noticed that human beings were set apart as the animals that could speak and reason, and thus argue with each other. Beyond the natural requirement of sexual union for reproduction of the species, their capacity for language drew human beings to each other in an engagement to exploit this special talent by conversing endlessly, trying to figure things out. Thus human beings are naturally political. Yet reasoning, talking, and arguing also distance us from each other because in reasoning, talking, and arguing we produce conflicting opinions; we do not see eye to eye. Our natural sociability is a source of tension and conflict. Our special blessing is also our special curse.

The task is to make the curse into a blessing, or at least to keep things in perspective and to conduct our debates with moderation. This was, Aristotle insisted, to be done through politics. For him, politics was that intense civic exchange of differing opinions for the purpose of eventually defining, and then maintaining, a way of life citizens could enjoy in common and willingly share by finding a way to fit their opinions to the way of life of their city. Aristotle could accept that the capacity for seeking this resolution is universal to human beings, but the accomplishment is not universal and is most likely, if Aristotle is correct, to come about only in a city small by any modern standard both in geographical scope and in numbers of citizens, and composed of free individuals, that is, those individuals who are not easily disturbed by endless argument and are willing to live with endless argument.

Since Aristotle's time, we have increasingly emphasized the potential universality of the human conversation, replacing Aristotle's emphasis on the polis or city with the idea of a cosmopolis, the city of universal scope and membership. Today we even speak of the global community. In the modern era, we have spoken often of progress and enlightenment, expressing thereby the conviction that somehow—either by providential design, an iron law of history, or sheer human will—a harmony of all the human differences would emerge and that the tension of history would be supplanted by the tranquillity of final fulfillment in universal community.

A typical argument has been that history is the testing ground on which we shall finally discover which opinions are true and that these truths shall, in the long run, be acknowledged. There is a profound urge in the modern era to use politics (the Machiavellian urge) in order to get beyond politics into a moralized world of perpetual peace (the Kantian urge). But the Kantian urge seems never quite able finally to overcome the Machiavellian urge. This fact haunts every modern revolution.

There are modern versions of natural law arguments that support the outlook I have just described. There are also older versions of natural law that proclaim the universal human community without aspiring to perfection in this world.

Each of these views has its advantages and disadvantages: the modern version energizes us with the conviction that we can make visible the hitherto invisible spiritual-intellectual unity by radically transforming the world. The inspiration to active idealism, which makes the human condition into a series of problems to be solved by our own ingenuity, is flattering to us and seductive; it seems to give us a sense of purpose and a direction. This is the advantage. Its disadvantage is that it is hostage to disillusionment and disenchantment induced by the extraordinary resistance of the human condition to its own perfection. This fact constantly calls into question the claims of idealist activism. The claim of enlightenment carries with it the prospect of disillusionment.

The old version has the advantage of sobriety and modesty in its claims for this world and, in this sense, is more genuinely appreciative of the actually prevailing diversity of human practices than any modern version. The modern version, for all of its emphasis on cultural diversity, has a deep and profound distrust of plurality even as it celebrates diversity rhetorically. But the old approach appears to its disadvantage in the extraordinary philosophical and spiritual demands that are placed upon us when we must try to see that unity which will neither replace on earth the empirical diversity of our historical existence nor produce final and perpetual peace. We are bidden in the old approach to take our bearings from what is seen only dimly and intermittently and what cannot be turned into a historical project for immanent perfection. The old version seems to give us less to do and counsels a certain resignation toward imperfection.

There was a moment in our tradition when we stood poised between the older contemplative and the newer activist outlook. One thinker who lived in this moment and whose thinking traversed the struggle for understanding engendered by this was John Locke in the seventeenth century. Locke was profoundly influenced by the thought of Aristotle and of Thomas Aquinas, while he was also of the age of Francis Bacon, Thomas Hobbes, and Isaac Newton. Locke thought a great deal about natural law, and evidence of his thinking on that topic is to be found scattered throughout his writings.

What I propose to focus on here is his extended philosophic reflection in a work variously called "Questions Concerning the Law of Nature," or "Essays on the Law of Nature." Locke never published this work. It only came to light in this century and now exists in two different editions.[1] The editors of the two editions disagree with each other over what Locke was trying to say in this work. The dispute is of great interest. I encourage you to pursue it for yourselves.

For now, I am going to ignore the scholarly controversy, present my own interpretation of this little known work, and say why it should interest us. That it is little known is not decisive because what the work helps us to see is the acuteness with which Locke anticipated some of the fundamental intellectual anxieties of the modern age, and thus it sheds light on the intention of his work as a whole. Moreover, what he says here can certainly be connected to his famous works, which, no one will deny, have profoundly affected modern intellectual life.

The work is organized around a series of questions that Locke poses to himself and then tries to answer. It is in the form of a scholastic disputation. A question is posed, Locke gives his answer to the question, and he summarizes the arguments for and against the answer he gives. Locke starts by pointing out that, if there is a law that is *natural*, then we must be able to understand it apart from revelation, through our own reason and experience. Otherwise, it would not be natural. Also, we must separate anything we might call natural from what we have merely acquired culturally from our family and society. A cultural acquisition is artificial and alterable, not natural. Locke clearly suspects that a lot of things that, in the past, were called natural were not natural.

What comes through is Locke's painful intellectual honesty about what can be said about natural law and what can be said against it. Locke safeguarded himself from easy answers by cataloguing the astonishing, if not horrifying, variety of human practices. Locke's survey of them is, metaphorically, a pilgrimage through them. This is a sophisticated philosopher's pilgrimage, to be sure, but it has affinities with the well-known literary pilgrimages of his time such as John Bunyan's *Pilgrim's Progress* or John Comenius's *Labyrinth of the World*. What Locke is hoping to find after this intense and painful journey will have been earned through the refining heat of a fiery intellectual furnace. Here we can sympathize immediately. If Locke was horrified at the variety of human practices in his time, what are we denizens of the late twentieth century to say about what we find in our time?

Locke is also facing the problem philosophy has in reaching any affirmative conclusions when it does not rely on revelation. This is not as such a modern problem, but in our age, which is often called secular, we can understand it very well.

Locke is not addressing those who have the gift of a simple and humble faith in God's providence. His audience is those for whom the shaking of the universal authority of Christendom in the Reformation, and the new awakening of that era to the variety of the world's non-European cultures, caused a crisis of intellectual confidence. Here too we can immediately sympathize.

Locke's first question is, "Is there a law of nature?" His answer to this is guardedly affirmative as we shall see in a moment. He approaches the question philosophically, presupposing no foundation that assures what the answer will be. He admits that although there is widespread affirmation of natural law, there are also those who deny natural law. Philosophically, therefore, we have a disputed question. Locke must then explain to himself what people mean when they assert that there is a natural law.

Some refer to natural law as "moral good," or "moral virtue," or "right reason." But everyone may claim to reason rightly, and this leads to sectarian wars and to asserting personal opinions as right reason. Thus, claims to morality and virtue foster the equation of one's interests or pleasures to virtue, and promote immoral imperialism. Locke, of course, does not approve of this equation. Yet he wants to defend the existence of natural law. Natural law should be universal, not divisive, but one can see how natural law is regularly employed divisively. Locke must reconcile natural law to the vast diversity of actual human conduct; and he must circumvent self-righteous appeals to natural law. Locke's concern is for the unity in diversity that is a fundamental practical issue for any thinker in the post-Reformation world who wants to establish principles of civility suffused by a liberal temper and spiritual toleration amidst contested moral and religious authorities.

Thus Locke locates the meaningful encounter with natural law in each individual human being. The "law of nature" refers to what "each individual can discover by that light alone which is implanted in us by nature . . . demanding a rational account of his duty." The law of nature is "the command of the divine will, knowable by the light of nature, indicating what is and what is not consonant with a rational nature." Human reason does not create this law but discovers and articulates a law made by a higher power that is somehow implanted in us. Reason becomes aware of and interprets this law which reason did not make. What reason gets from this natural law are the conditions necessary for making human laws. Natural law contains "the conditions requisite to obligation" and can be known by the light of reason alone and known directly by individual human beings without any intermediary.

The particular, diverse laws and customs across the world presuppose a concept of law as such or that there are conditions of lawfulness that are universal. Locke states it this way: "By the foundation of natural law we understand that which supports and upon which are erected, as upon a foundation, all the other precepts of this law . . . [a] fundamental law, which is the rule and measure of all the other laws. . . ."[2]

Human reason is universal. Human beings have the capacity to reason practically in the same way or from the same background considerations of the foundation of law despite their diversity of circumstances in time and place. Despite the diversity of practices, human beings could, in principle, understand each other if given time for deliberation and discussion. They could come to understand each other's laws even if they did not agree with the decisions made by each other.

Locke is saying that human beings have a natural and universal tendency to establish limits to their conduct. In establishing such limits, people are also marking out what they accept as the area in which freely chosen action should occur. Human beings, on Locke's view, are not actually desirous of acting against nature, but they are diverted by private interests and pleasures. The existence of conscience—the fact that human beings engage in self-judgment—supports this conclusion. It is natural, therefore, for the human mind to distinguish between interests and pleasures on the one hand and duty on the other. Even those who deny the law of nature cannot get rid of the distinction between duty and desire. Does man alone of all species have no function? No purpose to serve? Is man alone isolated from nature? Locke cannot countenance this conclusion.

Now Locke asks himself what can be said against the arguments he has put forth. The objectors to natural law deny that most men live orderly lives or seem to know the light of reason as proclaimed in doctrines of the law of nature. We disagree greatly over conduct; thus are we not free to disregard the law of nature? How can we disagree with each other and disregard moral duty if there is a natural law? Clearly, this law is not natural in the sense that animal and vegetable behavior is natural because it cannot be contradicted.

Locke responds to this objection by saying that some men are blind: they resist the law of nature. They cannot see it because they refuse to see it or have impaired mental abilities. But, we ask, if a law of nature is implanted in

us, how can we not see it? We can fail to see it if there is
in us a power to resist as well as a power to apprehend
the precepts of the law of nature. The law of nature must
compete against self-interest and pleasure. It is natural to
want law but it is also natural that duty and desire conflict. Thus the universal knowability of the law of nature
does not mean that it is actually universally known or
admitted. Rather, there will be degrees of knowledge of
the law of nature. That the law of nature is knowable
does not mean that it is inevitably known. Vice can
obscure virtue even though the distinction between
virtue and vice necessarily arises in human discourse.
Consciousness, for Locke, seems to require the possibility
of contradicting as well as submitting to law. Thus, Locke
argues, we must "consult not the majority of mankind,
but the sounder and more perceptive part." By "the
sounder and more perceptive part," I think Locke means
those who are able and willing to go through this painful
exercise of inquiry that he himself is attempting to exemplify in his reflections.

What if there is disagreement over the law of nature
even among the sounder and more perceptive part of
mankind? The fact that the debate is always there, Locke
argues, shows that the idea of natural law is always there.
The difficulty of grasping natural law in the right way
actually proves its importance to human beings.
Disagreement excites a desire for agreement. But the
desire for agreement produces a conflict of interpreta-
tions, each of which may appeal to the very law of nature
as the ground of its interpretation.

Implied in the debates, then, is the refusal (perhaps the
inability of human beings) to accept the conclusion that

might makes right. The authority of law in society derives from its compatibility with the general concept of duty found in the law of nature. Compulsion by force does not truly bind anyone, nor does one's calculation of possible advantage. Such calculations can lead to any conclusion if the sense of duty is absent. Utilitarian calculation must then also be grounded in the natural sense of duty, the belief that there is a right way for human beings to be human.

Humanity is tied necessarily to a sense of law. Wherever there are human beings there has to arise a distinction between virtue and vice. We are not governed by the law of nature in the sense of an inevitable force that we cannot depart from or resist. What governs us is awareness of a rational consideration that is never completely lost from sight, but that becomes effective only through active response to its demands. We must make a decision to act in accord with it. A decision to act against natural law assumes that there is something against which action is possible. In rejecting natural law, we come face-to-face with it.

The light of nature makes law accessible to human beings by stimulating their efforts, but there does have to be an effortful response on our part. We participate in the natural law actively. It is in us as something that elicits a response from us. The quality of that response, however, is not predetermined by the implanted awareness of natural law.

These thoughts of Locke show us how he understands what it means for us to be moral beings. If we were predetermined in our conduct by natural law as a kind of biological or mechanical process, we could not exhibit moral conduct. If, on the other hand, there were no law to which to respond, the standard of humanly chosen conduct would be arbitrary or relative to each chooser. We must choose and yet also accept that our choices are responses, not solely free creations.

Responses to what? To begin with, we are taught the precepts of the natural law by parents, teachers, and others. It is extraordinarily difficult to figure out the difference between what is naturally known and what is handed down. Locke, nevertheless, thinks the effort to separate the two is necessary. Locke wants us to grasp the natural law for ourselves, directly, and not just grasp what we have been taught. In this sense, we begin to see that for Locke the sounder and more perceptive human beings must be those who are capable of genuinely independent thought and reflection—the true individuals. Even if we get our initial moral knowledge through upbringing, we must somehow break through to a resolve of our own about moral virtue, reaching the point of steadfast certainty about our duty.

Why did Locke think this? Perhaps part of the answer is that as he became more familiar with the staggering variety of customs, practices, and cultures, he anticipated the growing inadequacy of appeal to tradition to justify morality. Once a traditional manner of conduct is questioned in the face of the dizzying variety of alternatives, the question of natural law becomes a matter of serious concern, and the basis of conduct becomes a matter requiring investigation. Tradition is destabilized because the vast variety of the world's practices makes possible a challenge to a tradition at any moment. Those who think only traditionally will find it hard to respond adequately.

I think Locke feared a division between those who, in the moment of moral crisis, would cling tenaciously to their received opinions, and those who would assert that there is no basis for duty, that all is arbitrary and everything is permitted. I think Locke anticipated a world that would not be allowed to escape this issue, and to this extent he was already trying to face what has become the all-too-obvious problem of subsequent centuries. His speculation on the need for a philosophic community of opinion thus turns on a fear that modern thinking may be inadequate to the problems it will face. From the perspective of our time, when liberal thinking is under attack for its abstract universality, Locke's readers are entitled to remind the critics of liberalism of the unruly sectarian alternatives that spring up, and also to remind liberals themselves both of what they need to defend and the intellectual courage it will take to defend it.

Controversy over the natural law can be explained only if we accept that what is inscribed in our hearts is the capacity to formulate general principles of conduct, but not (1) an equal ability or willingness among human beings to undertake the task to formulate the principles adequately nor (2) equal capacities to judge well what are the fitting responses to contingent conditions. As Locke says, only those who "gird themselves for work" can do this since it is not possible for the "idle and indolent. . . ."[3] The work we must do means rejecting both unthinking habit and the temptation to exploit uncertainty with sophistry. The vision of unity is something we must seek as our goal. Moreover, we have to figure it out because we cannot find it by looking back into the past. We can see here the seed of the orientation toward the future of modern activist idealism. What keeps Locke from becoming simply the modern activist idealist is the chastening honesty of Locke's awareness of the difficulties and a sobriety that is often lost in modern excess.

What are we girding for? We must try to let the light of nature guide us on the path of life, to avoid, as Locke puts it, "the rough stretches of vice and there the maze of error."[4] In principle, Locke is saying, there can be a symbiotic relation between reason and the senses. There is nothing in our experience that is inherently contradictory to rational ordering. The diversity of experience does not destroy the unifying power of reason, but the unifying power of reason cannot succeed by denying or suppressing the diversity of our experience. We must seek principles of conduct consistent with the appreciation of that diversity. Locke calls reason the "discursive faculty of the soul" through which we can work our way toward the formulation of the law of nature we did not know at the start but which is the conclusion of properly conducted inquiry.

Sense experience does not prevent us from having ideas but actually stimulates the possibility of ideas. Sense and ideas are not the same, but they are interrelated and, in principle, cooperative within us. The result of this symbiosis will be an awareness of God, of one's neighbor, and of oneself. We have duties toward all three, although there is no fixed ordering in the way we respond to those duties. Practical reasoning must relate and order our respective duties in each situation according to the situation's peculiar features.

Still, we do not know what we are actually to do. We can see that the relation of these duties is worked out in different ways for different political communities, but there is something universal beyond these orders that are the product of habit or force. No one of the earthly orders can be simply equated with the realization of the natural law. If there is a natural consensus that goes beyond the specific political orders, it is not a civil association but the precondition of all civil associations. Implicit in Locke's argument is a cosmopolitan point of view that as yet has no way to realize itself in a concrete, earthly order. Locke, moreover, finds no basis to assure human progress beyond our current degraded state in our various parochial orders. Locke finds it hard to assert that any law appears universally sacred in actual practice apart from the law of self-preservation. Even that law is regularly violated, however, by those who rush willingly to death for all sorts of causes. There appears to be no principle or proposition that cannot be contradicted in action—and that has not been contradicted—by someone, somewhere. There is a gulf between what the mind sees as the human possibility and what we actually achieve.

This sad catalogue forces upon us the elusiveness of the law of nature. Each reflective individual will have to make a decision on the law of nature in full knowledge of the difficulties. Reflection on the question of natural law leads us in one way to despairing of humanity but simultaneously brings us back to the quest for the way out. The desire of men for law and their capacity to perceive the difference between law and sheer force suggest the necessity of distinguishing between power and authority. We do not want to be ruled by sheer strength but by laws. Rulers do not want to rule by sheer force but by right. This is true even while it is also true that a large proportion of human relations continue to depend on force.

These contradictions at the heart of human experience are the ultimate test of one's tenacity to seek and acknowledge the law of nature. What Locke has done is translate the story of the fall of man in disobeying God into the modern idiom of promiscuity in conduct. Locke wants to insist that it is always wrong to murder, steal, or deprive others of their property through force and fraud. He wants to insist that we must always revere God, honor our parents, and respect our neighbors. In our common life, we ought to converse openly and candidly, in friendship, neither gossiping nor meddling. These are the verities he glimpses at the end of his pilgrimage road through the promiscuity of the world.

Finally, Locke affirms the natural law as the means to making human individuality manageable and fruitful. Practical virtue is reconciling our desires with our duties. Our freedom demands acknowledgment of our dependency. Freedom and responsible conduct are complementary and made explicit when we exercise obedience to law. It falls to us to enact this complementarity in practice—to make real the complementarity. If we do so, Locke assures us, we shall find that the harmonious economy of nature conduces to the increase of both our wealth and our community.[5] In Locke's *Second Treatise of Government*, his work on natural law is reformulated as the argument in defense of property and productiveness as the keys to human improvement. These things, far from being signs of secularism, are actually evidences for Locke of our cooperation with the providential design for human beings to fulfill themselves through the right use of their reason.

It is the rectitude of our conduct that clarifies and defines our advantage, not our advantage that clarifies and defines our rectitude. The law of nature is not antithetical to the individual or to diversity. It is the support without which individuality cannot find its appropriate happiness. Locke's view is, in the end, a prototype of an ideal moral life for what we have come to call the liberal tradition. It carries no guarantee of realization, and Locke is profoundly troubled about its actual possibility of success. He knew that theories of conduct do not finally determine the actual doings of humanity, even though theories of conduct significantly shape the way we characterize our difficulties and how we should respond to them. Locke emphasized the effort of response that we must make in subscribing to ideals of conduct that we must take responsibility to enact. Moreover, we cannot do without moral theorizing, especially in an age that has broken its link with a tradition of conduct and can no longer accept any tradition of conduct without skepticism and distrust. After Locke, theorists increasingly scrutinized history for signs of an inevitable historical development towards a new agreement or even a culminating fulfillment of human aspirations. To do so, thinkers increasingly had to detach themselves from Locke's intellectual agonies and presuppose the probability of the outcome they hoped for. To the extent this has happened, Locke's philosophical task has been replaced by an ideological quest. One may well wonder if in doing this we did not make it less likely rather than more likely that what Locke hoped for would come to pass. It is Locke's very honest uncertainty coupled with the tenacity of his moral commitment that exemplifies what he meant by the philosophic community for the liberal age, and one has to wonder if our current intellectual condition proves that he was right to be skeptical about the prospects for the success of an age in which intellectual life tends to divide itself between moral dogmatism and moral nihilism.

ENDNOTES

1. The two editions are *Essays on the Law of Nature,* ed. W. Von Leyden (Oxford: Clarendon Press, 1954) and *Questions Concerning the Law of Nature,* R. Horwitz, J. S. Clay, and D. Clay, eds. (Ithaca: Cornell University Press, 1990). References in the text are taken from the latter edition.

2. *Questions . . . , op cit.,* p. 237.

3. Ibid., p. 135.

4. Ibid., p. 153.

5. Ibid., p. 243.

Chapter 5

Theories of Natural Law in the Culture of Advanced Modernity

ALASDAIR MACINTYRE

Ours is a culture dominated by experts, experts who profess to assist the rest of us, but who often instead make us their victims. Among those experts by whom we are often victimized the most notable are perhaps the lawyers. If you as a plain person take yourself to be wronged and you wish to achieve redress, or if you are falsely accused and you wish to avoid unjust punishment, or if you need to negotiate some agreement with others in order to launch some enterprise, you will characteristically find yourself compelled to put yourself into the hands of lawyers—lawyers who will proceed to represent you by words that are often not in fact yours, who will utter in your name documents that it would never have occurred to you to utter, and who will behave ostensibly on your behalf in ways that may well be repugnant to you, so guiding you through processes whose complexity seems to have as a central function to make it impossible for plain persons to do without lawyers.

Plain persons, that is to say, can only hope to learn what the content of our law is from those who have undergone a specialized professional training. Plain persons are thereby made recurrently dependent upon lawyers and, if their interests in what the fundamental content of law is are more theoretical, upon professors of law. The thought that, instead, professors of law and lawyers need to learn what the fundamental content of law is from plain persons and that all plain persons— even including lawyers and professors of law, insofar as they remain plain persons—have within themselves the capacity to understand and to recognize what the fundamental content of law is (a resource more basic than anything that can be taught at any law school) is a thought that is alien to everything dominant and fashionable in our contemporary culture. But just this thought is central to older conceptions of natural law and especially to the conception that modern Thomists inherit from Aquinas.

On this Thomistic view, we all of us—except in certain exceptional, albeit very important, types of situations— know what the fundamental precepts of the natural law are and that they are true: that it is true that we ought not to take innocent life, that we ought to tell the truth and to keep promises, that we ought to respect the property of others, although not quite unconditionally, and so on. We also all know, on this Thomistic view, that all positive laws that conform to what reason requires by way of justice—

and only laws that conform to reason and justice are genuine laws—either give expression to these precepts or
provide for their application to a variety of concrete situations. We as plain persons know, on a Thomistic view,
what must seem a surprising amount.

Yet this is not all. It is not just that exponents of these
conceptions of natural law claim that plain persons all
have within themselves an authoritative knowledge of
the content of law. They also claim that plain persons are
all in agreement as to the fundamentals of law and
morals. But no fact seems to be plainer in the modern
world than the extent and depth of moral disagreement,
often enough disagreement on basic issues. So that once
again we find a remarkable difference between how matters are or were conceived by the exponents of these
older views of natural law and the beliefs dominant in
modern cultures. It follows that we should not expect
those older conceptions of natural law to continue to
flourish in the modern world. And they do not. What we
find instead, for the most part, are very different theories
of natural law, theories that have come to terms in greater
or lesser degree with cultural modernity.

I am going to argue that these latter theories all fail and
that they fail in just those respects in which their adaptation to what is distinctively modern in modern culture is
most evident. Such theories propose an understanding of
natural law that is in the sharpest contrast to the understanding of it proposed in the high Middle Ages by
Aquinas and revived in the last hundred years by his
Thomistic followers, most notably by Jacques Maritain.
The Thomistic account of natural law which is of course
still held by a minority of our contemporaries, including

me is, on the view that I am going to take of it, unlike its modern rivals precisely in that it is on the one hand, as I shall contend, true and, on the other hand, unacceptable by the dominant standards of modernity.

It must at first sight seem paradoxical and even perhaps insulting to suggest that out of a range of rival views on a particular subject-matter, the more nearly one of such views approaches to the truth, the less likely it is to be acceptable to modern persons. And an obvious objection at once arises. If knowledge of natural law is indeed a resource of plain persons, then how can it be the case that anyone at all should reject the precepts of the natural law? Or, to put matters another way, if it is the plain person who is the authority, and if we are all more or less plain persons, then surely the rejection of a particular account of natural law by some significant set of plain persons ought to be sufficient to show that that account is false. These are important questions and any defensible account of natural law will have to provide some adequate way of responding to them. But such a response must come at the end of my inquiry. Where should that inquiry begin? Clearly it should commence with a statement of what I mean by a theory or account of natural law.

Every account of natural law, no matter how minimal, makes at least two claims: first, that our human nature is such that, as rational beings, we cannot but recognize that obedience to some particular set of precepts is required, if we are to achieve our good or goods, a recognition that is primarily expressed in our practice and only secondarily in our explicit formulation of precepts; and, second, that it is at least one central function of any system of law to spell out those precepts and to make them mandatory by providing for their enforcement. But in specifying these claims further, natural law theorists disagree among themselves in important ways. They differ concerning the extent and nature of the claims they make about human nature. They differ in their conceptions of human rationality. They differ consequently as to why it is rational, given our nature, to obey the relevant set of precepts. They differ concerning what those precepts are to which obedience is thus required. And they differ about the function of law.

Let me begin with a distinctively modern theory of natural law, a minimal theory, advanced and defended by that most distinguished of recent legal theorists, H. L. A. Hart (1907–92). Hart was in most respects a legal positivist, and this fact makes it striking that he should have advanced anything even resembling a theory of natural law. For, traditionally, legal positivists have rejected any conception of natural law, and indeed some of the founders of legal positivism, such as Jeremy Bentham and John Austin, made their rejection of natural law central to their theorizing. What then is legal positivism?

A legal positivist distinguishes sharply between questions about what a legal system is and what makes some particular rule a law in some particular legal system, on the one hand, and questions about what it is for a law to be just or unjust, on the other. What makes a law a law in a particular system is no more than that it has been enacted by an appropriate authority. The question of whether a particular rule is or is not a law is then a quite different question from that of whether it would be just or unjust to enforce that same rule. Justice is one thing, legality another. Traditional natural law theorists, including Aquinas, had argued that a certain conformity to justice is a necessary condition of any rule or precept being genuinely a law. Such theorists had looked back to Aristotle, who had argued that in any legal system we can distinguish between that which is natural, that is, binding upon all human beings as human beings, and that which is merely conventional, local and peculiar to this or that particular legal system, binding only those under its authority. They had also followed Aristotle in recognizing the authority of unwritten laws, that is, of laws not acknowledged within some particular legal system by having been enacted, but nonetheless binding upon human beings. Legal positivists are of course committed to denying that there can be such unwritten laws, and it might well seem that all legal positivists would have to deny any distinction whatsoever between the natural and the conventional. But matters are a little more complicated than this, as Hart's theory of natural law demonstrates.

In his book *The Concept of Law,* Hart developed a thesis deriving from Hobbes and Hume, according to which it is certain very general features of nature and of our human nature that make law necessary and that determine a minimal function for any legal system.[1] It is a fact about the nature of human beings that they seek to preserve their own lives, and it is also a fact that they are limited in their regard for others, that they are limited in their own strength of will, and that they are as individuals roughly equal to each other in natural strength. The resources human beings need are also limited, and we are all more or less vulnerable to harms and dangers arising both from other humans competing for scarce resources and from nature. We therefore need enforceable laws as a protection against violence; we need a power capable of securing social stability; and we need rules that regulate the distribution of resources. Given that human beings have the goal of self-preservation and that their situation is otherwise thus, that systems of law should have this type of content is a matter of "natural necessity," and not just of convention.[2]

Hart also argued that if there are any moral rights, then there is one natural right, the equal right of all human beings to be free.[3] The details of his argument do not matter so much for our present purposes as do two features of his conclusion. The first is that his claim is a purely conditional one; it does not assert that anyone in fact has any natural rights. The second is that, even if they do possess such a natural right, Hart's conclusion is consistent with the natural right to freedom being a right only to the most minimal freedom.

There is an important parallel between Hart's argument concerning natural rights and Hart's arguments for his particular conception of natural law. In both cases the only premises from which he believes we can argue soundly are such as to deny us any substantive moral content in our conclusions. Just as we are provided with no grounds for believing that there actually are any natural rights, so the function of legal systems, according to Hart's account of natural law, could be adequately discharged by fundamentally unjust legal systems. All that is required for adequate discharge of function is that some human group should have met its needs for the preservation of life, for security, and for stability in the distribution of property by instituting a system of law. Such a group could allow its laws to sanction the persecution of minorities or the protection of slavery without those laws failing in any way to discharge their proper function for that particular group. So Hart's theory of the natural function and core content of law does not provide a standard for evaluating legal systems except in terms of their effectiveness or ineffectiveness in certain limited ways.

Hart thus remains a legal positivist in that he separates questions about what the law is for a particular group from questions about how and why it would be just for that group to act in one way rather than another. (We should of course notice that Hart himself was second to none in asserting that laws ought to be in conformity with justice; justice had no better friend than Herbert Hart.) But there are sufficient grounds for rejecting such versions of legal positivism on just this issue, and these grounds also provide a reason for concluding that Hart's theory of natural law is inadequate. What are they? Consider the kind of claim that spokespersons for any particular legal system seem bound to make to those over whom that system claims jurisdiction. Can we in fact realistically imagine such spokespersons saying, "This legal system is entitled to authority over you, but do not expect to receive justice from it" or perhaps "Considerations of justice happen to be irrelevant in this legal system"? Such remarks are of course entirely intelligible, if uttered either by someone criticizing some particular legal system or by some legal theorist, perhaps one making a point in favor of legal positivism. But such remarks would be markedly odd and puzzling, if uttered by official representatives of some particular legal system. I want to suggest that this puzzling character arises from a characteristic of legal systems that we commonly and rightly use to distinguish them from another very different type of system.

We make laws providing penalties for performing certain types of action and for failing to perform others only if and when we believe that there are good reasons, prior to and independent of our lawmaking, for judging it to be good or right that such types of action should be done or left undone. We also believe that those good reasons by themselves provide sufficient grounds for people in general to perform or to refrain from performing the relevant types of action. When by enacting laws we attach penalties to failure to perform or to refrain from performing, we provide additional grounds for those insufficiently motivated by such good reasons because of some deficiency of character. But our assumption is that anyone whose moral character was sufficiently educated would not need the motivation afforded by those additional sanctions for obeying the law.

Contrast with this a situation where either there are no good reasons for those subjected to it to obey the laws, apart from the penalties prescribed by those same laws, or those who make and enforce the laws do not care whether there are such reasons or not. Such a system is by intention and in effect purely coercive. Those who exercise authority in and through it rely exclusively upon and are seen to rely exclusively upon threats of force and the use of force. One example of such a system is the German Government-General of Occupied Poland between 1939 and 1945; another is that enforced by Al Capone during his reign of terror in parts of Chicago. It is important for theoretical and explanatory as well as moral reasons to distinguish such systems from legal systems. But legal positivists and Hart, insofar as he is a legal positivist, albeit a somewhat atypical one, have in the past ignored the theoretical importance of this distinction.

A contemporary heir of legal positivism, however, need have no difficulty in recognizing the importance of this point; and Neil MacCormick, whose philosophy of law is strongly indebted to Hart's, has spelled it out in some detail[4] speaking of "the essential moral aspiration of law-giving," while also continuing to insist that "for moral reasons we should seek to avoid confusing legal and moral issues, and that we should abstain from using the law simply to enforce whatever we hold to be of moral value".[5] It is worth noting that few, if any, theorists of natural law have held that we should use law "to enforce whatever we hold to be of moral value."[6] This shift in ground—perhaps only in emphasis—from Hart to MacCormick is highly significant. For if the question of how we are to understand the relationship between law and morality is primarily a moral question, then perhaps it is the case that a theory of natural law need be no more than a theory that first explains how the relationship between law and morality is to be understood from some particular systematic moral standpoint and then provides grounds for assenting to that particular standpoint rather than to its rivals. By a systematic moral standpoint I mean not only a set of moral judgments about different types of action, but also a set of philosophical judgments justifying the ascription of authority to the standards to which those moral judgments appeal. Indeed, this type of theory of natural law is now widely current. Consider two very different examples of just such a theory.

For Lloyd L. Weinreb, the relevant understanding of morality is one that focuses on the notion of the personal responsibility of individuals, asking what conditions must be met if someone is to be regarded as a responsible person. His answer begins from the assertion that "rights are specifications of a morally constituted individual," and he goes on to conclude that "[h]aving his rights, a person is responsible for his actions. But also, a person is not (properly regarded as) responsible unless, with respect to the conduct in question, he has his rights."[7] What particular rights are recognized within any particular society will depend on a number of factors. But each of us can appeal to those rights whose recognition accords responsibility to persons in arriving at our own "coherent vision of personal freedom."[8]

Weinreb distinguishes his position from that of legal positivists by arguing that the nature of appeals to rights provides a ground for denying the positivist contention that legal obligation is one thing, moral obligation quite another. We can require of a legal system that it should not disregard the fact "that it is intelligible and correct to regard a person as endowed with rights."[9] Weinreb takes his theory to be a natural law theory, but he has no illusions about how different his standpoint is from that of many ancient and medieval natural law theorists. He is curtly dismissive of the ontological claims about the foundation of law in nature and human nature advanced either by Greek philosophers or by Christian theologians. And he does not think that a sound theory of rights can yield an identifiable set of natural rights that can be justly claimed by any rational person. But Weinreb maintains that in appealing to the nature of human beings as responsible persons as the basis for evaluations of legal obligation, he is extending one strand in traditional natural law theory, and it is hence that he derives his claim to be a natural law theorist.

By contrast, Michael S. Moore begins by asserting not only that the "justness of a norm is necessary to [but not sufficient for] its status as law,"[10] or as he puts it elsewhere, that "law cannot be too unjust and still be law,"[11] but also that moral propositions, including propositions about justice, are to be understood in terms of some version of contemporary moral realism.[12] So he says that "moral facts are as factual as any other fact" and that a moral property "not only gives us reason to believe that it exists, like any other property," but also "gives rational actors an objective reason to act."[13] Being a moral realist is, in Moore's view, a necessary condition for being a natural law theorist. Hence all natural law claims would have to be denied, if moral realism were refuted.

Moore then proceeds to discuss the functions that law has. The feature of his discussion to which we need to attend is his conclusion that the purpose and function of particular statutes must be understood consistently with the thesis that "laws must be obligating to be laws" and that laws "must be just to be obligating."[14] Everything that makes Moore's thesis a natural law thesis depends on his moral realist claim that there is one true objective account of justice. Moore is well aware that radical disagreements about justice in our culture are persistent, and he never suggests that his version of moral realism can provide the resources for resolving such disputed questions. His claim is only that there is indeed some fact of the matter about which the participants in those disputes are disagreeing. And Moore is also well aware that all versions of moral realism, including his, are regarded as highly debatable within contemporary philosophy.

But this conjunction of moral and philosophical disagreements perhaps creates more of a difficulty for his type of standpoint on natural law than he acknowledges. The difficulty is one that arises equally for Weinreb's view and for any other view according to which a right understanding of natural law amounts to no more than this, that legal obligation is partially founded on moral obligation and that the relevant set of moral obligations are those upheld by that particular theorist. As to what that relevant set is and as to why it should carry weight in legal matters, this type of theorist is in unresolvable disagreement, not only with other natural law theorists of the same type, but also with a wide range of exponents of rival contemporary moral philosophies.

Why do such disagreements matter? They matter because they deprive appeals to natural law of what was traditionally one of their two central features, features that gave such appeals their distinctive point and purpose. What the natural law was held to provide was a *shared* and *public* standard, by appeal to which the claims of particular systems of positive law to the allegiance could be evaluated. But a shared and public standard of this kind must be one that is able to secure widespread, if not universal, rational assent. The other central feature of traditional appeals to natural law is that to which I alluded at the outset, that its appeals are to the judgments of plain persons and not to those of professional specialists. Hence a condition of appeals to natural law not being empty and vain is that they should secure the widespread rational assent of plain persons. The moral views advanced by such theorists as Weinreb and Moore notably fail to secure agreement, not only at the level of philosophy by their fellow theorists, but more importantly at the level of practical judgment by many plain persons.

To this it is open to such contemporary theorists to reply that older, traditional forms of natural law theory failed precisely because they too could no longer secure either philosophical or moral assent, so that contemporary theory of this kind is at least in no worse a condition than traditional theory. This is an important rejoinder, for it suggests the possibility that nothing worth calling a natural law theory may be viable anymore. So how should those of us who regard a substantive conception of natural law as indispensable respond to this damaging suggestion? We have, I believe, only one way to proceed.

No theory of natural law can any longer be regarded as defensible that does not satisfy two conditions, over and above its provision of an account of the content of the natural law and of the kind of authority that its precepts possess. Those two conditions are, first, that it must furnish an adequate explanation of the failure of the natural law to secure widespread assent in some cultures, especially in the cultures of advanced modernity such as our own, and, second, that it must identify the grounds for assent to the precepts of the natural law, which are in fact available to all rational persons, even in our own culture, even if those grounds are in very large part either flouted or ignored.

An acknowledgment of the importance of the first of these two conditions, even if not a fully adequate one, has recently been made by some adherents of another very different contemporary influential theory of natural law, that advanced by Germain Grisez and John Finnis. This theory was originally developed in part as an interpretation of the thought of Aquinas. But its differences from Aquinas's standpoint, especially as that standpoint has been understood by most modern Thomists, are as noteworthy as its resemblances. It does not, for example, rely upon an Aristotelian conception of essential human nature, defining goods in terms of the flourishing of such a nature and of the satisfaction of its various, hierarchically ordered inclinations. Instead it defines integral human fulfillment in terms of respect for and the achievement of a set of basic goods. It does not understand human individuals as essentially parts of larger wholes—of the family and of political community, for example—wholes apart from membership in which the human individual is incomplete. According to the Grisez/Finnis theory, individual goods are not understood in terms of a prior notion of the common good. Instead their theory defines the common good in such a way that the common good is nothing other and nothing more than one aspect of the set of fundamental human goods.[15]

The notion of a determinate and well-defined set of basic human goods is thus fundamental to this theory and to its central claim that the goodness of these goods is evident. No intelligent human being is unable to grasp that these particular goods are goods that are to be valued for their own sake and as final ends. John Finnis has listed them as the goods of life, of knowledge, of play, of aesthetic experience, of sociability (friendship), of practical reasonableness, and of religion.[16] These goods are incommensurable; they cannot be weighed against one another. The precepts that enjoin us to respect and to achieve them are exceptionless in what they prohibit as well as in what they enjoin. How do we know which goods to include in the list of goods? Reflection upon each of them and upon our own relevant experiences will, so it is claimed, show that we could not intelligibly deny them their status as such goods. Inquiry into the empirical findings of anthropology and psychology will confirm that others treat these goods as having just this status; and arguments designed to show that these are not basic goods all fail.

These considerations have not in fact seemed compelling to many critics of Grisez and Finnis. Even less compelling has been the claim that, because these goods are incommensurable and because all of them must be respected, no one of them can ever be sacrificed, or needs to be sacrificed, for the sake of another. To such critics, one reply, proposed by Joseph Boyle,[17] is that the errors of those who deny what Grisez, Finnis, and Boyle take to be evident truths about the basic goods and their incommensurability can in fact be plausibly explained. But it is at this point that their theory needs an important resource that Thomists have inherited from Aquinas: Aquinas's revised and unified Aristotelian account of human nature and of human flourishing. Grisez, Finnis, and other exponents of their position emphasize that their view—that our knowledge of human goods is not and cannot be derived from our knowledge of human nature, but rather is knowledge of what is self-evident to intelligent persons—does not mean that the goods of which they speak are not fulfilling of human nature. But they do repudiate all arguments of the form: Human nature's essential and ordered inclinations are such-and-such; the achievement of so-and-so would be the achievement of that to which human nature is inclined and ordered; therefore so-and-so is a good for human nature; and therefore we ought to respect and to achieve so-and-so. Thomists, by contrast, assert what Grisez and Finnis deny, that there are sound arguments of this form, arguments whose conclusions coincide with those uninferred and evident judgments that, in Aquinas's view, every rational person makes for himself, judgments concerning the truth of the precepts of the natural law.[18] But of what advantage is it to Thomists that they are able to invoke a revised Aristotelian conception of human nature in support of their natural law claims?

One answer likely to be suggested is that it can be of no advantage at all but only a source of disadvantage. Since this particular conception of human nature is widely rejected in modern culture, to annex to a set of already controversial theses about natural law an even more controversial claim—that human nature is very much what Aristotle and Aquinas said that it is—may seem to make the cause of commending and justifying the Thomist's view of natural law an even more hopeless one. But this pessimistic response ignores one crucial resource that the Thomist's account of human nature provides. What that account does enable us to understand is why, if the Thomist's view of natural law is true, we should expect that under certain types of circumstance it will be widely rejected. An Aristotelian Thomism has implicit within it a theory of moral and legal error, a theory that explains why what is at one level evident to every plain person may nonetheless be expected to be ignored or flouted by significant numbers of those same plain persons, let alone by legal theorists and moral philosophers.

What then is the Thomistic account of the natural law and how, in a Thomistic view, is that law grounded in human nature? I follow Jacques Maritain's exposition of it in *Man and the State*[19] and *La personne et le bien commun*.[20] Two ideas are central to that exposition. The first is that the precepts of the natural law are those rules of reason which a human being obeys, characteristically without explicitly formulating them, when that human being is functioning normally. Natural law, says Maritain, "is the ideal formula of development of a given being."[21] When we are functioning normally, we find ourselves inclined in certain directions and toward certain ends. The precepts of the natural law tell us what are or would be deviations from those directions.

The second central idea—like the first, it is primarily Aquinas's and only secondarily Maritain's—is that human beings are essentially sociable, that I achieve whatever I achieve as an individual by being and acting as an individual who is bound to others through a variety of familial, social, and political relationships expressed in joint activity aimed at achieving our common good. My good therefore is the good of someone who is a part of an ordered set of social wholes. My own good can only be achieved in and through the achievement of the common good. And the common good is that toward which we are inclined when we are functioning normally and developing as we should be. The precepts of the natural law thus direct us toward the common good.

What then is it to know the natural law, if we are functioning normally and are developing in a way that at least approximates our ideal development? Here I go beyond Maritain, although remaining close to Aquinas, by replying that it is to inquire of ourselves and of each other "What is my good? What is our common good?" and to answer these questions by our actions and our practices as much as by our judgments. The life that expresses our shared human nature is a life of practical inquiry and practical reasoning, and we cannot but presuppose the precepts of the natural law in asking and answering those fundamental questions through our everyday activities and practices. Generally and characteristically, the social relationships through which we are able to learn how to identify our individual and common goods correctly and adequately are those relationships governed and defined by the precepts of the natural law. I have to learn about my good and about the common good from family and friends, but also from others within my own community, from the members of other communities, and from strangers; from those much older than I and from those much younger. But how can I have relationships of adequate cooperative inquiry and learning except with those whom I can trust without qualification? And how can I trust without qualification, unless I recognize myself and others as mutually bound by such precepts as those that enjoin that we *never* do violence of any sort to innocent human life, that we *always* refrain from theft and fraud, that we *always* tell each other the truth, and that we *always* uphold justice in all our relationships. Throughout a life spent asking and attempting to answer questions about our own good, usually practically, but sometimes theoretically, we are recurrently vulnerable to a variety of harms and dangers from other human beings as well as from the vagaries of our natural environment. It is this vulnerability that makes obedience to the natural law necessary for the normal and right functioning of human nature.

Yet what often does and always can function well is always liable to function badly on occasion. Just as functioning well for human beings partially consists in individuals understanding themselves in a particular way, as engaged together with family, friends, and others in a shared discovery of what their individual goods and their common good are, so the malfunctioning of human nature is characteristically expressed in some kind of systematic misunderstanding. In the cultures of advanced modernity, and most notably in contemporary North America, the form often taken by this misunderstanding is one in which the individual is misconceived as someone who has to *choose* for himself what his good is to be. This conception of the sovereignty and central importance of individual choice is generated by several different but mutually reinforcing features of our dominant contemporary social and moral modes. Consider just one of these.

During our upbringing, morality is commonly presented to us in terms of two distinct sets of principles, self-regarding principles and other-regarding principles.

The individual is therefore commonly taught to ask not, "How should we in our familial and communal relationships act together?" but "How far should I regard only the promotion of my own happiness and the protection of my own rights, and how far should I also have regard for the happiness of others and the rights of others?" Underlying this latter question is a conception of society as primarily constituted, not as a web of familial and communal relationships, but as a set of individuals to each of whom everyone else is an 'other.' Once social life is thus conceived, individuals are bound to pose the question of how they are to decide between the competing claims of the self and of others. But there is in fact no rational way to make that decision, as we should have learned from Henry Sidgwick long since. There are only sets of competing principles between whose rival claims individuals each have to make their own choice. So individual choice itself becomes morally sovereign.

On a Thomistic view, this is not surprising. On that view, individuals who have not or not yet developed an adequate conception of the good, perhaps because through social mischance they have had no opportunity to do so, and who, perhaps because of miseducation, have not or not yet recognized themselves as engaged in a cooperative attempt to discover the human good, can be expected to find themselves confronted by the competing claims of a variety of passions and appetites, claims that, lacking an adequate conception of the good, they do not and cannot as yet know how to order. If they then try to decide between those competing claims, without joining in action and inquiry with others, in a way that would require them to attend practically to the injunctions of the natural law—that is, if they try to decide between those competing claims from the standpoint of an isolated nonsocial individual for whom there can be no such thing as the common good—then they will find themselves with no resource for decision, beyond their own individual choices. On a Thomistic view, it is to be expected that under certain social conditions in which adequate moral education is unavailable, the place of individual choice in the moral life will be misunderstood in precisely the way it has been misunderstood in the dominant cultures of advanced modernity.

The exercise of individual choice thus understood, that is, not choice as governed by principles but choice as prior to and determining our principles, is often identified in the contemporary world with the exercise of liberty. Liberty is therefore thought to be threatened whenever it is suggested that the principles that ought to govern over our actions are not in fact principles that are up to us to choose, but principles that we need to discover. But since a Thomistic understanding of natural law commits those who possess it to asserting that human nature is such that rational practical principles are antecedent to and govern choice in rational well-functioning human beings, and that therefore those principles have to be discovered, not chosen, any defense of a Thomistic understanding of natural law is very easily construed as a threat to liberty.

While the Senate was engaged in considering the nomination of Clarence Thomas to the Supreme Court, a rumor circulated that Thomas held something close to a Thomistic view of natural law—a rumor for which there was and is no foundation whatsoever in any judgments of Justice Thomas—and Senator Joseph Biden at once expressed the fear "that natural law dictates morality to us, instead of leaving matters to individual choice."[22] Senator Biden's instantaneous reaction, presupposing as it did widespread agreement among the general public with his own view, was a symptom of just that kind of social and moral attitude that needs to be understood in Thomistic terms.

Senator Biden, of course, was correct in supposing that he was articulating what would be felt—and 'felt' is the right word—by a very large number of North Americans. Such modern persons are all too likely to reject any Thomistic understanding of natural law, and most of all what that understanding, or more fundamentally the account of human nature upon which it relies, says to them about their own condition, as one giving expression to a distorted view of the moral life. It therefore turns out to be the case, as I wrote earlier, that if my arguments are sound and my conclusions are true, then many people will reject them. Notice, however, that for so doing you will pay a certain price.

What these people will have deprived themselves of is the only account of natural law that not only is able to explain its own rejection, but also justifies plain persons in regarding themselves as already having within themselves the resources afforded by a knowledge of fundamental law, resources by means of which they can judge the claims to jurisdiction over them of any system of positive law. In the United States today, we inhabit a society in which a system of positive law with two salient characteristics has been developed. At a variety of points, it invades the lives of plain persons, and its tangled complexities are such that it often leaves those plain persons no alternative but to put themselves into the hands of lawyers. It is notorious that ours has become a society of incessant litigation, in which plain persons can all too rarely hope to resolve matters of dispute by appeal among themselves to evident and agreed moral principles—for the loss of an adequate understanding of the natural law has resulted in a widespread belief that there are no such principles—but instead must resort to the courts and therefore to lawyers. Of course, in any society, there cannot but be some need for positive law and for litigation as a last resort. But it is an index of great moral deprivation in a culture when litigation so often becomes a first resort. Perhaps it has done so because the dominant culture of North American modernity is inimical to any adequate conception of the natural law.[23]

ENDNOTES

1. H. L. A. Hart, chap. 9, sec. 2 in *The Concept of Law* (Oxford: Clarendon Press, 1960).

2. Ibid., 195.

3. H. L. A. Hart, "Are There Any Natural Rights?" *Philosophical Review* 64, (1955): 175–91.

4. Neil MacCormick, "Natural Law and the Separation of Law and Morals" in *Natural Law Theory: Contemporary Essays*, ed. R. P. George (Oxford: Clarendon Press, 1992), 118.

5. p. 129.

6. See on this Aquinas, *Summa Theologiae* 1a–2a, q. 96, a. 2.

7. Lloyd L. Weinreb, "Natural Law and Rights" in *Natural Law Theory: Contemporary Essays*, 290–91. See also L. L. Weinreb, *Natural Law and Justice* (Cambridge, Mass.: Harvard University Press, 1987).

8. Weinreb, "Natural Law and Rights," 297.

9. Ibid., 298–299.

10. Michael S. Moore, "Law as a Functional Kind" in *Natural Law Theory: Contemporary Essays*, 198.

11. Ibid., 199.

12. Ibid., 190–192.

13. Ibid., 195–196.

14. Ibid., 226–227.

15. Germain Grisez, *The Way of the Lord Jesus*, vol. 1, *Christian Moral Principles* (Quincy, Ill.: Franciscan Herald Press, 1983), 270.

16. John Finnis, *Natural Law and Natural Rights* (Oxford: Clarendon Press, 1980), 85–90.

17. Joseph Boyle, "Natural Law and the Ethics of Traditions" in *Natural Law Theory: Contemporary Essays*, 3–30.

18. For an exposition and defense of what Grisez and Finnis say about human nature, see R. P. George, "Natural Law and Human Nature" in *Natural Law Theory: Contemporary Essays*, 31–41.

19. Jacques Maritain, *Man and the State* (Chicago: University of Chicago Press, 1951), 84–94.

20. Maritain, *La personne et le bien commun* (Paris: Brouwer, 1947), 44–56.

21. Maritain, *Man and the State*, 88.

22. *Washington Post*, 8 September 1991.

23. I am indebted to Martin P. Golding and Paul Weithman for constructive criticisms of earlier drafts of this essay.

Part II

Topics in Natural Law
Theory

Chapter 6

What Dignity Means

VIRGINIA BLACK

> *Natural law has primacy in all things, both in time and in dignity. For it began with the beginning of the rational creature and does not vary with time. It stands immutable.*
>
> —*Gratian*

Losing one's dignity is not difficult to imagine. In Western cartoon culture, slipping on a banana peel is the ultimate example. This kind of losing one's dignity is called "being undignified." If personal poise evokes the respect that goes by the name "dignified," and if slipping on a banana peel makes one lose one's poise, then one loses one's dignity as well, and so is "undignified."

In his book *Beyond Freedom and Dignity*, the famous behavioral psychologist B. F. Skinner has a funny paragraph about losing one's dignity.

> The general does his best to maintain his dignity while riding in a jeep over rough terrain, and the flute player continues to play although a fly crawls

over his face. We try not to sneeze or laugh on
solemn occasions, and after making an embarrassing
mistake we try to act as if we had not done so . . . we
eat daintily though ravenous . . . and we risk a burn
by slowly putting down a hot plate. (Dr. Johnson
questioned the value of this: spewing out a mouth-
ful of hot potato, he exclaimed to his astonished
companions, "A fool would have swallowed it!")[1]

We can think of examples of lost dignity more trau-
matic than a fly crawling over our face when we're trying
to play an instrument. In quarreling with parents or
friends, we can lose our dignity through excessive anger
that afterwards we realize was unjustified. Career uncertainties can make us lose our dignity—we are out of sorts
if we go too long without really knowing what we're aim-
ing at or whether there's a chance to reach these aims,
especially if our friends have their own career aspirations
worked out. Dating uncertainties can lack dignity. So can
unsettling personal finances—they can make us feel
undignified, especially if our friends seem to have
enough to meet their needs.

When questioned, some of my students thought dignity meant standing up for one's beliefs, having no
shame in one's actions, not being made a fool of, and not
answering embarrassing questions. I suppose any time
we're in some undefined transition period, we feel some
degree of awkwardness and indignity. All these
instances, though, refer to our feelings. They are
instances of what we can call lack of dignity from a psychological perspective. They refer back, I think, to lack of
self-confidence. Such instances touch our sense of unity
and capability; we can *feel* whether or not we're confident

and decisive and at-one. This kind of dignity, or lack of it, is empirical because it's sensory and can be described. Shortly we shall contrast empirical dignity with moral dignity and its opposite: being treated by others who ignore or abuse our moral dignity.

Psychological or empirical "undignity," though, has a bearing on moral dignity. Lacking a sense of ourselves and our capacities and strengths means lacking boundaries, not knowing our limits and structures, and this can play into our moral choices. An unhealthy ego cannot even make moral choices for it cannot know when its will is free and rational.

This is the place to mention that other psychological dimension, "false dignity." The mistake arises from ignorance as to what true dignity is, from thinking that undignified means lacking in dignity, so that anything that looks undignified is avoided at all cost. The unfortunate outcome is that people who fear being undignified lose their dignity anyway, trying to avoid awkward situations, often by deceiving themselves and thereby thinking they're also deceiving others. Consider a Polish gentleman I know. We might say of him because of the way he handles himself, "He's a very dignified person." He smokes cigarettes off the end of a very long holder, stands tall like a straight rod, and makes an excuse to go around kissing the ladies' hands at all the international conventions. It is hard to know whether deceit or genuine cultural innocence inhabits this man.

False dignity is having no income, yet refusing to take a menial job in the interim, with "menial," of course, being defined by the person himself, for nothing is inherently menial if we respect the dignity of work. False dignity is taking offense at the slightest remark. It is feeling humiliated when one is not introduced in the right away or given the credit one thinks one deserves. False dignity is substituting what money will buy for developing one's character, reading the book at the top of the list instead of a book one would enjoy, and giving a dinner party only to show off whom you know or where your dishes came from. False dignity is making sure your Rolex is showing on your wrist.

Behind false dignity is an attitude of one-upmanship. It presupposes that other people do not regard you highly, and so it becomes necessary, because the inside feeling is so low, to put on the outer garments of respectability— that is to say, to avoid at all costs appearing undignified by one's own subjective measure of this trait, tied superficially only to the appearances of things.

Let us look a little longer at the various meanings of dignity already resident in our vocabulary and see where they lead. Let us explore their "departments"— Ralph McInerny's term for the various kinds of concrete goods we know—so as to make clear what the abstract word "dignity" refers to when we employ it in particular situations.

Being a speaker of natural English since childhood, I had some idea, even though vague, of what dignity means. Here are some of the things I heard when I kept my ears and eyes open for the English vernacular.

"The last decade," said Bill Clinton (when he was the Democratic presidential candidate), "took the dignity out of the blue collar worker."

"The poor are struggling with dignity." (I heard this on TV.)

A student of mine said, "Dignity plays a role in all my decisions." And another said, "I have dignity in my family and where I come from."

"Prejudice," someone said, "demeans the other's dignity." And another statement someone offered was, "Dignity is found in the ability to endure suffering courageously."

A correspondent of mine thought the Clarence Thomas hearings lacked dignity. And then he went on to say, "Even a murderer or a rapist has a right to his dignity and a clear name."

Someone used this expression: Communism is ". . . the total loss of dignity visited upon the population." Of course I agree.

Finally, here is a sample of the use of dignity from a context no one would guess. "As we reflect on our 1992 resolutions to continue to find more ways to respect nature and human dignity, we want to thank you . . ." This is an ad! It comes from a very sophisticated toothpaste manufacturer called Tom's, and Tom makes his toothpaste of pure, natural ingredients up in Kennebunkport, Maine.

Our survey would not be complete if we did not acknowledge that those who think more profoundly about the ideas that play on the edges of common knowledge, and so the ideas that often become central to our thinking about various matters, influence us mightily. "Dignity," in fact, has become so familiar a term and so pervasive in the media, it is difficult not to find it spinning around in all kinds of texts having to do with morals, religion, law, politics, and society in general. Here, then, are a few uses of the term from philosophers and legal thinkers who have dipped into the philosophic bottle.

"[T]he death penalty must comport with the basic concept of human dignity at the core of the [Eighth] Amendment," reads the Supreme Court's minority opinion in *Gregg v. Georgia* (on interpreting the cruel and unusual punishment clause regarding whether capital punishment is constitutional). Writing for the minority, Justice Thurgood Marshall put it this way: ". . . the objective in imposing it must be [consistent] with our respect for the dignity of [other] men. . . . [Capital punishment] has as its very basis the total denial of the wrongdoer's dignity and worth."[2]

In his book *Natural Law,* John Finnis holds that human action has dignity because human acting is acting for a reason, that is, deliberately with an end in mind.

Philosopher Martin Schlag, a young Austrian, believes that dignity is a "first principle." "If dignity is negated, the legal system is negated." These are powerful words.[3]

And Mary Ann Glendon, Harvard law professor, in her important book *Rights Talk,* refers to ". . . the dignity and uniqueness of every single human person [within] the social nature of human life."[4]

Here is one more, this one very different. I find it poignant and sad. "I survived in concentration camp because I lost my dignity. I didn't try any longer to keep up my dignity." This poor man had lost everything.

Social policy makers use "dignity" in this way, neither as a psychological nor moral term, but referring only to externalities. They claim that people live without dignity when they're homeless, unclothed, or uneducated, and ignored by society. And so it follows that when this concentration camp victim lost a normal and hospitable environment, and lost his political freedom, he believed he also lost his dignity. Tragically, he lost something within himself too. He lost his incentive and his will to try even to hang onto his dignity.

What is this dignity that we try to hang on to, no matter what? We will come to this. But I think we have to acknowledge merit in the view that our circumstances, that externalities, do sometimes relate to dignity, even though indirectly. Believing that people's circumstances count tends to draw our attention to compassion for our fellow beings, because their worldly condition is often exactly what we must motivate ourselves to try to repair, like the medical healing Albert Schweitzer did in Africa and Mother Teresa did in India, and like refugee and disaster workers do everywhere. These are meaningful pursuits, and the expression "restoring people's dignity" is appropriate to them. The thought humbles us: but for luck and contingencies over which we have little control—and but for God—any of us could be destitute.

I do not think we exercise compassion appropriately toward people's disadvantaged worldly conditions, however, when we institute vast social policies in order to "dignify man," because these policies seldom work. Government is good at protecting us, someone said, but not good at all at providing for us. Government must be regarded as a last-ditch effort, the end-of-the-line used only when social organizations, those thousands and thousands of service and aid societies created by people's voluntary associations, fail to resolve the problem. Political programs enhance the staying power and self-aggrandizement of the politicians who work these schemes. Over time they deteriorate and tend to make conditions worse.

I think the way to dignify the disadvantaged is to believe William James when he writes, "I am done with great institutions and big success, and I am for those tiny, invisible . . . moral forces that work from individual to individual." But this wretched concentration camp prisoner, ignored in both his physical and spiritual needs, and no doubt tortured as well, thought of his dignity in just the opposite way: If he could get himself to forget his dignity and not try to resurrect it, he thought he might survive, and this is what he most wanted to do. He rejected one of our common meanings of dignity, which is to respect oneself no matter what one's situation. He thought dignity is what is left over when your self-respect is *taken away from you*. And in one sense of "dignity," it surely can be taken away from you when your circumstances are reduced to those of a pig.

B. F. Skinner would probably approve of this government-policy approach to dignity because it externalizes everything through what he calls "contingencies of reinforcement," as if inexorable causal lines run from an improved bathroom faucet in a leaky tenement, as cause, to our happiness and dignity, as effect.[5] There is a connection, I believe, between aesthetic living surroundings and a sense of well-being, but I do not think "dignity" is the right word to describe this condition, or euphoria quite what is meant by moral dignity. There are too many nasty people living in aesthetic living surroundings—and no one has identified a single law of nature in which environmental reinforcements regularly and singularly bring about in ourselves or anyone else a dependable, predictable, human action.

When Rodney King, suspected by the police of reckless driving, was taken forcibly out of his car and so mercilessly kicked and clubbed, I think people felt that something about his dignity was also mercilessly abused. All kinds of "outside-of-us" things—slander, cruel gossip, public humiliation, unjust punishment, legal conviction paraded in public—all of these ego-shattering events and circumstances do have some relationship to our dignity, even though there is another meaning of the word "dignity" which, as someone said, "cannot be taken away." As another of my students explained, "Dignity is that which is held onto when everything else is lost."

There is another way to avoid dignity, and it, too, is unfortunate. An African-American man I heard in a television documentary on the Civil War, talking about slavery, said, "If you tried to show normal dignity, you were accused of being uppity."

I want now to discuss another meaning of dignity referred to only briefly above. It has persisted through time; its meaning is still in use, and it relates closely, as we shall see, to inherent moral dignity, which we will discuss later. During the Roman Republic, *dignitas* was a term of praise for the high and mighty, primarily for the patrician senators and others holding political office or inherited status. It was a role term, an institutional term, denoting honorary position or office—fully the contrary condition of our wretched prisoner, the lowest of the low.

Dignitas connoted as well—and significantly—possessing a certain set of virtues. We can call them Stoic virtues for shorthand since some of the Stoic philosophers articulated, systematized, and placed great emphasis on them, and Roman gentlemen preparing themselves for political and legal office educated themselves through studying the Stoics. (The Stoic philosophers had no monopoly on the virtues of dignity, however, for Confucius had talked about dignity as uprightness in the ruler 300 years earlier.) These virtues had, in a sense, to be earned; acknowledging their presence was justified if they were merited by the actual conduct expected of a man of honor. So besides status and the duties that political office carried with it, *dignitas* quite naturally connoted the virtues that conscientiously carrying out these duties required: personal responsibility, sacrifice, loyalty, self-discipline, trust, good faith, dependability, reasonableness, honesty, and so on—traits we can sum up as giving someone personal integrity.

Dignitas therefore meant something earned and hence bestowed only when merited. In the sense of something earned or merited through achievement, dignity is a very significant idea. Having dignity, in this meaning, is receiving what is deserved, after deserving what is to be received. And earning or deserving something and not getting it is suffering one's dignity to be neglected or abused. Such a condition is demeaning. To win a contest and have the honor or the prize withheld from one, or given to someone else, is degrading—it is a loss of face, of dignity.

But so, too, is receiving praise or an award that one does not earn. Under this condition, the shame one feels is psychological. But when we inquire why one feels this shame, moral meaning inevitably appears: Lacking integrity toward the rules, lacking cooperation or personal effort, or failing to achieve the goal, we simply have not earned it.

In its modern philosophical origin, dignity is tied to the thought of Immanuel Kant, the eighteenth-century German moral philosopher who used the idea of dignity synonymously with "respect." He meant by it "the inherent worth of persons," a central idea developed in his well-known *Foundations of the Metaphysics of Morals.* "So act," he wrote, "as to treat humanity . . . as an end withal, never as a means only."[6] One does not have, in other words, to be useful to anyone, or even to oneself, to have inherent moral worth, that is, dignity. Dignity and meaning in one's life transcend mere usefulness. Kant wrote:

> Socrates lived in a state of wretchedness; his circumstances were worthless; but though his circumstances were so ill-conditioned, yet he himself was of the highest value. Even though we sacrifice all life's amenities we can make up for their loss and sustain approval by maintaining the worth of our humanity. We may have lost everything else and yet still retain our inherent worth.[7]

Clearly, Kant rejects that other idea noted above, namely, that our worldly state determines, even to a small extent, our dignity. And so he calls moral dignity "inherent." It belongs intimately to the person and is an attribute of our "interior" self. Nothing external to us qualifies our inherent dignity. No worldly condition, however demeaning, degrades our inherent dignity.

This idea of being inherent is not difficult to grasp; it simply denies that psychological states or externalities, whatever they be, define or diminish our dignity. Low circumstances neither cause nor justify diminishment of our dignity because dignity is always there, no matter what happens. Nor does an elevated social status enhance our dignity—we have no more or less dignity than the next person. Likewise a low mood or diminishing self-esteem does not define our dignity. The idea that dignity is inherent to our person rules out expedience, self-serving, and instrumentality as reasons for others treating us in a certain way. It denies that these are motives for humane treatment, and it denies that they are motives for anything other than humane treatment. Inherent dignity also rules out mere agreement, or social consensus, as a reason for treating people humanely. Like the inalienability of our rights, the inherent nature of our dignity attaches to our persons as persons. But inherent dignity is stronger than inalienability because the latter idea can be compromised or conditioned if two or more inalienable rights come into conflict. Inherent dignity comes into conflict with nothing because, like truth, it is whole and indivisible. It is a unitary idea; no competitors are possible.

Now that inherent dignity has been made explicit, given systematic treatment within the body of Kant's ethical philosophy and used by nearly every moral philosopher who came after him as something that is within us without qualification, affixed to our nature and to ourselves as agents of our moral actions, dignity will never, I think, disappear from the literature. Too much use is now made of the term. It has affixed itself to pervasive moral and legal argumentation.

It is this idea of inherent moral worth with which we have to come to terms. It carries with it the notion of universality; moral necessity demands that we ascribe or impute inherent dignity to all persons, that is, impute it to persons as equals because reasoning recognizes our common capacity for moral agency and moral responsibility, and our common capacity to benefit from the benevolence of others and to return this benevolence in service to or respect for others. No good reason can be given for excluding any person from these goods because treating others humanely rests minimally on something we cannot deny. This is our common nature. And so the moral equality that inherent dignity logically entails ignores people's differentiating psychologies and circumstances. By the definition of "inherent dignity," no one, not even he who lives in up-beat quarters, enjoys high status, has accomplished his ends, or deserves the praise of millions has more dignity than another.

Our lives are so easily degraded—by others, by the powerful, by the state—that we need something that cannot be touched, tarnished in the least, or lost. Our inherent moral worth is antecedent to government and to everything else except our existence; and so, spelling it out, our inherent dignity implies human beings' fundamental rights, those that governments—and every party—are morally obligated to respect. Because of our inherent dignity, we are, as morally equal persons, rights-holders. To talk about persons having rights makes no sense unless moral value is antecedently attached to our very personhood. Inherent dignity—our equal individual worth—is our human rights in implicit, abbreviated form: the right, in short, to be treated with respect. It encompasses having our own rights respected and it also encompasses our moral obligation to see that others' rights are respected.

Some people have denied that this idea of inherent worth has meaning. B. F. Skinner is one of these deniers. Let us face his challenge. What exactly is it, he asks, to take that concept called worth and apply it to persons when there is no clear measure or standard involved by which to measure worth? We know what monetary worth means. We know what an official status may be worth. We know what the worth of some creative production is, especially if criteria have been set out for it. We know when, through a contract, something is owed to someone. But what does that ephemeral "moral worth" mean? And what does it mean to say that our dignity is "inherent"? In what contexts is this disembodied, abstract ascription meaningful? By what logic, asks Skinner, do we impute a moral quality to a mere creature of nature? When should we, and to whom? And to do what? And of what use is it?

I believe the answer to Skinner and to others, such as materialists who disbelieve in the reality of anything intangible and nonsensory (and that certainly includes morality) lies in an elucidation of both ideal and effective rights as criticisms and as legal weapons against powers that throughout history have wreaked havoc upon the lives of ordinary people, like the concentration camp victim who could live only by forgetting his dignity. Everyone can witness the consequences of rights abuses. The story of human rights abuses is history itself. And everyone can discern an increasing humaneness in moral ideas and their influence as we have moved through time, from the crudities and evils of ancient times—random, mindless, barbaric—to our present upset even about trees and animals. Certainly there are plateaus and setbacks in which we seem not to be making moral progress. But ideas have consequences, and now we have the ideas. Today one is expected to apologize if he treats others without dignity.

We have need of this greater humaneness, for I think a global phenomenon is just ahead of us—and I do not mean an Armageddon—for which we will need strenuous zeal to draw upon whatever sense of the equal dignity of persons we can conceive or will to exist. I will explain what I think this phenomenon is at the end.

Almost two centuries after Kant, one of his students, the ethical scholar Leonard Nelson, also a German and one of the only philosophers to renounce Hitler and leave Germany as soon as he was able, translated Kant's injunction about not using other people ulteriorly as means, as instruments to our own ends, like this:

> We ascribe dignity to whatever the law protects from our discretion. Consequently, the dignity of the person is the condition to which the moral law restricts our action. Subjection of our will to the condition that the dignity of the person must be upheld is what we call "respect." Hence, we may express the condition we have just established in the form of this imperative: "Respect personal dignity!" I call this postulate "the principle of personal dignity."[8]

Nelson makes human dignity a first principle—inviolable. Upon it, everything moral about our actions toward other persons rests. Then Nelson goes on to insist that having interests is not enough even to justify our being treated as beings with equal rights. It is only our "true interests" that count. That is, it is *proper values* that count. It is not enough to have the capacity or power, or even the right, to choose what we want or desire. To have a natural right, says Nelson, we must choose *worthy things*. We must not just desire things but desire *desirable* things—at least in one sense of the term "right." Professor Edward McLean thinks so too. In the article "Natural Law as the Defense for Human Life and Dignity," he has written that abstract rights alone cannot defend dignity. Liberty alone allows us to do anything we want to do. This is not what dignity means.[9]

The important thing about identifying personal freedom with natural law is not what our freedom enables us to do. It is what freedom logically implies. It implies responsibility for our choices and commitments. But in any case, people without even personal freedom may yet be proper subjects of inherent dignity. Psychopaths, criminals, babies, and old men with Alzheimer's disease have dignity in the moral sense—and these beings have no capacity rationally to choose anything. They even have no coherent, stable sense of self-individuation. Prisoners, victims of oppression, and victims of tragic circumstances and degrading life situations also have inherent dignity; and these beings not only suffer undignified circumstances, they do not even have the political liberty to try to do something about their circumstances.

So it may be true that natural rights depend to some extent on persons choosing wise values, that is to say, on persons choosing and acting on natural law, which furnishes the necessary restraint on their actions. Doing this is respecting others' dignity. But the inherent dignity of all persons equally that they are respecting depends, as we saw, on nothing.

A fifteenth-century medieval philosopher, Giovanni Pico della Mirandola, a count and churchman, when he was not yet even thirty years old, wrote a short treatise that he called "Oration on the Dignity of Man." Pico got into trouble with the Church because he denied that man had any fixed character. This is Christian heresy. If man has no nature, then God did not create man after His own essence. What then is man? And what is his relation to God? "Man is a creature of indeterminate nature," wrote Pico. Man is completely free. "He determines by free choice his [own] form and value." But Pico was not an Existentialist, affirming the morality only of personal freedom and denying the existence of objective moral truth. Clearly, man has an obligation to pursue moral truth. Moral truth, said Pico, is man's "obligation to make the best possible choices and to elevate himself to the life of angels." We, in other words, are to aspire to the godly life as we understand it. Moral freedom is understood as our obligation to aspire upward, but it is the aspiration that imparts dignity to life.[10]

Let us draw some conclusions regarding the definition of dignity. "Dignity" is a many-sided word. This may be good, because we want to do so many things with it; dignity plays such an important and pervasive role in our thinking about ourselves and others, and about the meaning and value of life. "Dignity's" plurality of meanings is bound to an extent by the contexts in which the word is found and the linguistic history through which these contexts of usage evolved. But because of these multiple meanings, some of them seem contradictory. How can this be?

We say, for instance, that our circumstances can lack dignity and yet dignity is something we never lose no matter what. We say that our dignity can be abused and yet it can never be taken away from us. We say that dignity must be earned to be received, and yet however lowly, ineffective, and undeserving we are, we still retain dignity. One of my students said, "Buying a house and owning a car helped build my dignity." But another, contrariwise, said, "Some people compromise their dignity for material gains." The concentration camp victim found it best not to think about his dignity, yet another prisoner of war kept himself going by remembering that he still had something left that no one could take away: his dignity.

Consider the familiar arguments for and against the right to help decide one's time of death. Both positions make contradictory statements by using "dignity" in opposite ways. Remember the Nancy Cruzan case in 1988. She was alleged to have a right "to refuse...artificial death prolonging procedures." Advocates of euthanasia talk about the indignity of suffering or of maintaining life under the undignified conditions of being hooked up to artificial tubes when we know death is imminent. Their persuasive literature reads, "Every person has the precious right to a dignified, timely, pain-free death."[11] Opponents talk about the dignity of living despite suffering, because, they argue, our death is something God decides. Advocates are looking at the external circumstances. Opponents are looking at what they believe is inherent and unchanging in the person.

Looking carefully at all these meanings of dignity, we discover that they can be classified in at least a rough-and-ready way. (1) There are what we can call *empirical meanings* that by and large have to do with how people feel about their dignity and its abuse and about the tangible circumstances people find themselves in. (2) There are what we might call *semi-empirical meanings*. These have to do not with our circumstances but with what we earn or deserve. I use *semi-empirical* because in describing why we have earned something, we report our actual efforts and visible accomplishments. But the idea of *deserving something because we have earned it* points at the same time to what we think is of value and worth. In these contexts, "dignity" takes on both empirical and valuative meaning at once. We shall see that the availability of this double meaning is important, for it allows us to impart an empirical element to an otherwise abstract moral idea, that of inherent dignity. It brings together moral meaning with reality. (3) There is an *institutional meaning* of dignity, too, that has to do with status or office, as the term *dignitas* and its modern ramifications designate. (4) Finally, there are the *purely moral meanings* of "dignity." One is virtue, and we stressed the classical virtues associated with philosophic Stoicism because this is one moral meaning associated with dignity. The other moral meaning is inherent dignity. This is the sense of dignity that nothing whatsoever, under any circumstances that we can think of, can discredit. We saw that this meaning of dignity implies freedom from interference in our daily, ordinary, and nonharmful pursuits, and freedom from abuse of our person. Ascribed to us for being the kinds of beings we are, human beings, it is the source and font of the unity of morals and the sacredness of individual personality.

Having done the definitional homework, I can proceed to my own contribution, to what I believe to be true and important about dignity and the reasons why I think this belief is true.

We have recognized half a dozen or so ideas about dignity already lodged in our everyday speech. I think I can tie some of these ideas together and bring unity to them, because some ideas about dignity bear critical relations to others. By introducing into our survey of dignity what I call a *bridging concept,* we can perhaps reach an overarching perspective that organizes and elevates our understanding. We have dignity—we keep our dignity, or we do not lose our dignity—when we show dignity to others. This is the idea about dignity that I'd like to consider. I call it *reflexive dignity.*

When we consider how it operates on us psychologically and morally, inherent dignity is a kind of reflexive idea itself: it harkens back to the giver. Even while it is inherent in us, when we ascribe dignity properly to other beings by respecting others' rights, showing them hospitality, relieving their distress, and so on, we receive in return more dignity ourselves. And to acknowledge another's dignity and receive it, we do not even need to have a clear sense of "self." We owe dignity to other beings even when *they* lack a clear sense of self. We owe it, in short, to everyone. And when we recognize the inherent dignity of others, we receive it back even if *we* do not have a clear idea of our own self, and even if we have not been treated reciprocally with dignity.

We receive dignity even if sometimes we do not think or know that we are receiving it. Sometimes we receive dignity even when we think we're being denied dignity or when we think that some of the things other persons do defy our dignity—neglect it, harm it, withhold it, bruise and abuse it. Drawing upon the idea of dignity as something we have earned or merited through moral action imparts to our moral actions what we called before an empirical element, because we can see, and so can others, what we have done. Certain parts of actions—not, of course, our motives or purposes—can be observed. And so too, often, can the results of our actions. Also, the feeling of being uplifted by moral action, our own and that of others, is a sensory, though subjective, state; and so again, both our effort to do right toward others and the exhilaration we often feel upon doing so, are knowable through our introspective sense. Even our disappointment upon not receiving the dignity we believe is our due, being a psychological condition, is an empirical fact.

Coupling these facts about ourselves with those very basic notions of justice, that is, with the idea of what is due or what we have merited or earned, we find we cannot fully separate the factual, empirical element from the moral element of dignity. They belong together, almost like a single idea.

Reflexive dignity is a demand on us to go outside our subjectivity and empathize with the subjectivity of the other person—of the "thou"—treating that person with respect as an equal, and to be especially solicitous about doing this when that person's way of life, his conduct, his beliefs and values, differ from our own. Patience and tolerance are ways of showing dignity to others even when their actions and values differ radically from our own.

Reflexive dignity comes into existence when we treat others as ends, as worthy beings in themselves; when we assume an absolute equality of persons all the way from the *dignitas* of the senator to the homeless, helpless being dwelling in a cardboard box under the town bridge; when we reverse roles and imagine ourselves on the receiving end as the object of others' treatment of us; when we exercise the Stoic virtues even though we are not patricians and these virtuous traits are not reciprocated; when we show forgiveness and compassion in placing understanding before explaining; when we extend hospitality, like the almost holy Huguenots of Le Chambon in France during World War II, who, at great risk to themselves, housed and rendered hospitality to about 6,000 Jewish orphans whose parents had been murdered in the brutalizing Nazi killing camps of central Europe. And always, always—as spoken by that deep thinker Václav Havel, former president of the Czech Republic—show ". . . humility in the face of the mysterious order of Being."[12]

Reflexive dignity, by definition, means that our dignity, in this context and with respect to this special meaning, *is a matter of degree.* It rests on, and presumes, that we and all others have inherent dignity, and this is absolute, not a matter of degree at all. But to the extent that we acknowledge and act on the inherent dignity of others, *so much* as we show to others, *so much—to that degree*—we receive back. Thus do we receive—and keep, or lose—our dignity. Our inherent dignity we never lose. But the dignity that reflexively accrues to us upon acting toward others as if *they* had inherent dignity can be lessened or lost. Thus, reflexive dignity is earned. It is earned in accordance with, and is conditioned upon, the respect we show for the inherent dignity of the other person. If we gain reflexive dignity in proportion as we do good, we lose it in proportion as we do wrong.

It is hard for me to imagine anyone exemplifying the virtuous traits, habits, and conduct that I have described, who would not, in turn, feel an enormous sense of dignity, uprightness, self-worth, and self-respect within himself. And not in a self-righteous way, but in a humble way, almost wondering what he could do next to uphold the inherent dignity of another person. There is a sense that with reflexive dignity—the kind of dignity that grows or diminishes, increases or disappears; the dignity that can be kept or lost—we discover a relationship to that other important meaning of dignity that refers to what is merited or earned by our accomplishments. In the case of reflexive dignity, our accomplishments are measured by how well we respect the transcendence of a person by treating him as someone with inviolable worth. But instead of earning a gold star, a blue ribbon, or a prize for our accomplishment, we earn back a measure of dignity.

The principle of reflexive dignity is reflected in that poignant, biblical message in Leviticus: "The stranger that sojourneth with you shall be unto you as the home-born among you, and thou shalt love him as thyself." Here is a clear example of reflexive dignity, and one with an empirical counterpart; for psychologists have vindicated—and our own experience confirms—that those whom we care for and love tend to care for and love us in return.

There is something else, I think, that helps us define both inherent dignity and the reflexive dignity that I believe rests on inherent dignity, neither being complete without the other. This is what we can call the spiritual, or transcendent, dimension of dignity that some people associate with religion. The heart of it is allegiance to some higher, unitary reality.

I suppose we can say that this spiritual or transcendent concept of dignity, if not explicit in language, is represented by the ancient—almost 25,000-year-old—tombstone of a slave that was found in Egypt. The master presumably had inscribed on the stone that his slave had been a good man. Why should anyone have cared to do this unless dignity or some sort of transcendent glorification was recognized even in the slave in his wretched earthly condition, especially after death when nothing resembling gratitude can be shown? Even subservience for the flattery of being said to be good cannot be shown. Some early, primitive burial sites reflect respect for the bodies of the dead; their burial positions are tenderly laid out, and remnants of bouquets of flowers appear.

The Bible is full of allusions to the dignity of man, even when the term is not used. When the Hebrews insisted that the opening flaps of their tents not be facing each other, the privacy that was intended reflects an idea of dignity. In Deuteronomy, we can readily read the dignity of the individual into the equitable procedural rules for the administration of justice. And when Isaiah tells the errant Hebrew people that if they cannot follow God's law, then he will put the law in their hearts, isn't this an idea of the dignity of the individual? Laws and rules are meant for groups—they evolve out of our interpersonal relations and customs—but the heart is a private matter and belongs to individuals. The individual has to put this social commodity called the law in his heart.

Belonging to *individuals*, this responsibility to conform to the moral law is reflexive dignity because responsibility is something returned to us: it is something we cannot get rid of after we have chosen to act in a certain way. It belongs to us in the way that our actions belong to us and the way that natural rights and inherent dignity belong to us. Insofar as one treats his fellows with dignity, he conforms to the moral law; and insofar as he does this, he possesses, or there accrues to him like a boomerang, reflexive dignity.

When Moses gave the Hebrews God's Law, he gave them dignity. How can dignity accrue to anyone for any length of time if one's fellow men are not, to quote Leonard Nelson, "constrained in their discretion by the law"?[13] And what, finally, is a more magnificent appeal to the dignity of the individual, no matter how low his station, than the Sermon on the Mount in Matthew? "Blessed are the meek: for they shall inherit the earth." If the meek are those who humbly respect the dignity of others without appearing prideful for their actions, then we are promised that morality shall inhabit the earth.

Reflexive dignity also makes sense in relation to the situational meaning of dignity we examined. When we offer assistance to someone who is in need because his circumstances are in one way or another disabling or wretched, we receive dignity back. All of life's experience informs us of this truth. This is not an esoteric notion difficult to grasp; the giver who tries to overcome the incommodiousness of the one who does not have what he needs is in every sense of the word also the receiver. And in proportion as he gives, so does he receive the dignity he merits. He measures this dignity himself, and so he knows, even if Skinner does not, how much it is worth.

Herein enters yet a third meaning of dignity that we can unify with the other meanings of dignity by using the bridge concept of reflexive dignity. This third meaning is the Stoic concept of dignity as acting on certain virtues. The character virtues named before, like reliability, honesty, and self-restraint, are exactly those we have to engage if we are to offer compassion and assistance to others. This requires forgetting our personal concerns and sometimes postponing our efforts at self-enhancement. In turn, acting virtuously correlates with what we already said about freedom: freedom in personal choice is not enough to dignify our autonomy. Freedom has to be used rightly; our choices have to take proper aim. The satisfactions we choose have to be set in motion by worthy desires, that is, they have to fulfill our truest interests.

We can also tie *dignitas*, that attribute signifying that certain men of affairs held important offices, into reflexive dignity and into natural law as well. By losing his office or legal status, a Roman citizen lost his *dignitas*, by definition. Analogously, in losing the Stoic virtues that the man of *dignitas* is supposed to exemplify through using these virtues to regulate the actions and proprieties of his office, we can say that he fails to conform to natural law. It is important to have some way of saying, "No natural law, no dignity," and failing to develop one's character is an apt way of making this claim. Reflexive dignity is just the idea we need here because it works by degrees; it works through more or less. We can keep or lose our reflexive dignity by degrees. We can increase or diminish it by our actions.

Reflexive dignity really is not new. It is an old, familiar friend; it has merely been hiding in our vocabulary. "Dignity," said an unusually insightful friend, "is the only thing you can offer to anyone." So dignity is not only something we inherently own. It is also something that we can, without loss, like love and truth, give away. But I think we always are in danger of losing this idea of reflexive dignity, this measuring of ourselves through the dignity we recognize in others. Why is this, and can we do anything to firm it up and keep it in use?

I have set down a meaning for reflexive dignity, tried to show how such an idea helps to unify various other pervasive concepts of dignity, and highlighted how central this idea of reflexive dignity is in our everyday lives. But there is one more set of relationships I would like to examine in order to reinforce how dignity concretely operates on us. There are certain relationships between reflexive dignity and what has come to be known as *natural law*.

We hinted at this relationship when we spoke earlier of dignity implying our fundamental rights. The clear connection here is that violating our rights is one way to abuse our dignity—dignity, of course, in the sense that can be damaged by others, like the damaged dignity of Rodney King.

There is controversy over whether natural rights are natural laws. I think that they are, but only if we understand a natural right as a freedom that has to be completed by right choices. And if right choices are those that show respect for the dignity of others, then it follows that natural rights are a kind of natural law. The abuse of natural rights, then, is an abuse of someone's dignity.

In the quotation at the opening of this paper, the Roman Emperor Gratian speaks of natural law as "having primacy in dignity." I presume this means that dignity is the first principle of natural law, and this surely entails that if persons had no inherent dignity, then affording them rights or acting morally toward them would make less sense than it otherwise does.

It seems, then, that without the idea of persons' inherent dignity as a presupposition, acting morally makes much less sense. We can still act morally, but our actions will be ad hoc and whimsical; they will depend on mood, personality, and whom we're acting toward; and they will be difficult both to censure and to justify. We can never build a moral tradition or habituate civilization to acting virtuously on these kinds of contingencies.

I like to think of natural laws as making dignity explicit, as formulating or breaking down dignity into its principled parts. Because the concept of dignity is condensed and abstract, we need to operationalize it somewhat as we did before. When we do this, we discover that natural law ideas inhere in the various ways in which both the moral and empirical uses of "inherent dignity" come together in the idea of reflexive dignity. If dignity is a moral and psychological attribute of persons, then natural laws are the principles that this attribute exposes when we analyze it, and that exercise themselves when we commit ourselves to it. They are the principles it is morally natural, reasonable, and responsible to act on if we take reflexive dignity seriously.

Let us broadly define natural law first in terms of its form, that is, as that moral law pertaining to what is foundational, universal, and unchanging about ethical life, and let us rest this formal definition of moral law mainly on three related ideas that most natural law thinkers have thought essential. These three ideas all refer back to the nature of ethical life at its unchanging foundations as universal, that is, as true everywhere and always. These are (1) being a human person; (2) being a human person who can feel, reason, and will; and (3) being a human person who tends, through using his reason and will, to lift himself above the ordinary and the *merely natural* in aspiring to an elevated moral and intellectual status, something one has the potential to be, higher and better than one actually is—whatever noble ideal this is.

If this is an acceptable working definition of the form and direction that natural law traditionally takes, then natural laws are the substantive, content-filled ways in which this ideal of the person gets carried through. We see that running throughout this entire moral ideal is the idea of *the person with dignity*. Without dignity, our aspiring toward higher actions and conduct does not make full sense and can be explained only on the ground that we are having fun doing this but we know not why. Pointless actions, unreasoned and without purpose, stop short at the impenetrable gates of chance and accident.

Nor, in carrying out our conduct, does the use of only our reason and will, the formal elements in choice, make sense; for without virtue, we cannot be said even to *conduct ourselves*. Rather, we merely act and react in a random, mindless fashion without responsibility and commitment of will *toward something of value*. And finally, without positing the criterion that denotes our human-ness, we cannot know why we ought to act as we should act. For this knowledge, we have to make reference, even though indirectly, to our human species. Why can we not simply act like any indiscriminate organic or living being? The answer is because we are a *specific* living being: we are *human beings*. And so, as the philosopher Martin Schlag put it, we have to be treated in accordance with our dignity as *living, human beings*.

If the Stoic virtues are the substance of natural laws (natural laws now understood as the moral habits with which we direct our character), then once again dignity is in agreement with natural law since these virtues are exactly what enable us to act consistently on natural law principles, that is, to act as if persons had inherent dig-nity. According to the idea of reflexive dignity, when we do this, then dignity comes back to us and is enhanced. What we called earlier the form of natural law is involved here too; for we never, all at once, achieve perfection in treating others with dignity. We have to work at this, improve it, aspire to it as a higher purpose.

For me, the choice is clear: either we reach for spiritu-ality and hence conduct ourselves as if reflexive dignity mattered, or we do not care to reach for spirituality and hence our consciousness makes itself indifferent to the choice. If we follow the natural, that is, the moral law, reflexive dignity accrues to us. If we do not care about fol-lowing the natural law, then as we saw, because dignity carries its own kind of internal wisdom and measure, it does not reverberate in our direction.

I close with one very practical thought that is an appli-cation of what I have examined in this essay. It is my opinion that there are certain upcoming and very real waves of global magnitude that we and subsequent generations will critically be subject to in a very short time. These waves, of such magnitude that we can scarcely comprehend them, are the global interactions of peoples of radically different cultures who, geographically, are moving in any direction toward which they think they can find life and hope. Each of us, I believe, is going to experience the outcome of vast migrations of peoples: the shifts, wanderings, and desperate searches of immigrants, refugees, and disaster victims that result for many reasons, in many ways, and with many and variant consequences, both good and not good. If this is the irreversible trend of our current times, then it seems clear which choice we have to make. We have to bring our personal inclinations, resources, patience, and virtue to bear on treating with dignity people who belong to groups we are not familiar with and may not even like, that is, treating them as moral equals. If we do not, I think we shall all go under. And the conflicts of intolerance and hatred preceding our destruction will not even be worth engaging in because both the means to resist and the end that is not resistible are unworthy of our dignity.

ENDNOTES

1. B. F. Skinner, *Beyond Freedom and Dignity* (New York: Alfred A. Knopf, 1972).

2. *Gregg v. Georgia*, (1976), USGa, 96 SCt 2909, 428 US 153, 49 LEd 2d, 859, stay gr, 96 SCt 3235, 429 US 1301. Selections reprinted in *What is Justice*, eds. N. C. Solomon and M. C. Murphy (New York: Oxford University Press, 1990).

3. Martin Schlag, "The Revolution in Human Dignity," presented at Fourteenth World Congress of International Association of Philosophy of Law and Social Philosophy, Edinburgh, Scotland, 1989. *Vera Lex*, V. XIII, Nos. 1 & 2, pp. 19–22, 1993.

4. Mary Ann Glendon, *Rights Talk* (New York: Free Press, 1990).

5. B. F. Skinner, *About Behaviorism* (New York: Alfred A. Knopf, 1974).

6. *Grounding for the Metaphysics of Morals,* trans. James W. Ellington (Indianapolis, Indiana: Hackett Publishing Co., 1981).

7. Immanuel Kant, "Proper Self Respect," *Lectures on Ethics,* trans. Louis Enfield (New York: Harper & Row, 1963).

8. Leonard Nelson, *System of Ethics,* trans. Norbert Guterman (New Haven: Yale University Press, 1956).

9. *Vera Lex,* V. XIII, Nos. 1 & 2, pp. 23–25. 1993.

10. Giovanni Pico della Mirandola, "Oration on the Dignity of Man," in *Renaissance Philosophy of Man,* Ernst Cassirer, Paul Oskar Kristeller, and John Herman Randall, Jr. (Chicago: University of Chicago Press, 1956).

11. J. B. Quinn, "A Living Will Is the Best Way to Avoid Spending Last Days Attached to Tube," *Washington Post,* nd.

12. Philip Hallie, "From Cruelty to Goodness," reprinted in *Vice and Virtue in Everyday Life,* ed. C. H. Sommers (New York: Harcourt Brace Jovanovich, 1985).

13. Leonard Nelson, op cit.

Chapter 7

Natural Law and Positive Law

ROBERT P. GEORGE

As I understand the natural law, it consists of three sets of principles.[1] First, and most fundamentally, a set of principles directing human choice and action toward intelligible purposes, i.e., basic human goods that, as intrinsic aspects of human well-being and fulfillment, constitute reasons for action whose intelligibility as reasons does not depend on any more fundamental reasons (or on subrational motives such as the desire for emotional satisfactions) to which they are mere means. Second is a set of "intermediate" moral principles that specify the most basic principles of morality by directing choice and action toward possibilities that may be chosen consistently with a will toward integral human fulfillment and away from possibilities inconsistent with such a will.[2] Third are the fully specific moral norms that require or forbid (sometimes exceptionlessly, sometimes with exceptions) certain specific possible choices.[3]

The first and most fundamental principles of natural law are not, strictly speaking, moral norms. They do not resolve questions of which option(s) may be uprightly chosen in situations of morally significant choice. Indeed, the multiplicity of these most basic practical principles *creates* situations of morally significant choice and makes it necessary for us to identify norms of morality in order to choose uprightly in such situations.

The most basic practical principles refer to ends or purposes that provide noninstrumental reasons for acting. These principles identify intrinsic human goods (such as knowledge, friendship, and health) as ends to be pursued, promoted, and protected, and their opposites (such as ignorance, animosity, and illness) as evils to be avoided or overcome.

Of course, not all ends to which action may be directed are provided by reasons, much less noninstrumental reasons. All of us sometimes want things we have no reason to want. Such desires, though not rationally grounded, are perfectly capable of motivating us to act. One may, for example, experience thirst and desire a drink of water. It may well be that no intelligible good is to be advanced or protected by one's having a drink. One desires a drink not for the sake of health, or friendship, or any other intelligible good that would provide a *reason* for going to the water fountain. Still, one has a motive, albeit a subrational motive, to have a drink. One's acting on this motive is perfectly explicable and may, depending on other factors, be perfectly reasonable.[4]

In addition to the distinction between reasons and nonrationally grounded desires (and other subrational motives), there is the distinction between instrumental and noninstrumental reasons for action. Instrumental goods provide reasons for acting only insofar as they are means to other ends. Money, for example, is a purely instrumental good. It is of value only insofar as one can buy or do things with it. Intrinsic goods, on the other hand, though they may, to be sure, also have considerable instrumental value, are worthwhile for their own sakes. As ends-in-themselves, intrinsic goods provide reasons for action whose intelligibility as reasons does not depend on more fundamental reasons (or on ends ultimately provided by subrational motives) to which they are mere means.

Following Germain Grisez, I (and others) refer to intrinsic goods as "basic human goods." We do so to stress the point that such goods are not "platonic forms" somehow detached from the persons in and by whom they are instantiated. Rather, they are intrinsic aspects of the well-being and fulfillment of flesh and blood human beings in their manifold dimensions (that is to say, as animate, as rational, and as agents through deliberation and choice). Basic human goods provide reasons for action precisely insofar as they are constitutive aspects of human flourishing.

Taken together, the first principles of practical reason, which direct action to the basic human goods, outline the vast range of possible rationally motivated actions, and point to an ideal of "integral human fulfillment." This is the ideal of the complete fulfillment of all human persons (and their communities) in all possible respects. The first principle of morality, which is no mere ideal, directs that our choosing be compatible with a will toward integral fulfillment. The specifications of this principle in, for example, the Golden Rule of fairness or the Pauline Principle that evil may not be done even that good might come of it take into account the necessarily subrational motives people may have for choosing or otherwise willing incompatibly with such a will.

Moral principles—whether the most basic and general principle prior to its specification, or those specifications which are intermediate between the most basic principle and fully specific moral norms, or the fully specific norms themselves—are intelligible as principles of action and relevant to practical thinking only because, at the most basic level of practical reflection, rational human beings are capable of grasping a multiplicity of intelligible ends or purposes that provide reasons for action. Paradigmatically, moral principles govern choice by providing conclusive second-order reasons to choose one rather than another, or some rather than other, possibilities in cases in which one has competing first-order reasons, i.e., where competing possibilities each offer some true human benefit and, thus, hold some genuine rational appeal.[5] Paradigmatically, moral norms exclude the choosing of those possibilities which, though rationally grounded, fall short of all that reason requires.

This conception of the role of moral norms in practical reasoning is captured in the tradition of natural law theorizing by the notion of *recta ratio*—"right reason." Right reason is reason unfettered by emotional or other impediments to choosing consistently with what reason fully requires. Often enough, a possibility for choice may be rationally grounded (i.e., for a first-order *reason* provided by the possibility of realizing or participating in some true human benefit, some basic human good), yet, at the same time, be contrary to *right* reason (i.e., contrary to at least one conclusive second-order reason provided by a moral norm that excludes the choosing of that possibility).

Of course, most of our choices are not between right and wrong options, but rather between incompatible right options. Where a choice is between or among morally acceptable possibilities, one has a reason to do X and a reason to do Y. Yet sometimes the doing of Y is incompatible here and now with doing X, and no conclusive reason is provided by a moral norm to do X or not to do X for the sake of doing Y. In situations of this sort, one is considering possibilities made available by the practical intellect's grasp of the most basic principles of practical reason and precepts of natural law. These pertain to the first set of principles of natural law I identified earlier. Yet practical reason is unable to identify principles in the second and third sets (i.e., second-order principles or norms) to determine one's choice. One's choice, then, though rationally grounded, is in a significant sense rationally underdetermined.[6] Doing X or not doing X in order to do Y are both fully reasonable, are both fully compatible with *recta ratio.*

As choosing subjects, or "acting persons," we make the natural law effective by bringing the principles of natural law into our practical deliberation and judgment in situations of morally significant choice. This task is not merely a job for the natural law theorist or for believers in natural law. It is something that every rational agent does to some extent, and every responsible agent does to a large extent.

Even in the most mundane aspects of our lives, in matters of no great moral moment, we regularly and effortlessly identify and act upon the first-order reasons that constitute the most basic principles of natural law. In fact, countless choices in which these principles centrally figure are so commonplace that ordinary people would be shocked to learn that they were acting on principles at all. They would characterize their choices as merely "doing what comes naturally" or even "doing what I like." And, in a sense, they would be absolutely right. They are choosing and acting, with minimal reflection or deliberation, for the sake of reasons (and, thus, on principles) that are so patently obvious, that are grasped so effortlessly, that fit into the established patterns of their lives so easily that they require hardly any thought at all.

Beyond this, everyone who deliberates among competing possibilities each or all of which have at least some rational appeal, and who, upon reflection, identifies a principle of rectitude in choosing—that will enable him to judge correctly that one of these options is, uniquely, right (and should therefore be chosen) and that others are wrong (and therefore, despite their elements of rational appeal, should not be chosen)—makes the second and third sets of principles of natural law effective in his own willing and choosing. In cases of this sort, one is acting not only on the *prima principii*, the most basic precepts of natural law that are, as it were, the foundations of any sort of rational action (whether morally upright or defective), but also on the basis of moral norms that distinguish fully reasonable from practically unreasonable, morally upright from immoral, choosing.

Now, here it is worth pausing to avert a misunderstanding. By saying that the choosing subject "makes the natural law effective," I do not mean to imply that the subject creates the natural law or confers upon it its moral bindingness or force. No one should infer from my willingness to put the choosing subject in an active role with respect to the natural law ("making it effective") that the natural law, as I understand it, is somehow subjective. On the contrary, the reasons constitutive of each of the three sets of principles of natural law are, in a stringent sense, *objective.* They are grasped only by *sound* practical judgment and missed only when inquiry and judgment miscarry. They correspond to aspects of the genuine fulfillment of human persons, as such, and to the real (and strictly nonoptional) requirements of reasonableness in human willing and choosing (i.e., the norms of morality) that obtain for human beings, as such, and that do not depend upon, or vary with, people's beliefs, wishes, desires, or subjective interests or goals. The principles of natural law possess and retain their normative and prescriptive force independently of anyone's decision to adopt or refuse to adopt them in making the practical choices to which they apply.[7]

That being said, it remains true that we make the natural law effective in our lives precisely by grasping and acting on these principles. In doing so, we exercise the human capacity for free choice. A free choice is a choice between open practical possibilities (to do X or not to do X, perhaps for the sake of doing Y) such that nothing but the choosing itself settles the matter.[8] The existence of basic reasons for action (and, thus, of the primary principles of natural law) are conditions of free choice. If there were no such reasons, then all of our actions would be determined—determined either by external causes or by internal (subrational) factors such as feeling, emotion, desire, et cetera.[9] The denial of free choice, which is central to the various modern reductionisms in philosophy, psychology, and the social sciences, is, then, closely connected to the denial of the possibility of rationally motivated action. To deny free choice and the existence of the basic goods, reasons, and principles that are its conditions is to suppose that people are nothing more than animals with a well-developed capacity for theoretical and instrumentally practical rationality. If people were nothing more than that, then natural law could never be effective for them and would, indeed, hardly be intelligible conceptually.

Because persons can make free choices, they are self-constituting beings. In freely choosing—that is, in choosing for or against goods that provide noninstrumental reasons—one integrates the goods (or the damaging and consequent privation of the goods, i.e., the evils) one intends into one's will. Thus, one effects a sort of synthesis between oneself as an acting person and the objects of one's choices (i.e., the goods and evils one intends—either as ends-in-themselves or as means to other ends). One's choices perdure in one's character and personality as a choosing subject unless or until, for better or worse, one reverses one's previous choices by choosing incompatibly with them or, at least, one resolves to choose differently should one face the same or relevantly similar choices in the future.[10]

Of course, ethical theory is a complicated business in part because different types of willing bear on human goods and evils in interestingly and importantly different ways. Thus, it is necessary to distinguish, as the tradition of natural law theorizing does, as distinct modes of voluntariness, *intending* a good or evil (as an end or as a means to some other end) and *accepting as a side effect* a good or evil that one foresees as a consequence of one's action but does not intend. Although one is morally responsible for the bad side effects one knowingly brings about, one is not responsible for them in the same way one is responsible for what one intends. Often, one will have an obligation in justice or fairness to others (and thus a conclusive moral reason) not to bring about a certain evil that one knows or believes would likely result, albeit as an unintended side effect, from one's action. Sometimes, though, one will have no obligation to avoid bringing about a certain foreseen bad side effect of an action one has a reason (perhaps even a conclusive reason) to perform.

Communities, like individual persons, make choices. Their choices have to do with the ordering of the common lives of members of communities. Sometimes, especially in small communities, many of these choices or decisions are made by consensus, by achieving unanimity about what to do. It is the rare community, however, that can rely exclusively on unanimity. Most communities must rely on authority to coordinate the actions of individuals and subcommunities within the larger community for the sake of the common good. This is obviously true of political communities. Although there are many different forms of government, all political communities must create and rely upon authority of some sort.[11]

Political authorities serve the common good in large measure by creating, implementing, and enforcing laws. Where the laws are just (and expedient), authorities serve their communities well; where they are unjust (or inexpedient), they serve their communities badly. The moral purpose of a system of laws is to make it possible for individuals and subcommunities to realize for themselves important human goods that would not be realizable (or would not be realizable fully) in the absence of the laws. Hence, according to Aquinas, "the end of the law is the common good."[12]

It is tempting to think of authority and law as necessary only because of human malice, selfishness, inconstancy, weakness, or intransigence. The truth, however, is that law would be necessary to coordinate the behavior of members of the community for the sake of the common good even in a society of saints. Of course, in such a society legal sanctions—the threat of punishment for lawbreaking—would be unnecessary; but laws themselves would still be needed. Given that no earthly society is a society of saints, legal sanctions are—quite reasonably—universal features of legal systems. They are not, however, essential to the very concept of law.

But, someone might object, certain familiar laws would not be necessary in a society of saints—laws against murder, rape, theft, etc. The actions forbidden by such laws are plainly immoral—contrary to natural law—and would never be performed by morally upright beings. True. And since the moral point of law is to serve the good of people as they are—with all their faults—laws against these evils are necessary and proper. The natural law itself requires that someone (or some group of persons or some institution) exercise authority in political communities and that those in authority fulfill their moral function by translating certain principles of natural law into positive law and reinforcing and backing up these principles with the threat of punishment for law-breaking. Thus, those exercising legistlative authority, in a sense, derive the positive law from the natural law or, as I have said, translate natural principles of justice and political morality into rules and principles of positive law.

Aquinas, following up a lead from Aristotle, observed that the positive law is derived from the natural law in two different ways. In the case of certain principles, the legislator translates the natural law into the positive law more or less directly. So, for example, a conscientious legislator will prohibit grave injustices such as murder, rape, and theft by moving by a process akin to deduction[13] from the moral proposition that, say, the killing of innocent persons is intrinsically unjust to the conclusion that the positive law must prohibit and punish such killing.

In a great many cases, however, the movement from the natural law to the positive law in the practical thinking of the conscientious legislator cannot be so direct. For example, it is easy to understand the basic principle of natural law that identifies human health as a good and the preservation and protection of human health as important purposes. A modern legislator will therefore easily see, for example, the need for a scheme of coordination of traffic that protects the safety of drivers and pedestrians. The common good, which it is his responsibility to foster and serve in this respect, requires it.

Ordinarily, however, he cannot identify a uniquely correct scheme of traffic regulations that can be translated from the natural law to the positive law. Unlike the case of murder, the natural law does not determine once and for all the perfect scheme of traffic regulations. A number of different schemes—bearing different and often incommensurable costs and benefits, risks and advantages—are consistent with the natural law. So the legislator must exercise a kind of creativity in choosing a scheme. He must move, not by deduction, but rather by an activity of the practical intellect that Aquinas called *determinatio*.[14]

Unfortunately, no single word in English captures the meaning of *determinatio*. "Determination" captures some of the flavor of it; but so does "implementation," "specification," or "concretization." The key thing to understand is that in making *determinationes*, the legislator enjoys a kind of creative freedom that may be analogized to that of the architect. An architect must design a building that is sound and sensible for the purposes to which it will be put. He cannot, however, identify an ideal form of a building that is uniquely correct. Ordinarily, at least, a range of possible buildings, differing in a variety of respects, will satisfy the criteria of soundness and usability. Obviously, a building whose doors are no more than three feet high ordinarily fails to meet an important requirement for a usable building. No principle of architecture, however, sets the proper height of a door at six feet two inches as opposed to six feet eight inches. In designing any particular building, the conscientious architect will strive to make the height of the doors make sense in light of a variety of other factors, some of which are themselves the fruit of something akin to a *determina-*

tio (e.g., the height of the ceilings); but even here he will typically face a variety of acceptable but incompatible design options.

It is meaningful and correct to say that the legislator (including the judge to the extent that the judge in the jurisdiction in question exercises a measure of law-creating power) makes the natural law effective for his community by deriving the positive law from the natural law. The natural law itself requires that such a derivation be accomplished and that someone (or group or institution) be authorized to accomplish it. Because no human individual (or group or institution) is perfect in moral knowledge or virtue, it is inevitable that even conscientious efforts to translate the natural law into positive law, whether directly or by *determinationes,* will sometimes miscarry. Nonetheless, the natural law itself sets this as the task of the legislator, and it is only through his efforts that the natural law can become effective for the common good of his community.

Of course, the body of law created by the legislator is not itself the natural law. The natural law is in no sense a human creation. The positive law (of any community), however, *is* a human creation. It is an object—a vast cultural object composed of sometimes very complicated rules and principles, but an object nonetheless. Metaphysically, the positive law belongs to the order Aristotle identified as the order of "making" rather than of "doing." For perfectly good reasons, it is made to be subject to technical application and to be analyzed by a kind of technical reasoning—hence the existence of law schools that teach students not (or not just) moral philosophy, but the distinctive techniques of legal analysis, e.g., how to identify and understand legal sources, how to work with statutes, precedents, and the often necessarily artificial definitions that characterize any complex system of law.

At the same time, the creation of law (and a system of law) has a moral purpose. It is in the order of "doing" (the order, not of technique, but rather of free choice, practical reasoning, and morality—the order studied in ethics and political philosophy) that we identify the need to create law for the sake of the common good. The lawmaker creates an object—the law—deliberately and reasonably subject to technical analysis, for a purpose that is moral, and not itself merely technical. To fail to create this object (or to create unjust laws) would be inconsistent with the requirements of the natural law; it would be a failure of legislative duty precisely in the moral order.

The fact that the law is a cultural object that is created for a moral purpose generates a great deal of the confusion one encounters today in debates about the role of moral philosophy in legal reasoning. The vexed question of American constitutional interpretation is the scope and limits of the power of judges to invalidate legislation under certain allegedly vague or abstract constitutional provisions. Some constitutional theorists, such as Professor Ronald Dworkin, who wish to defend an expansive role for the judge, argue that the conscientious judge must bring judgments of moral and political philosophy to bear in deciding hard cases.[15] Others, such as Judge Robert Bork, who fear such a role for the judge and hold, in any event, that the Constitution of the United States does not give the judge such a role, maintain that moral philosophy has little or no place in judging, at least in the American system.[16]

Some people who are loyal to the tradition of natural law theorizing are tempted to suppose that Professor Dworkin's position, whatever its faults in other respects, is the one more faithful to the tradition. This temptation should, however, be resisted. While the role of the judge as a law-creator reasonably varies from jurisdiction to jurisdiction according to each jurisdiction's own authoritative *determinationes*—that is to say, each jurisdiction's positive law—Judge Bork's idea of a body of law that is properly and fully (or almost fully) analyzable in technical terms is fully compatible with classical understandings of natural law theory.[17]

Natural law theory treats the role of the judge as itself fundamentally a matter for *determinatio,* not for direct translation from the natural law. It does not imagine that the judge enjoys (or should enjoy), as a matter of natural law, a plenary authority to substitute his own understanding of the requirements of the natural law for the contrary understanding of the legislator or constitution-maker in deciding cases at law. On the contrary, for the sake of the rule of law, understood as ordinarily a necessary (albeit not a sufficient) condition for a just system of government, the judge (like any other actor in the system) is morally required (that is, obligated as a matter of natural law) to respect the limits of his own authority as it has been allocated to him by way of an authoritative *determinatio.* If the law of his system constrains his law-creating power in the way that Judge Bork believes American fundamental law does, then, for the sake of the rule of law, he must respect these constraints, even where his own understanding of natural justice deviates from that of the legislators or constitution-makers and ratifiers whose laws he must interpret and apply. None of this means that Judge Bork is more nearly correct than Professor Dworkin on the question of what degree of law-creating power *our* law places in the hands of the judge; it merely means that the question whether Dworkin or Bork is more nearly correct is properly conceived as itself a question of positive law—not natural law.

Bork, who is understood by some of his critics as denying the existence of natural law or any type of objective moral order, has clarified his position:

> I am far from denying that there is a natural law, but I do deny both that we have given judges the authority to enforce it and that judges have any greater access to that law than do the rest of us.[18]

If Bork's view is sound (and subject, perhaps, to one or two minor qualifications, I am prepared to believe that it is sound), that leaves us with the question whether the natural law itself—quite independently of what the Constitution may say—confers upon the judge a sort of plenary power to enforce it. One of my central aims in this essay has been to suggest that the correct answer to this question is no. To the extent that judges are not given power under the Constitution to translate principles of natural justice into positive law, that power is not one they enjoy; nor is it one they may justly exercise. For judges to arrogate such power to themselves in defiance of the Constitution is not merely for them to exceed their authority under the positive law; it is to violate the very natural law in whose name they purport to act.

ENDNOTES

1. For a fuller account of the understanding of natural law set forth in this paragraph, see Joseph M. Boyle, Jr., Germain Grisez, and John Finnis, "Practical Principles, Moral Truth and Ultimate Ends," *The American Journal of Jurisprudence,* Vol. 32 (1987), pp. 99–151. I have defended this understanding against various criticisms in "Recent Criticism of Natural Law Theory," *University of Chicago Law Review,* Vol. 55 (1988), pp. 1371–1492; "Human Flourishing as a Criterion of Morality: A Critique of Perry's Naturalism," *Tulane Law Review,* Vol. 63 (1989), pp. 1455–1474; "Does the Incommensurability Thesis Imperil Common Sense Moral Judgments," *American Journal of Jurisprudence,* Vol. 37 (1992), pp. 185–195); and "Natural Law and Human Nature" in Robert P. George, ed., *Natural Law Theory: Contemporary Essays* (Oxford: Clarendon Press, 1992), pp. 31–41.

2. Examples of moral principles in this category are the "Golden Rule" of fairness and the "Pauline Principle," which forbids the doing of evil even as a means of bringing about good consequences.

3. Examples of norms in this category are those forbidding such specific possible choices as willfully refusing to return borrowed property to its owner upon his request (which is a good example of a moral norm that admits of exceptions) and directly killing an innocent person (which is a good example of an exceptionless moral norm). NB: "Direct" killing refers to the intending of death—one's own or someone else's—as an end in itself (as in killing for revenge) or as a means to another end (as in terror bombing the civilian population of an unjust aggressor nation). It is sometimes, though not always, morally permissible to accept the bringing about of death—one's own or someone else's—as the foreseen and accepted side effect of a choice in which one does not intend death (either as end or means).

4. To act on one's subrational motive is not necessarily unreasonable or morally wrong. Moral questions arise only when one has a reason not to do something that one has a nonrationally grounded desire to do. So, to stay with the example, where one is thirsty and has no reason not to slake one's thirst, then there is nothing wrong with having a drink. Visiting the water fountain, in these circumstances, is an innocent pleasure.

5. I defend this conception of the role of moral principles in "Incommensurability Thesis."

6. See Joseph Raz, *The Morality of Freedom* (Oxford: Clarendon Press, 1986), pp. 388–389.

7. On the objectivity of the principles of natural law, see John Finnis, *Natural Law and Natural Rights* (Oxford: Clarendon Press, 1980), pp. 69–75; and *Fundamentals of Ethics* (Oxford: Oxford University Press, 1983), pp. 56–79.

8. For a thorough explanation and defense of this conception of free choice, see Joseph M. Bolye, Jr., Germain Grisez, and Olaf Tollefsen, *Free Choice: A Self-Referential Argument* (Notre Dame, Indiana: University of Notre Dame Press, 1976).

9. I explain this point at length in "Free Choice, Practical Reason, and Fitness for the Rule of Law," in Daniel N. Robinson, ed., *Social Discourse and Moral Judgment* (New York: Academic Press, 1992).

10. On the lastingness and character-forming consequences of free choices, see Finnis, *Fundamentals of Ethics*, pp. 139–144.

11. See Finnis, *Natural Law*, pp. 231–259.

12. *Summa Theologiae*, I–II, q. 96, a. 1.

13. Ibid. I–II, q. 95, a. 2.

14. Ibid. For a sound exposition and valuable development of Aquinas's understanding of *determinatio*, see John Finnis, *Natural Law and Natural Rights*, pp. 285–290. See also Finnis, "On 'The Critical Legal Studies Movement,'" *The American Journal of Jurisprudence*, Vol. 30 (1985).

15. For the most fully developed articulation of Dworkin's position, see his *Law's Empire* (Cambridge, Massachusetts: Harvard University Press, 1986).

16. See Robert H. Bork, *The Tempting of America: The Political Seduction of the Law* (New York: The Free Press, 1990), esp. pp. 251–259.

17. I am concerned here with the role and duty of judges in basically just legal systems, i.e., systems that do not deserve to be subverted and that judges and others would do wrong to subvert. Different considerations apply in sorting out the obligations of judges in fundamentally unjust legal systems. I do not take up these considerations in this essay.

18. Bork, *The Tempting*, p. 66.

Chapter 8

Natural Rights and the Limits of Constitutional Law

RUSSELL HITTINGER

If one is in search of a direct connection between (1) the language of moral duties and rights and (2) the art of making constitutions, one need only peruse the constitutions of the several states. State constitutions do not hesitate to display the moral premises of the positive law. The Oklahoma Constitution, for example, expressly prohibits polygamy, forbids primogeniture and entailments as violative of "the genius of a free government," and makes "excessive" use of intoxicating liquors by state officials an impeachable offense.[1] Oklahoma's fundamental law expressly affirms "the inherent right" of all persons "to life, liberty, the pursuit of happiness, and the enjoyment of the gains of their own industry."[2] Victims of crime enjoy "rights" to be treated with "fairness, respect and dignity." The Oklahoma Constitution is typical of state constitutions throughout our polity. First principles of justice and morals are invoked, and certain conclusions are drawn from those principles for particular matters of conduct on the part of the state and its citizens.

Yet the unamended Constitution of the United States, ratified in 1787, makes no mention of natural law or natural rights. In Article I, Section 8, Congress is delegated the power to grant temporary rights for useful discoveries.[3] Beyond that, there is no report of rights, natural or positive. Even when we take the most morally fraught amendment to the U.S. Constitution, the First Amendment, the contrast with state constitutions on the same subject is telling. Whereas the First Amendment to the U.S. Constitution simply declares a want of power on the part of Congress to make any law "respecting an establishment of religion" (with no mention of God or conscience), the Virginia Constitution declares that religion is the "duty which we owe to our Creator." From this premise, the Virginia Constitution goes on to infer a set of duties and rights, including "the mutual duty of all to practice Christian forbearance, love, and charity towards each other."[4]

In *The Natural Law*, Heinrich Rommen pointed out that wherever there is a bill of rights, there is a "strong presupposition" that the human law must be in harmony with natural law.[5] While Rommen is certainly correct that bills of rights usually presuppose the existence of certain inviolable principles of justice, when we descend into the concrete and particular frame of constitutions, we notice that even bills of rights differ in how they give expression to this "strong presupposition" in favor of natural law. As we have already said, within our own polity, state constitutions give much more ample and detailed expression to the rights of citizens than does the U.S. Constitution—and this, despite the fact that, in the founding generation, these constitutions were often drafted by the same men. The American creed of natural rights, summarized in the Declaration of Independence, is expressly affirmed in the state, rather than federal, constitutions.

In this essay, we shall attempt to frame at least the beginnings of an answer to the following question: Why is the U.S. Constitution so abstemious in its reference to the moral grounds of positive law? The first set of points will be chiefly institutional in nature, for in order to evaluate the relative absence of moral language in the U.S. Constitution, we first must know precisely the nature and limits of that constitution. The second set of points will be more philosophical. Here, we will consider the dangers to limited government when constitutions and courts speak too directly about natural principles of justice. In particular, we will look at the problem of under-specified rights, such as often appear in lists of rights and in judicial dicta.

At the outset, it is important to insist that it is not the object of this essay to question the importance of natural justice for legal reasoning, much less to disparage the existence of natural law or natural rights. Rather, we shall consider the practical problem of how such principles are given expression in human law, and what the U.S. Constitution might teach us about that problem.

If one surveys the great treatises on natural law, from Thomas Aquinas to Hugo Grotius, one will be struck by the fact that philosophers and jurisprudents have taken it for granted (1) that natural justice is of primary interest to legislator and (2) that lawmakers legislate for a government of general jurisdiction, having moral police powers.

Given the conviction that there exist rules and measures of justice antecedent to the positive law of the state, it would seem to follow that whoever makes law is most immediately responsible for ensuring that statutes and policies are in harmony with the natural law. This is not to say that judicial and executive powers in a polity have no interest in the natural law. Rather, it is only to make the obvious point that human law first connects or disconnects with the natural law in the act of legislation. Without a legislative act, there is nothing to execute and nothing to adjudge. The great theoreticians of the natural law also assumed that the legislative power is responsible to the whole of the common good—that kind of "whole" characteristic of a polis or *civitas*—namely a political community. Thomas Aquinas insisted that lawmaking presupposes a political community, in contrast to the family, tribe, or economic corporation. A political community is a *communitas perfecta;* that is, a community that includes within itself all of the resources for human flourishing.[6] Though the legislative power has justice as its direct object, it has *in potentia* an indefinite scope of objects and issues, for its end is the temporal happiness of the whole people. A government of general jurisdiction, then, is interested in the defense of the people, education of the young, institutions of distributive and legal justice, and the protection of obligations and rights incurred by way of commutative justice at private law.

On the model of a government of general jurisdiction having moral police powers, it is not difficult to picture, in a general way, how political institutions are related to natural law. The human legislator has the task of making the natural law effective in the political community. In the first place, this will involve using principles of natural justice for remedial purposes. Some natural principles of justice will be represented, by way of codification. For example, natural law precepts forbidding murder and theft will be acknowledged in criminal codes. The fundamental law of the state will not neglect to include the power to enforce such principles. In the second place, the human law will recognize certain limits on its own power. At least in the Western constitutional polities, the rights and duties of persons at private law, the rights of the church, and the rights of persons (such as are spelled out in bills of rights) are typically recognized as setting some limits to the jurisdiction of the state. In the third place, the human legislator will use creatively the rules and measures of the natural law for the purpose of making more determinate rules and measures as needed by the people. In the right to enforce moral principles, in recognizing jurisdictional limits, and in making statutes and policies that serve the common good, the human legislator variously works with principles of justice that are antecedent to the positive law of the state. All three of these are quite evident in constitutions of the several states, because the states are (or were) governments of general jurisdiction.

The U.S. Constitution is a different kind of instrument because this government is not (or was not) a government of general jurisdiction, having police powers. As one of the framers, James Wilson, observed, the government created under the U.S. Constitution was "a system hitherto unknown."[7] For the U.S. government was not merely limited by rules of law or limited by a feudal-like system of customs and common laws; nor was it limited merely by the separation of powers. This government was limited by other governments, according to the principle of dual sovereignty. In *Democracy in America*, Alexis de Tocqueville contended that the entire genius of this new government is summarized in the following four sentences of Federalist 45:

> The powers delegated by the proposed Constitution to the federal government, are few and defined. Those which are to remain in the state governments are numerous and indefinable. The former will be exercised principally on external objects, as war, peace, negotiation, and foreign commerce, with which . . . the power of taxation will, for the most part, be connected. The powers reserved for the several states will extend to all the objects which, in the ordinary course of affairs, concern the lives, liberties, and properties of the people, and the internal order, improvement, and prosperity of the state.[8]

According to James Madison, the political rule of this new regime consists of two quite distinct kinds of government. Madison reiterated the point in Federalist 51: "In the compound republic of America, the power surrendered by the people is first divided between *two distinct* governments. . . . Hence a double security arises to the rights of the people."[9] On the one hand, there are governments of general jurisdiction, having moral police powers. As Madison said, their powers are "numerous and indefinable" because their objects extend to all of the things "in the ordinary course of affairs" that bear upon the common good. On the other hand, there is a government of delegated and enumerated powers. Many, if not most, aspects of human well-being—marriage, religion, education, crime—do not immediately fall under its direction.

From this, we can adduce two institutional reasons why the U.S. Constitution is so abstemious in its use of moral language. *First*, given a government of "few and defined" powers, one is first interested in whether that government has a power and only secondarily (but not unimportantly) in how it is used. In this respect, an abundance of moral language would prove counterproductive. To worry whether the use of a power is morally adequate to various objects and ends is to put the cart before the horse. The first question is whether that government has been delegated power over a specific object or end. *Second*, because it is not a government of general jurisdiction having moral police powers, many areas of human conduct that are most immediately and vividly related to moral considerations fall outside its jurisdiction. In the original Constitution, even slavery was left primarily to the states. The states, having "numerous and indefinable" powers, reach many more ends. Thus, it is entirely appropriate that the state constitutions should expressly include the moral axioms and theorems that guide these powers.

It should be emphasized, however, that this does not mean that the U.S. Constitution is not informed by moral principles; it is only to say that their exposition is indirect, in keeping with the nature of the instrument and its ends. This indirection represents a deliberate effort by the framers to discipline how we should think about the limits of governmental power. Rather than listing all of the moral norms that ought to guide the use of legislative, executive, and judicial powers, the Constitution tries to state as precisely as possible who has authority over a certain scope of objects. The Constitution does not provide us with a moral argument justifying every institutional limitation of power.

Enumerated powers do not necessarily tell us whether any particular law made in pursuance of a power satisfies or thwarts natural justice; nor does it immediately tell us whether a liberty exercised in the absence of a power is exercised rightly or wrongly, from a moral point of view. So, for example, Article I, Section 8, gives Congress authority to grant temporary rights to authors and inventors for their respective writings and inventions. This article does not, however, tell us whether or how this Congressional power ought to reach a Kevorkian suicide machine, much less which, if any, writings have redeeming social value. Unlike ordinary moral reasoning, which is only satisfied when the choice is fully adequate to the concrete particular, the articles of the Constitution make little or no effort to exhibit their moral presuppositions and how they are brought to bear upon concrete choices by the legislature. Considered very generally, there is no delegated power that is, in itself, contrary to the natural law. The power to grant rights to inventors is certainly congruent with fundamental principles of justice.

It is indeed a moral question whether Congress ought to underwrite inventions that are likely to serve immoral purposes. We can assume that, implicit in the grant of power, is a norm requiring those who use the power to use it reasonably, in accord with the common good. This level of reasoning, however, is not *constitutionalized* by the Constitution. It is left to the judgment of Congress and ultimately to the people who are represented therein. Principles of natural justice, therefore, are not excluded but rather are included at a different level.

From the very outset, critics of the U.S. Constitution complained that its lack of explicit moral language was a defect. Calvinist divines at Princeton College led a movement against ratification on the ground that the Constitution failed to recognize God. Anti-Federalists urged that the Constitution be adopted only if it included a bill of rights. In this century, Article III courts have come to believe that the sparse and lawyerly language of the U.S. Constitution contains hidden moral substance that courts must make explicit.[10]

At this juncture, we may turn to our second set of points. Heretofore, we have suggested that the Constitution's abstemious moral rhetoric is not a defect, nor an expression of some "positivist" ideology, but rather a carrying forward of the precise institutional character of a government of enumerated powers conjoined, in a novel way, to governments of general jurisdiction in the states. But there is another reason why the framers were hesitant about *constitutionalizing* the rhetoric of natural rights.

In his magisterial *Commentaries on the Constitution of the United States* (1833 edition), Chief Justice Joseph Story wrote:

> That a bill of rights may contain too many enumerations, and especially such, as more correctly belong to the ordinary legislation of a government, cannot be doubted. Some of our state bills of rights contain

clauses of this description, being either in their character and phraseology quite too loose, and general,
and ambiguous; or covering doctrines quite debatable, both in theory and practice; or even leading to
mischievous consequences, by restricting the legislative power under circumstances, which were not
foreseen, and if foreseen, the restraint would have
been pronounced by all persons inexpedient, and
perhaps unjust. Indeed, the rage of theorists to
make constitutions a vehicle for the conveyance of
their own crude, and visionary aphorisms of government, requires to be guarded against with the
most unceasing vigilance.[11]

Story's point is aimed at the Anti-Federalists, who (in
Story's view) misunderstood the nature of the U.S.
Constitution. But his deeper point touches upon an
important question of practical philosophy. Do vaguely
formulated principles of natural right really limit government in the ways their proponents imagine?

Before turning to the philosophical issue, it would be
useful to recall the historical context of the dispute over
the Bill of Rights. Story's remark was made in reference
to Alexander Hamilton's famous argument in Federalist
84, that a bill of rights is unnecessary. Hamilton contended that "the Constitution is itself, in every rational
sense, a Bill of Rights." Insofar as a constitution delegates
and enumerates the powers of the state (here, the U.S.
government), there is no need to limit the state by the
addition of natural rights claims, nor indeed any kind of
rights claims. Hamilton asked: "[W]hy declare that things
shall not be done which there is no power to do?"
Accordingly, the internal structure of the government

protects rights by spelling out precisely what the government cannot do. If Article I gives Congress no power to make laws respecting an establishment of religion, there is no reason to reiterate the want of power in an amendment. Hamilton concluded: "Here is a better recognition of popular rights than volumes of those aphorisms which make the principal figure in several of our State bills of rights and which would sound much better in a treatise of ethics than in a constitution of government."

The options presented by Hamilton are simple. We could, in the fashion of moral philosophers, first identify a body of moral rights and then erect institutions of government as so many implications of those rights. For example, from the proposition that individuals have an inalienable right of conscience, we could declare in the Constitution that government may not abridge the right of religious conscience. Or, we could, in the fashion of the framers, limit the institutions and activities of the government, from which there would flow certain liberties enjoyed by the people.

On the first model, the duties of government are derived and exposited from antecedent rights claims; on the second model, rights are enjoyed as liberties exercised in the absence or specification of a governmental power. On the second model, public and justiciable rights do not appear prior to the actual institutions of law and government. The same result can be generated by either starting point, for citizens cannot be molested or impaired in their religious duties whether we start from the want of power on the part of Congress to make such laws or whether we start from the right of citizens to religious conscience. However, the framers, eschewing the first model, avoided the problems characteristic of natural rights discourse: (1) there are no rights antithetical to the rule of law (2) there are no vague propositions about justice (3) there is no lack of clear and precise instructions to the government about the nature and scope of its powers, for the government is not being asked to interpret its powers as though they were implications of a list of human rights.

James Madison wrote in Federalist 51: "In framing a government which is to be administered by men over men, the great difficulty lies in this; you must first enable the government to control the governed; and in the next place oblige it to control itself." The Federalist argument was that while it is relatively easy to enumerate governmental powers, it is relatively difficult to formulate abstract principles of justice or of natural rights. A government that will not conform its activities to the powers delegated to it by the people is not apt to be a government that will limit is activities to the abstract aphorisms of natural rights. In fact, Hamilton warned that abstract rights, rather than limiting the government, "would furnish to men disposed to usurp, a plausible pretense for claiming that power." Once government is commissioned to secure the end of generally stated moral desiderata, government will not only claim the power to interpret the scope of these ends, but will also claim power over the means to achieve them. Since the former are general and indefinite, so too are the latter.

Here, we can recall Justice Story's criticism, supra, of state bills of rights, which

> contain clauses of this description, being either in
> their character and phraseology quite too loose,

and general, and ambiguous; or covering doctrines quite debatable, both in theory and practice; or even leading to mischievous consequences, by restricting the legislative power under circumstances, which were not foreseen, and if foreseen, the restraint would have been pronounced by all persons inexpedient, and perhaps unjust.

Examples of this problem are abundant, especially in the dicta of the courts. Consider *Planned Parenthood of Southeastern Pennsylvania v. Casey* (1992), where the Supreme Court tried to expound the principle of justice limiting the moral police powers of the state governments on the issue of abortion. The Court maintained that: "At the heart of liberty is the right to define one's own concept of existence, of meaning, of the universe, and of the mystery of human life. Beliefs about these matters could not define the attributes of personhood were they formed under compulsion of the State."[12] This particular right, without further qualification, would give citizens an immunity from virtually all positive law. So stated, it could mean anything. A right that can mean virtually anything does not limit the government. Rather, such a right authorizes the government both to meddle in social relations for the purpose of securing open-ended claims of justice and paradoxically to make constant exceptions to the alleged right whenever its open-ended character seems to conflict with some compelling governmental function. Vaguely formulated "rights" must prove extremely difficult to adjudicate in any fair, public way. Apropos of the *Casey* dictum, in the context of litigation, how can the right to define the meaning of the universe be ascertained by a judge, since the right is essentially a right to enjoy private, if not idiosyncratic, meanings? As Simone Weil said: "To set up as a standard of public morality a notion which can neither be defined nor conceived is to open the door to every kind of tyranny."[13]

Justice Louis Brandeis's dictum in *Olmstead v. United States* (1928) is familiar to every student of constitutional law:

> The makers of our Constitution undertook to secure conditions favorable to the pursuit of happiness. They recognized the significance of man's spiritual nature, of his feelings and of his intellect. They knew that only a part of the pain, pleasure and satisfaction of life are to be found in material things. They sought to protect Americans in their beliefs, their thoughts, their emotions and their sensations. They conferred, as against the government, the right to be let alone—the most comprehensive of rights, and the right most valued by civilized men."[14]

Once again, we can see that were such a "comprehensive" right claimed by individuals, the restraint on government, as Justice Story said, "would have been pronounced by all persons inexpedient, and perhaps unjust." There may well be a kernel of moral truth in Brandeis's dictum; but as it stands, the "right" is underspecified. Until it is further specified, no one can know who is bound to do (or not do) what to whom. And so long as that condition persists, there is no limit to the government.[15] On the one hand, we have a principle of unbounded individual liberty; on the other, a government responsible for enforcing that principle in a very arbitrary manner.[16]

The problem of underspecified rights claims is well known, if not always adequately appreciated. Let us see how one proponent of natural rights deals with the problem. In *Man and the State* (1951), Jacques Maritain argued that the political "madness" of the twentieth century can be traced to two general causes. The first is the ideology of "substantialism," or the doctrine that the state is a moral person in the proper and normative sense of the term.[17] According to Maritain, by conflating the common good with the juridical apparatus of the state, "substantialism" perverted the entire order of distributive justice. It canceled out the liberty and authority appropriate to social bodies other than the juridical state.

The second problem was the failure of European peoples to hold that state to "the objective order of justice and law." Europe strayed from one of the things it got right in the eighteenth century, namely, the doctrine of natural rights—a doctrine that brought "to full light the rights of man as also required by natural law." Maritain famously argued that a lack of theoretical consensus about human rights should not deter practical agreement. A "practical ideology," to use Maritain's own words, is feasible because the experiences and practices of modernity have contributed to a clearer moral sense of what belongs, of right, to individuals.[18] Despite the devolution of philosophical theory in modernity and despite the gross violations of human rights by modern states, there is nonetheless progress in consciousness—a kind of new *ius gentium* of human rights.

Maritain believed that these two principles of constitutionalism and natural rights are complementary. He thought so, among other reasons, because of the example afforded by the United States, where Maritain saw both a constitutionally limited government and a nonsectarian creed of natural rights. Why limit government only by constitutional enumeration of powers, when one can also limit it by compelling it to recognize the rights of man? In *The Rights of Man and Natural Law* (1943), Maritain approvingly cited Section 1 of the Fourteenth Amendment as the model for bringing government under the rule of rights.[19] Yet, even as he wrote, Section 1 of the Fourteenth Amendment was being used by the Court as a bottomless reservoir of new rights—rights that were to be secured against political authorities and societies lower than the national state. There could not have been a better example of how the principle of limited, constitutional government and the principle of rights (however harmonious in theory) were not always complementary in practice. Maritain was seemingly oblivious to the problem. Indeed, in 1958, he wrote of the Supreme Court: ". . . I think that the American institution of the Supreme Court is one of the great political achievements of modern times, and one of the most significant tributes ever paid to wisdom and its right of preeminence in human affairs.[20]

Maritain was certainly aware of the tendency to inflate rights claims. "We have especially a tendency to inflate and make absolute, limitless, unrestricted in every respect, the right of which we are aware, thus blinding ourselves to any other right which would counterbalance them."[21] "Even for the absolutely inalienable rights," he writes, "we must distinguish between possession and exercise—the latter being subject to conditions and limitations dictated in each case by justice."[22] Here, the problem of underspecified rights claims snaps into view. How can there be rights prior to the dictates of justice?

The problem is how to conceptualize the possession of a moral right antecedent to those very dictates of justice according to which the action can be said to be "right." To speak of a moral right that binds someone else, much less a right that binds the entire polity, ahead of the judgment that the action is "right" and ahead of the rules of law according to which and by whom that judgment is to be made, is to equivocate on the meaning of rights and, even worse, to breed precisely the sort of confusion that constitutionalism is meant to remedy. Can the distinction between possession and exercise rescue Maritain?

In order to sharpen our dubiety about the usefulness of the possession/exercise distinction as a way to handle the problem of inadequately specified moral rights, I shall give an example of a right about which it is meaningless to speak of the distinction between possession and exercise. Consider the due process clauses of the Fifth and Fourteenth Amendments. According to the Fourteenth Amendment, no state may take life, liberty, or property without due process of law; that is, without a fair finding of some guilt or obligation on the part of whoever has his life, liberty, or property taken. It hardly needs emphasis that the entire apparatus of the state's criminal law depends upon the truth of this right and its corresponding duty. In the case of the right of the innocent not to be punished, the possession and exercise are unified without remainder; for it is in the very nature of the thing that government could never use power directly and knowingly to punish the innocent or to punish the guilty without a fair finding of his guilt. One always has a right to exercise this right against government, and government has an obligation to give due process whether or not it is claimed by the citizen. No one would claim that the government has an obligation to give due process, except when it has a compelling interest to do otherwise. Correlatively, no citizen possesses a right to obtain due process which he cannot exercise. Of course, we will need additional determinations of an institutional and procedural sort for the purpose of regulating the finding of guilt or innocence. But the point remains. The possession/exercise distinction is irrelevant, for there is no gap between right and duty other than what needs to be filled in by a finding of fact.

The more honest and perceptive liberal theorists have known that broadly drawn rights often fail to include the principle of moral rectitude or obligation. William Galston, for example, writes: "Liberal practical philosophy has long excelled at the defense of individual choice; it must now learn how to provide standards for the right exercise of rights."[23] Galston continues: "What also emerges . . . is the incompleteness of the language of rights. There is a gap between 'I have a right to do X' and 'X is the right thing to do,' which can only be filled by a moral vocabulary broader than the language of rights."[24] Now, Galston could be right about this "gap" if he is referring only to legal rights. It is uncontroversial that a person *could* have a legal right to buy a $70,000 Corvette during a time of famine, without thereby claiming either (1) that the purchase is morally right or (2) that he has a moral right to purchase the car. Presumably, his right rests on the fact that the positive law gives no other person the right to stop him. So too, in the case of many other legal rights, the possession of a right and the morality of its exercise are not coimplicates in any strict sense. But Maritain is speaking of moral rights, not legal rights. And in the sphere of moral rights, Galston's notion of a "gap" between the possession of a right and its morally proper exercise is fatal. This sort of incompleteness stands at the level where the moral duty has to be located. Until it is located, it is not clear whether one can be said to have a moral right.

In short, no one has a moral right to do moral wrong; one doesn't possess such a right, and therefore the state cannot be said to restrict the exercise of it. Now, one might have a moral right that such and such a person not impede one's doing of a moral wrong; but this is not because of the merit of the action or choice, but because of the quite different principle that no government official is allowed to act beyond the powers given him. And even here, there is no relevant distinction between possession and exercise. If indeed one has a moral right that some other person not impede one's doing of a moral wrong, then this right is precisely what one is entitled to exercise. The prospective buyer of the Corvette might therefore have a moral right that the taking or restricting of his economic liberty be done only by those who have authority to redistribute wealth, just as the felon has a moral right not to be punished by a vigilante mob. None of these examples, however, requires us to follow Maritain down the path of affirming the possession of moral right ahead of whatever specification is needed to generate a duty on someone else's part.[25]

Inadequately specified moral, human, or natural rights claims have some very deleterious consequences for constitutionalism. First, generalized rights claims do not always limit the government, for government will inevitably have to make exceptions to the exercise of the alleged right. It is not merely coincidental that the Court invented the criterion of "compelling state interest" at the same time that the Court started down the path of interpreting the Constitution in the light of substantive rights rather than in the light of enumerated powers of government.

Second, even under optimal conditions of a government that sensibly deliberates about how to fill the "gap" between rights and rights exercised rightly, the government does not have a sufficiently precise idea of how to direct and limit its powers. For every underspecified or overspecified rights claim, we will have to commission the government to discover precisely what it is that the government must promote, protect, and secure. Since no one knows precisely who is obligated and what they are obligated to do or not do, the constitutional system will become dystelic and ultimately unjust. It is one thing to suffer morally confused individuals; it is far more dangerous to suffer a government that acts blindly, without direction—especially when the confusion stems from the fundamental law of the constitution rather than from a stupid or unjust policy or statute.

Third, whereas a crudely framed policy or statute can be corrected through the ordinary political process, a morally improper right at the constitutional level can generate a crisis of conscience for the entire polity. This problem surfaced in an especially critical way with the Dred Scott decision of 1857. With regard to the notion that owning slaves is a fundamental or natural right, Abraham Lincoln observed: "Its language is equivalent to saying that it is embodied and so woven into that instrument [viz. the Constitution] that it cannot be detached without breaking the constitution itself."[26] "If slavery is right," Lincoln said, "all words, acts, laws, and constitutions against it, are themselves wrong, and should be silenced, and swept away."[27] In the same vein, James Madison, a slaveholder, argued at the Constitutional Convention that it would be "wrong to admit in the Constitution the idea that there could be property in men."[28] With consummate clarity, Madison understood that to recognize such a right in the fundamental law would forever take the matter of slavery out of the sphere of governmental prudence and would bind the entire polity to the protection of a wrong. Such "wrongs" can enjoy a kind of legal immunity in the case of legislative toleration or in the case where a constitution does not delegate to government, or a certain sector of it, the power to address the wrong. But as both Madison and Lincoln understood, toleration and the want of power are entirely different than grounding the wrong in a claim of natural right.

The framers and ratifiers of the U.S. Constitution certainly believed in natural rights. But to their credit, they were exceedingly cautious about writing these principles directly into the fundamental law. Instead, they opted for a Constitution of enumerated powers, which spelled out precisely what the government cannot do and how it must do the things it can do. In framing this kind of fundamental law, they believed that the institutions of government would be broadly congruent with natural principles of justice. How the actions of government are to be made more adequate to the requirements of natural justice is deferred to the deliberative skills of ordinary legislators.

The framers understood that from unbounded individual liberty comes despotism and that one of the best ways to limit the despotic tendencies of government is to eschew broad and underspecified rights claims. Far from disparaging principles of natural justice, the framers took care to protect those principles from the exuberance of ideologues. The specific institutional character of the U.S. Constitution is one among many different kinds of constitutional order. It differs sharply from those constitutions which display the powers and ends of a government of general jurisdiction. To this extent, it is not necessarily a model for any other polity. However, its institutional wisdom about the problem of rights drawn too broadly has value for political and legal philosophers.

Endnotes

1. Oklahoma Constitution, art. 2, sec. 2 & 11.

2. Ibid., sec. 34.

3. "To promote the Progress of Science and useful Arts, by securing for limited Times to Authors and Inventors the exclusive Right to their respective Writings and Discoveries."

4. Virginia Constitution, art. 1, sec. 16.

5. Heinrich Rommen, *The Natural Law* (St. Louis: Herder, 1947), 261.

6. "[I]t should be said that as one man is a part of the household, so too a household is a part of the state, and the *civitas* is a perfect community, according to *Politics I*. Therefore, as the good of one man is not the last end, but is ordered to the common good, so too the good of the one household is ordered to the good of a single state, which is a perfect community." St. Thomas

Aquinas, *Summa Theologiae,* trans. Fathers of the English Dominican Province (New York: Benzinger Brothers, 1948), 1–2, q. 90, a. 3, ad. 3.

7. James Wilson, "Opening Address at the Pennsylvania Ratifying Convention," 24 November, 1787, in *The Debate on the Constitution,* ed. Bernard Bailyn (New York: Library of America, 1993), 791, 793.

8. Alexis de Toqueville, *Democracy in America,* ed. J. P. Mayer (New York: Doubleday-Anchor, 1969), 115.

9. Emphasis added.

10. The Fourteenth Amendment (1868) created federal supervisory and enforcement powers over some of the police powers of the state governments. Although the amendment did not make the federal government a government of general jurisdiction, it sowed the seeds for that transformation. Having the power to supervise police powers is, at least operationally, the same as having the police powers, since the police powers of the government of the United States will be enlarged accordingly. Once the Article III courts got into the business of incorporating the Bill of Rights against the states, it is not surprising that judges would feel compelled to introduce substantive moral principles.

11. Joseph Story, *Commentaries on the Constitution of the United States,* Bk. 3, Ch. 44 (1833; reprint, Durham: Carolina Academic Press, 1987), 979.

12. *Planned Parenthood of Southeastern Pennsylvania v. Casey,* 112 S. Ct. 2791, 2807 (1992).

13. Simone Weil, "Human Personality," in *Selected Essays,* trans. Richard Rees (Oxford: Oxford University Press, 1962), 9–10.

14. *Olmstead v. United States,* 277 U.S. 438, 978 (1928) (Brandeis, J., dissenting).

15. Take as another example, the recent United Nations Convention on the Rights of the Child. Article 12 asserts "that the child who is capable of forming his or her own views has the right to express those views freely in all matters affecting the child." Article 13 asserts "that the child shall have the right to seek, receive and impart information and ideas of all kinds, regardless of frontiers, either orally, or in writing or in print, in the form of art, or through any other media of the child's choice." *Convention on the Rights of the Child,* November 20, 1989, 28 I.L.M. 1448, 1461. Moral desiderata are not the same thing as morally binding prescriptions, even if one tries to compel these desiderata into the rhetoric of moral prescriptions.

16. On the evolution of such generalized rights claims in United States constitutional law, see Russell Hittinger, "Liberalism and the American Natural Law Tradition," in *Wake Forest Law Review,* vol. 25, issue 3 (1990).

17. Jacques Maritain, *Man and the State* (Chicago: University of Chicago Press, 1951), 14, 16 n. 11.

18. Ibid., 78.

19. Jacques Maritain, *The Rights of Man and Natural Law,* trans. Doris C. Anson (New York: Charles Scribners, 1943; reprint, New York: Gordian Press, 1971), 115.

20. Jacques Maritain, *Reflections on America* (New York: Charles Scribner's Sons, 1958), 171.

21. Maritain, *Man and the State,* 103.

22. Ibid., 101.

23. William Galston, "Between Philosophy and History—The Evolution of Rights in American Thought," in *Old Rights and New,* ed. Robert A. Licht (Washington, D.C.: The AEI Press, 1993), 74.

24. Ibid., 52.

25. It should be noted that the failure of an underspecified claim to generate a duty does not imply that such a claim fails to call attention to the fundaments of a right. The fact that someone is a human being, entitled to inclusion within the moral community, is an ontological principle that precedes any properly specified rights to claim. Indeed, any properly specified moral rights claim will specify that very fundament of nature. Senator Joseph Biden voted against the confirmation of Robert Bork, among other reasons, because Bork expressly rejected judicial uses of natural law. Against Bork, Biden declared: "I have certain inalienable rights because I exist. . . ." This statement is true, but it still fails to specify a right. See Russell Hittinger, "Natural Law in the Positive Laws: A Legislative or Adjudicative Issue?" 55 *Review of Politics* 5 (1993).

26. Abraham Lincoln, Speech at Columbus, Ohio, 16 September 1859, in *Lincoln: Speeches and Writings* 1859–1865, ed. Don E. Fehrenbacher (New York: The Library of America, 1989), 53.

27. Lincoln, Address at Cooper Union, 27 February 1860, in *Lincoln: Speeches and Writings,* 129.

28. In vol. 2, ed. Max Farrand (New Haven: Yale University Press, 1966), 417.

Chapter 9

Natural Law and Sexual Ethics

JANET E. SMITH

I am honored to have my essay included in this series on natural law. Many of the other contributors are among my heroes and friends. One of my heroes, Alasdair MacIntyre, uses one of his favorite terms in his essay: he writes of "plain persons" and their grasp of morality and natural law in contradistinction to the experts and professional philosophers and their grasp of these matters. A few years ago in Dallas, Alasdair MacIntyre gave a talk entitled "Do plain persons need to be moral philosophers?" When I was asked to give the response to his talk, I was most honored because I consider Professor MacIntyre one of the foremost moral philosophers in the world, and it was a thrill to comment on his work. I felt dreadfully underqualified—I felt like a high school student going up against Larry Bird—until I realized that I did not need to respond as an expert, as a moral philoso-

pher of his caliber, but that I could respond as the quintessential plain person—for that is what I am. After all, I
am Janet Smith, daughter of John and Anne Smith; I grew
up at 5 Hill Street and went to Home Street School. I
could write more, but it is all very plain.

The point I am making here is not merely a flip one—
designed to ease us into more serious matters through an
attempt at humor. There is a serious point here—natural
law is the plain person's morality—in a sense it is simply
plain old common sense. There are profound and sophisticated ways of explaining natural law, but the *practice* of
reasoning in accord with natural law principles, according to the theory itself, is natural to plain persons—that is,
natural to all mankind. Natural law holds that many of
the most fundamental principles of moral reasoning are
obvious, that is, easily known by all. Yet, in spite of the
plain commonsensicalness of natural law, it can seem
shocking and provocative in many ways, for like natural
law, plain old common sense does not command a lot of
followers these days and can be shocking when juxta-
posed to the values of our times.

This essay is very basic in several respects. It reviews
some of the basic principles that other contributors have
covered, reviewing some in depth, some more in passing.
It also is very basic because it attempts to apply natural
law to concrete moral issues, specifically issues in the
realm of sexual ethics. My job is not to justify natural law
ethics but to explain it and apply it. On these matters, I
will largely follow the thought of Thomas Aquinas and of
Aristotle from whom Aquinas learned many of the principles that informed his teaching on natural law. I shall
also incorporate into my arguments the thought of

another stellar natural law theorist, still alive and well: I shall make use of the work of Karol Wojtyla, now known as Pope John Paul II. I will refer to him as Wojtyla simply because I do not want to be perceived as invoking his authority as Holy Father; I cite him simply as a philosopher who has made great advances in our understanding of natural law, particularly in regard to sexual ethics.[1]

Let me begin with a review of the principles of natural law. Aquinas maintains that the first principle of natural law is "do good, avoid evil." As he notes, that is a self-evident principle and obvious to all; if we want to be moral, we should do good and avoid evil. There is no controversy here. The questions are, of course, what is good, what is evil, and how do we come to know which is which? Some think we cannot know what is good and evil, so the best we can do is live by the conventions of our times. Others think it best to let our passions be our guide to whatever we want to do. Others think only revealed religion can give us absolutes. These three positions capture the predominant views of our times.

Aquinas holds none of these positions.[2] He argues that reason should be our guide to morality. Not only does he hold that the first principle of natural law—"do good, avoid evil"—is self-evident, he argues that there are other self-evident first principles, such as "Harm no man." These, he says, are imprinted in the minds of all by God. I believe other precepts such as "Provide responsibly for your offspring," "Give to each man his due," and "Seek knowledge" would qualify as precepts that Aquinas thinks all men know. Men (I use the term generically here and throughout) may act against these precepts out of passion or because of ignorance of some fact operative in a situation, but all would agree that such principles are moral truths. Aquinas goes on to say that what he calls primary precepts of natural law are *naturally* and immediately known by man; he cites the Ten Commandments as examples of these types of precepts. These precepts are justified by the primary principles. From the most general principle "Give to each man his due" and from an understanding of what one owes to one's mother and father, it is clear that one "should honor one's father and mother."

This is not to imply that one discovers the moral law by discovering these precepts in a deductive manner, moving from the most general to the more particular. Rather, it seems that moral discovery, as the discovery of other general truths, often moves from the particular to the universal. That is, an individual could witness or participate in a transaction and quite immediately make the moral judgment that the act is good or bad. For instance, an individual could witness someone honoring or dishonoring his parents and judge the action to be good or bad; from this action and others of the same sort one may come to formulate the "law" that one should give each man his due. But it is because we already naturally know—in an unexpressed and unformulated way—that one should give each man his due, that we are able to see readily that honoring one's parents is good. Much in the same way that we, without musical training, can judge certain tones to be off pitch, we have moral "perceptions" that some actions are good and some bad, without having any explicit training about such kinds of actions. I speak of these as moral "perceptions" not because they are equivalent to sense perceptions, but because of their immediacy and their unformulated quality; indeed, I believe them to be rational in several important respects, not least because they are cognitive acts and they are in accord with reality.

Now consider rationality and the Thomistic claim that "one should act rationally." Indeed, one could formulate the first principle of natural law not only in the most basic formula, "do good, avoid evil"; in Thomistic terms, several formulas serve to express the same truth. For Aquinas, the following phrases are synonymous: "Act in accord with nature"; "Act in accord with reason"; "Act rationally"; "Act in accord with virtue"; "Act in accord with the dignity of the human person"; and "Act in accord with a well-formed conscience." Indeed, "Act in a loving way," properly understood, serves as well.

While it would be of great profit to elaborate how each of these phrases is synonymous with the other, I want to devote most of my efforts to explaining how "Act in accord with nature" and "Act in accord with reason" are synonymous and worthy guides to moral behavior.

First we must clarify as much as possible what it means to say "Act in accord with reason" or "Act rationally." In our day, reason often gets undeserved criticism. This is a fault not of Aristotle or Aquinas, but of Descartes, Kant, and their followers. Since they retreated into the mind and abandoned the senses, emotions, and nature as guides to truth, they made reason seem coldly logical, impersonal, abstract, and completely devoid of experiential and emotional content. In their view, mathematics and geometry are the quintessential rational acts; to be rational is to operate totally within one's mind and be completely unemotional. Another view of rationality that dominates modern times is the view that only that which can be measured scientifically deserves any recognition as objective truth. No truths other than those substantiated by scientific proofs—truths that can be quantified largely in the laboratory—count as truth. No proof other than scientific proof counts as truth; only science and that which approximates scientific truth are truly rational.

Neither view is the view of reason and rationality held by the ancients and medievalists—those who defined the view of natural law I am defending here. The ancients and medievalists did not think rationality was possible without the senses and the emotions, for both are tools to reading reality; they provide the intellect with the material needed to make a good judgment. The etymology of the word "rational" is rooted in the word *ratio*, which means measure or proportion. One is being rational when one's thought and action are measured to, are proportionate with, or correspond with reality (which itself is measured or governed by discernible laws). The thought that leads to acting in accord with reality is called rational. This thought need not be and perhaps only rarely will be the kind of abstract, cold, logical reasoning of a Descartes, Kant, or research scientist. This thought can be intuitive, creative, poetic, inductive, deductive—indeed, whatever human thought can be. It is all called rational thought not because it proceeds by syllogism or because it is subject to certain scientific tests; it is called rational because it corresponds with reality—and this includes all of reality, the spiritual and the transcendental as well as the logically provable and the scientifically measurable reality.

Such thought cannot proceed without abundant data from our senses and our emotions. The intellect processes such data and orders it; it determines what values are important in the data and decides on the appropriate response. If one acts rationally, one then acts in accord with the ordering done by the intellect. While the intellect should govern the emotions, it is not a natural law teaching that all rational behavior will be devoid of emotion. Again, the emotions can provide essential data to the intellect. Emotions that are well habituated may lead one quite spontaneously to respond correctly to situations. One may spontaneously get angry at witnessing some act of injustice, and if one knows one's emotions to be well ordered, one could respond quite immediately and correctly—and even angrily—to the situation. Indeed, at times it may be an appropriate response to reality to rant and rave. Someone doing so is properly called rational, in spite of our common parlance.

This talk of the mind and of rationality as something that is measured to reality suggests, as mentioned above, that reality is a thing that can be grasped. Natural law depends upon such. It rests upon the claim that things have natures and essences that we can know and to which we correspond our actions. There are many reasons for making this claim. One is the fact that things act in a predictable fashion; when we learn the properties of oil and water, for instance, we can predict certain things about their behavior. The fact that we build bridges that stand, that we make artificial hearts that work, or that we put men on the moon also indicates we are able to measure our thoughts to the external world and to act in accord with it.

Moreover, natural law operates on the premise that nature is good, that is, that the way things naturally are is good for them to be; it holds that the operations of things and parts of things contribute to the good of the whole. The wings of different birds are shaped in certain fashions because of the sort of flying that they must do to survive; different digestive systems work in different ways because of what is being digested. Indeed, natural law holds that the natural instincts of natural things are good; they lead them to do what helps those things function well and helps them survive. Since natural things have an order, there is said to be a ratio or order to them; not one of which they are conscious but one that is written into their functioning. Natural law holds that we live in a universe of things that have a ratio to them, and that we shall get the best out of these things if we act in accord with the ratio or nature that is written into them.

Now man is a natural thing. He, too, has parts, operations, and instincts that enable him to function well and to survive. Man differs from other creatures in that he has free will; that is, he can either cooperate with his nature or act against his nature, whereas other natural things have no such freedom. What enables man to be free is his reason, his rationality; he is able to weigh and measure different courses of action and determine which actions are good or bad. According to natural law, those actions are good which accord with his nature and with the nature of other things. Since man is by nature a rational animal, it is good for him to act in accord with his reason. By acting rationally he is acting in accord with his own nature and with a reality that is also ordered. When he acts rationally, he acts in accord with his own nature and reality, and in accord with the nature and reality of other things.

Next, let us get concrete. Let us consider acting in accord with the nature of a few specific things. Take tomato plants, for instance. Tomato plants have a certain nature. In order to have good tomato plants one must act toward these plants in accord with their nature; one must water them and give them sunlight and good soil if one wants to produce good tomato plants. Such is acting in accord with nature in respect to tomato plants, such is rational behavior in respect to tomato plants. If one's tomato plants fail to produce tomatoes, one knows that one is doing something wrong; if one's tomato plants produce good tomatoes, one knows one is doing something right. In his book *Fifty Questions on Natural Law,* Professor Charles Rice speaks of the rationality of putting oil and not molasses in the engine of a car.[3] One needs to act in accord with the nature of things if one wishes them to perform well.

Moving quickly, let us now move to human nature. If a human being wishes to function and perform well, what does his nature require of him? Let us begin with his physical nature. There is a considerable consensus about what makes for physical health and what is conducive to physical health. Those who do not get sick, who are able to function well in their daily activities, who are not overweight, we call healthy. We know how to produce such individuals. We are regularly and rightly advised to eat well, exercise regularly, and get plenty of sleep. Those who do so generally flourish physically— because they are acting in accord with nature, with reason, and with reality. Psychological health is also understood to some extent; we know we need friends, rest, and interests to sustain our psychological health; that is our nature; that is reality.

Nor are we in the dark about what makes for moral health or moral goodness. We recognize the goodness of the various virtues such as self-discipline, reliability, justice and fairness, kindness, truthfulness, loyalty, etc. Those who exhibit these qualities we generally recognize as being good—that is morally good—human beings. Parents who have children displaying such qualities are rightly proud of them; their "tomato plants" turned out well.

In regard to sexual behavior, sexual moral health, so to speak, what qualifies as acting in accord with nature, with reason? How do we determine what it is?

For Aquinas these are not difficult questions; though, apparently, they are extremely difficult questions for modern times. We are terribly confused about what proper sexual behavior is. College newspapers are filled with news of campuses that are devising codes of moral sexual behavior—codes that are designed primarily to stop or reduce the incidence of date rape on campus. These codes suggest or require that in sexual activity neither individual proceed to the next level of sexual activity without obtaining the permission of the other individual. These codes reflect what has been the principle governing sexual behavior in recent times: whatever one feels comfortable with and whatever one agrees to is morally correct. This is basically what we are teaching our young people, and they are doing what one would expect given that teaching. As long as it feels good and they have consented to it, there is no reason for them not to do "it."

Is this working? Is this principle leading to moral health or moral sickness? What can we say about the moral sexual health of our society? What does the fact that 68 percent of African-American babies are born out of wedlock suggest? The figure is now 22 percent in the white community and rapidly growing. This figure, of course, would be higher if it were not for the one and a half million abortions a year. One of two marriages is going to end in divorce. AIDS is decimating some portions of our population. Are there any hints here that we are violating nature, acting irrationally, failing to live in accord with reality? Are our tomato plants thriving?

Think about each one of these as a concrete moral fact: when we see the heartbreak and social dysfunction associated with out-of-wedlock births, don't our immediate and natural moral perceptions and judgments say, "Something is wrong here"? When we learn that a woman has had an abortion, no matter what our view of the morality of abortion, don't we say, "Something has gone wrong here"? When we hear of a divorce and all the surrounding heartbreak and dysfunctionality, don't we think, "Something has gone wrong here"? When we see young people dying of AIDS, don't we think, "Something has gone wrong here"?

The moral principle I am going to articulate may seem perfectly obvious to some and quite ridiculous to others. Before I articulate the principle, I would like to briefly consider the significance of the diversity of predicted responses to it. MacIntyre points out how curious it is in the modern age that we have so little consensus on the most straightforward claims of natural law; what seems obvious to some seems ridiculous to others. Whereas some take this lack of consensus to suggest that claims about the universality of natural law are false, MacIntyre takes this lack of consensus to indicate the moral corruption of our times. That is, we have become so corrupt that we cannot discern what is obvious. I am not going to try to analyze how this came about, but I do want to make a suggestive analogy with the physical senses. Just as our ears, when subjected to noises that are too loud and sharp, lose some of their ability to hear, so too does our moral "sense," when subjected to too much corruption, lose its ability to judge what is right and wrong. Much of what I am going to articulate will sound strange to modern ears because we have lost our moral sense to some considerable extent.

What is this obvious principle I am threatening to articulate? It is a principle readily justified by natural law reasoning. A natural law theorist reasons that man certainly has a natural inclination to engage in sexual intercourse and that that natural inclination is good for man—much in the same way that sunshine is good for a tomato plant. As for all animals, sexual intercourse leads to the perpetuation of the species, and that is good. Because man is rational, he can naturally and readily see that his natural sexual inclinations differ from those of animals who copulate and reproduce willy-nilly. Human sexual intercourse is clearly for much more than simple reproduction of the species. Sexual intercourse conduces to the well-being of human beings in many ways. For instance, sexual intercourse can expand the opportunities for humans to love—not only to love their sexual partner but also to love the offspring they may have. It allows spouses to build a family together and to have a meaningful life.

It would be profitable for us to consider a little more how human sexual behavior does and should differ from animal sexual behavior. Certainly, for both animals and men, sexual intercourse is extremely pleasurable. But for humans, that pleasure is not an uncomplicated pleasure. First, we have a powerful sense of the power and mystery of sexual intercourse. We sense that we are dealing with something fraught with emotional risks, fraught indeed with serious responsibilities. These responsibilities are twofold, at least; they are the responsibilities that come with the babies that naturally result from sexual intercourse and with the bonding between the partners that naturally comes with sexual intercourse. So here is the key for natural law ethics. Since sexual intercourse has this twofold natural purpose that must be respected—the purpose of bringing forth new lives and the purpose of uniting men and women together—whoever participates in sexual activity must do so in a way that protects these natural goods of sexual intercourse.

Let us speak of babies first. Again, as with animals, the extremely pleasurable act of sexual intercourse naturally, though not always or even usually, can lead to the birth of an offspring. Unlike most animal offspring, a human baby needs years of prolonged and devoted care to come to maturity. The evidence is overwhelming that such care is best given by the parents of the baby. And here is where the first major moral principle of sexual behavior becomes manifest. Given the nature of human babies, given this reality, is it not right to posit the moral principle *"Rational behavior requires that those who are not prepared to be parents ought not to engage in sexual intercourse"*? Although that principle sounds shocking and strange to modern ears, I believe that it is plain common sense; indeed, that it is obvious.

Let me elaborate. Most individuals want to be good parents. They see that being a good parent is part of being a good human being and living a full and good human life. They recognize that children need parents with at least some degree of maturity. They agree that those who are not ready for babies ought not to have them. They even agree, for the most part, that being ready to be parents means being married, for only those who are willing to commit to marriage have the kind of commitment needed in parents. (Even those men who are sexually promiscuous are generally uncomfortable with the idea that they may have fathered children they do not know or care for, or that some of the babies they have fathered may have been aborted.) In spite of this consensus and plain common sense, in our times these insights do not translate into seeing that one ought not to have sexual intercourse until one is ready for babies. We think it is perfectly all right for those who are not prepared to have babies to have sexual intercourse. We think so because we rely upon contraception to sever the natural connection between having sexual intercourse and having babies. We think we are being responsible if we contracept; that is, after all, what responsible sex is, is it not?

Some readers might think that my first principle of sexual morality, "Don't have sexual intercourse until you are ready to be parents" (or more precisely "Don't have sexual intercourse until you marry—for only the married are truly ready to be parents"), is the surprising and provocative part of my plain, commonsensical position. However, some readers might be further surprised. I contend that in spite of our modern practices and views about sexual responsibility, contraception is not a rational or natural act. In fact, I think that contraception is one of the great evils of modern times, for it has been the fuel that has allowed the sexual revolution to rage. And the sexual revolution has led to the sexual chaos of our culture, which I sketched earlier: millions of babies aborted or born out of wedlock, millions of divorces, tens of thousands dying from AIDS. And this chaos, as we know, leads to multiple other social ills.

Contraception is at the center of this reality and a major contributor to it because it severs having sex from having babies and allows millions of people to participate in an act whose consequences they are not prepared to face. Millions are involved in relationships that are not prepared for the eventuality of a baby; when a baby is conceived, abortion or out-of-wedlock birth is the most common result. In my reading, contraception does not foster responsibility; it fosters irresponsibility by promoting the view that one need not be prepared to be a parent in order to have sexual intercourse responsibly.

The consequences of a contraceptive culture are abundantly clear to us. I think that once one ponders how unnatural contraception is, how out of accord with reality it is, the sexual chaos that characterizes our culture should not surprise us. Why would I say that someone who uses contraception is not respecting the nature and reality of sexual intercourse? First, consider the reality of contraceptives, what they do to a woman's body. The Pill is the most popular form of contraception. Furthermore, when does one generally take a pill? Obviously, when one is ill. But is fertility a sickness? Isn't fertility a healthy, natural condition? Doesn't The Pill treat fertility as though it were an illness, a defect, not a natural good? And think of the side effects of The Pill. The insert that comes with The Pill lists a large number of contraindications or bad side effects. It can cause blood clots, strokes, and infertility in a small percentage of cases—to be sure, but when millions of women are using The Pill, the small percentages can add up to large numbers. Think of the everyday, common side effects. It is common for women who use The Pill to complain of increased irritability, depression, weight gain, and a decreased libido. Isn't The Pill something every woman wants—something to help her be more irritable, to be more depressed, to gain weight, and to have a decreased desire for sexual intercourse! Why would any man want the woman he cares for and maybe even loves to take such a chemical monstrosity? In our age, when we have discovered how foolish it is to dump alien chemicals into the environment, why do we think it is sensible for women to put so many alien chemicals into their bodies?

The most serious feature of The Pill, however, is that it can operate as an abortifacient. The Pill (and Norplant and Deprovera) works in three ways. It works by stopping ovulation; if a woman does not release an egg, she cannot get pregnant. It works by changing the viscosity of the mucus that either helps or hinders the sperm in getting to the egg. And it works by rending the uterine wall hostile to the fertilized ovum—or, in my thinking, to the new human being. A woman never knows how the hormones in The Pill are affecting her body; she does not know how it is preventing her from becoming pregnant. It could be preventing her from ovulating, but it also could be causing her to self-abort. The IUD, which has been taken off the market because it endangered women's lives, also operates as an abortifacient. It may stop ovulation, but more often it makes the uterine wall hostile to the fertilized ovum, the new human being. Thus, the same natural law arguments used to demonstrate the immorality of abortion can be used to demonstrate the immorality of The Pill, Norplant, Deprovera, and the IUD. Any man or woman opposed to abortion should have nothing to do with these contraceptives.

The barrier methods of contraception begin to disclose another feature of contraception that is against the goods of sexual intercourse. They reveal that contraceptives not only work against babies, a natural and good outcome of sexual intercourse; they also work against the uniting and bonding of the sexual partners. The very name "barrier" is revealing. A couple wishes to make love, but first they must get their barriers in place. They may decide to use a good spermicide to kill whatever sperm may approach the egg. This action is saying, "I want to love you and give myself to you and receive you, but I want to kill any sperm that may penetrate my being." Is there not a discordant note of hostility in this act that is meant to be a loving act? Does not the rejection of one's beloved's fertility also mean a rejection of one's beloved, as well, at least to some extent? All of contraception says, "I want to give myself to you and receive you, but I reject completely your fertility; it is not welcome here."

Here is where Karol Wojtyla's analysis of sexual ethics has made a major contribution. Wojtyla has written extensively on human sexuality; it is possible here to give only the briefest sketch of his thought. He observes that male and female are made for each other. Each sex is really incomplete without the other; physically and psychically the sexes complete each other. The story told by Aristophanes in Plato's *Symposium* comically portrays this reality. Aristophanes suggests that the first human beings at one time had two heads, four legs and arms, etc. Later they were cut in half, one-half male, the other half female and since then they have spent an enormous amount of energy trying to reunite.

Wojtyla maintains that we have a deep and natural need to give ourselves to another person, to make ourselves whole by giving ourselves to another. He says that this giving is most completely performed in the sexual act between male and female, an act that is meant to express the deep commitment and desire for union that we feel and wish to express. Wojtyla says that the attempt to thwart the fertility of the sexual act means that one is withholding one's fertility from the other—one is withholding something that belongs in the sexual act. To withhold it diminishes the meaning of the sexual act. One way of seeing Wojtyla's point is to think of the difference between the phrases "I want to have sex with you" and "I am open to having babies with you." The first phrase is one our culture utters with the greatest of casualness; contracepted sex is often engaged in with the same commitment that going out to dinner or playing tennis with another suggests—that is, not much. Being open to having a baby with another, however, bespeaks a very great commitment to another, the kind of commitment that should be made by those engaging in an act that might in fact result in a baby. It bespeaks the willingness to have one's whole life entwined with another's, to have breakfast together, to go to Little League games, to plan weddings.

Many in our culture cannot imagine life without contraception. They think the alternative means no sexual intercourse at all or lots of babies. Since our culture is so obsessed with sex and so hostile to babies, both possibilities seem unthinkable. Few have any idea how satisfying it is to wait until marriage to have sexual intercourse with someone with whom one has vowed to spend one's life. Few have any idea how deeply meaningful noncontracepted sexual intercourse is; how doable periodic abstinence is in marriage for those who have abstained before marriage. They know nothing about how methods of natural family planning work; they often refuse to believe, in spite of the most solid scientific evidence, that methods of natural family planning are more reliable and effective than any other form of birth control.[4]

Many fail to see any moral difference between contraception and methods of natural family planning. They think that since a contracepting couple and one using natural family planning both intend not to have a child and do intend to have sexual intercourse that does not issue in a child, what they are doing amounts to the same thing. The standard distinction between means and end is certainly operative here. Though they may have the same moral end—limiting their family size—one couple chooses the means of thwarting their fertility, of engaging in potentially fertile acts and simultaneously working to destroy that fertility; the other couple respects their fertility and when not prepared to accept a child, refrains from fertile acts. A standard example demonstrating the difference between contraception and natural family planning is the analogy with eating. Some who wish to avoid a weight gain eat and then force themselves to vomit; they wish to have the pleasure of eating but not accept the consequences. Others who wish to avoid a weight gain do not eat foods that would add weight. They abstain from rich foods and eat them only when prepared for the consequences. The parallels with contraceptive sex and natural family planning are clear.

The differences between the two means of birth control are much greater than the above too-quick argument portrays. As a simple indication that what contracepting couples and couples using methods of natural family planning are doing is remarkably different, I ask: If they are so similar why are contraceptors so reluctant to switch to a method of natural family planning and why do those who use natural family planning find contraception so revolting? Both couples recognize that to switch would be to adopt a whole new view of sexuality, of one's relationship with one's spouse (or sexual partner, in the case of contraceptors), and indeed perhaps a whole new lifestyle. Actions that are morally equivalent rarely are perceived to be so different in so many respects.

The differences between contraceptive sex and sex governed by the principles of natural family planning (NFP) are very many; there is not room here to enumerate them all. Let me, however, note just a few features of NFP that may suggest how it is eminently human and draws upon fully human resources. There is something radically antifemale in contraceptives: they suggest it is better to have a male body that can engage in sexual intercourse and not get pregnant. Many women resent contraceptives for the unpleasant side effects and also resent the male who wants them to use contraceptives. Women who use NFP, on the other hand, are generally very positive about it, because it does not in any way threaten their health; it reveres their fertility whereas contraception, as noted above, treats their fertility as a liability. They have confidence in the love of their husbands, who revere their fertility to the extent that they do not wish to interfere with it. They understand abstaining to be another form of love. After all, many abstained before marriage, precisely out of love for their beloved.

Let me mention one other thought on this issue: contraceptors divorce at the rate of 50 percent, while evidence shows that couples using natural family planning divorce at a rate of under 2 percent.[5] While several factors undoubtedly contribute to this disparity, that there is such a disparity suggests that the couples' relationships differ vastly in quality. I suggest the quality of the sexual relationships may be a major factor, and I suggest that the much greater meaningfulness of a sexuality that respects the baby-making power of sexual intercourse may be the key. The notion that children are an optional offshoot of sexual intercourse, and not a natural and good consequence that should be respected, leads individuals to make bad choices for marriage partners. Because our culture denies the intricate relationship between sexual intercourse, babies, and marriage, those who engage in sexual intercourse often have few thoughts of marriage or babies in their minds. When they do marry, they are often simply marrying a sexual partner that they have become accustomed to. Sexual attraction and sexual compatibility become the chief foundation for relationships.

Often when I suggest to young people that the primary question they should ask themselves when they are looking for a spouse is "Would this individual be a good parent to our children?" they are astonished by the question and realize that it would radically influence their choice of a spouse. They admit that such a consideration had been far from their minds!

Our culture is a mess, and it is largely young people, and particularly young women, who are suffering the consequences of this mess. We can hardly blame them for the choices they make since they are the choices that we have deemed "responsible." Most who contracept have little understanding of what damage contraception can do to their relationships and to society as a whole. But as any biologist knows, if one is ingesting poison, even if it is cleverly disguised as a good, one will still suffer the ill effects of the poison. No matter how reliant our culture is on contraception, no matter how good we believe it to be, the evidence is becoming clearer and clearer that contraception is not the good many hoped it would be. If Aquinas is correct that nature is ordered and ordered to what is good, and if flouting the natural law leads to things not functioning properly, the current situation should be no surprise. The reality of sexual intercourse is that it is intimately and naturally connected with having babies and with creating strong bonds between the sexes. Natural law ethics acknowledges that living in accord with reality and nature limits our choices and our actions, but it holds that it limits them in a way that promotes our human good.

ENDNOTES

1. Karol Wojtyla, *Love and Responsibility* (Polish first edition published in 1960. Revised edition published in English in 1981 by William Collins Sons & Co. Ltd., London, and Farrar, Straus and Giroux, Inc., New York , 1960; reprint, San Francisco: Ignatius, 1993).

2. Statements I make about Aquinas's position are based upon questions 90–100 in *Summa Theologiae* I–II.

3. Charles Rice, *Fifty Questions on Natural Law* (San Francisco: Ignatius, 1993).

4. E. J. Ryder, "Natural Family Planning: Effective Birth Control Supported by the Catholic Church," British Medical Journal, 307 (6906). September 18, 1993. 723–726.

5. There do not as yet exist good studies on the relationship between NFP and divorce, but the anecdotal evidence from organizations that have taught NFP for decades is that reports of divorce among those who practice the methods are very rare. The reports of one nonscientific survey are reported by Nona Aguilar, "No-Pill, No-Risk Birth Control" (New York: Rawson Associates, 1986), 195. For the relation between contraception and divorce, see Robert T. Michael, "The Rise in Divorce Rates, 1960–1974: Age-Specific Components," *Demography* 15: 2 (May 1978): 177–82; "Determinates in Divorce," in *Sociological Economics*, edited by Louis Levy-Garboua (London: SAGE Publications, 1979); 223–54. and "Why Did the U.S. Divorce Rate Double Within a Decade," in *Research in Population,* (Greenwich: JAI Press, 1988) 361–99.

Part III

The Praxis of Natural Law

Chapter 10

Contract Law and Natural Law

EDWARD J. MURPHY

In preparing for a final examination, a student collected all of the notes which he had taken during the semester. Being a very industrious student, he had taken notes numbering in the hundreds of pages. Determined to put them into a more usable form, he began the process of condensing these materials. He was very good at it. So much so that on the day before the exam he had reduced everything to one page. But he was not content. One hour before the exam, one paragraph. Five minutes before the exam, three words. And just before the exam was to be written, he had captured it all in one word. He then began to write the exam and forgot that word.

If there is one word that captures the essence of contract law that word is "promise," for every issue respecting the legal enforcement of a promise is a contract issue. An authoritative definition is that of the American Law Institute's *Restatement of Contracts:* "A contract is a promise or set of promises for the breach of which the law gives a remedy, or the performance of which the law in some way recognizes as a duty."[1] In short, a contract is a legally binding promise. Thus, Arthur Corbin, a leading American contracts scholar described the purpose of this area of law as follows: "[T]he law of contracts attempts the realization of reasonable expectations that have been induced by the making of a promise."[2]

Contract law thus concerns the promises we make, and it takes but a moment's reflection to be impressed by the broad scope of the subject. Instances are legion in which we repose confidence in the promises of others. Limited to the commercial area alone, every employment agreement, sales contract, promissory note or check, rental or lease agreement, and so on, embodies a promise or contractual undertaking. And lest one conclude too hastily that mankind is totally unregenerate, consider that, in the vast majority of these cases, people keep these promises. They do what they say they will do. Goods are ordered, delivered, and paid for; work is performed and wages are paid; funds are deposited and returned with interest; and so on, through a myriad of economic transactions. There are, to be sure, enough cases where such promises are not kept to keep lawyers and law professors busy, but we should not forget that the real contract story is a *success* story.

Contemporary American law recognizes four types of contracts, each involving a transaction where something is added to a promise so as to make that promise legally binding. They are: (1) a promise plus consideration; (2) a promise plus form; (3) a promise plus an antecedent benefit; (4) and a promise plus unbargained-for reliance.[3]

The first of these is the bargain contract. Here the

promise is supported by an element called consideration, "something which is bargained for and given in exchange for the promise."[4] Almost all contracting is of this variety. The parties make a bargain; each exacts a price or payment, a quid pro quo, for their promises. For example, you promise to sell me your car in exchange for my promise to pay you five thousand dollars. Each promise is the consideration for the other promise, and a promise plus consideration yields a contractual obligation.

There are, however, additional instances where one may be obliged to perform a promise even though nothing was bargained for and given in exchange for that promise; i.e., where there was no consideration. For example, in a few cases, a promise is enforceable if it is in writing, quite apart from whether or not consideration was given.[5]

There are also times when a promise made in recognition of a prior benefit conferred by the promisee upon the promisor will be enforced. An example is where there is a debt against which the statute of limitations has run, leaving no more than a moral duty to pay. If the debtor later promises the creditor to pay that debt, this later promise, even though not supported by additional consideration, is enforceable.[6]

Finally, promissory liability may emerge because of a promise that engenders detrimental reliance by the promisee, a reliance not requested by the promisor. Treated under the rubric of promissory estoppel, this is an example of binding promise based upon unbargained-for reliance.[7] A nineteenth-century Nebraska case, *Ricketts v. Scothorn*, is illustrative.[8] Katie Scothorn worked as a bookkeeper in a store. Her grandfather came into the store one day and handed Katie his promissory note in the amount of two thousand dollars. He said: "I have fixed out something that you have not got to work any more. . . . None of my grandchildren work and you don't have to." Katie was overjoyed and proceeded to quit her job, remaining out of work for a considerable period. The court was careful to point out that the grandfather did not make a bargain with Katie; i.e., he did not promise to pay her two thousand dollars if she quit her job or agreed to do so. Rather, as the court noted: "[H]e exacted no *quid pro quo*. He gave the note as a gratuity and looked for nothing in return."[9] In holding that Katie could collect on the note, the court offered the following justification: "Having intentionally influenced the plaintiff [Katie] to alter her position for the worse on the faith of the note being paid when due, it would be grossly inequitable to permit the maker, or his executor, to resist payment on the ground that the promise was given without consideration."[10]

Why do people ordinarily fulfill their contractual obligations? No doubt the fear of a legal sanction helps to deter breach. But the matter surely goes beyond mere fear of the law. Indeed, the fear of an officially imposed sanction (e.g., a judgment for damages) may be a relatively minor deterrent in many situations. One thinks, for example, of the great law merchant tradition of the late medieval period, out of which much of our modern commercial law developed.[11] The merchants themselves administered a remarkably effective system that did not depend upon state enforcement mechanisms or procedures, but relied upon private sanctions such as refusal to deal or boycott.

Obviously, it is generally in one's self-interest to keep promises. If one is to have credibility in the future, one must perform one's promises today. Finally, most people believe that promises ought to be kept because it is the right thing to do. It is a part of right conduct, the way an honest person behaves. There is the widespread belief that a person is obliged, in justice, to render others their due, and a major part of their due derives from contract.

It is not surprising that there emerged in our legal tradition the notion of "sanctity of contract." One writer summarized the prevalence of this attitude as follows:

> The conclusion at which I have arrived during my study of the development of the general law of contract in England and of the remedies provided by English law for the redress of breaches of contract is that throughout the greater part of that development the giving of a promise or the conclusion of an agreement involved a solemn undertaking the breach of which amounted in the eyes of the Church to a sin and in the eyes of the general body of contemporary lawyers to an immoral or unethical act. With the special emphasis placed by the nineteenth-century philosophers and jurists on the importance of freedom and the manifestation and extension of an individual's freedom through contract, it was not surprising that contracts developed a juristic blessedness or halo and were so often regarded as sacred. Their sanctity is directly traceable to their early religious and ecclesiastical associations, their protection by the Court of Chancery as a court of conscience, . . . their importance to international merchants as the foundation of credit, and the prominent place that the individual freedom which they fostered held in the eyes of nineteenth-century jurists and political philosophers.[12]

Although there is no record of a legal system that has undertaken to enforce all promises, there is yet to appear an organized society that has repudiated altogether the concept of a binding promise or contract. To be sure, criteria of enforcement have varied. Moreover, the sanction imposed for nonperformance has at times been merely social or religious, rather than an official court command to perform the promise (specific performance) or a judgment awarding monetary damages. In addition, the extent of contractual recognition and development has depended heavily upon the degree of private autonomy accorded the individual to contract for himself or herself and upon the amount of commercial activity taking place in the society. Still, the modern person who insists "You gave me your word" or "A bargain's a bargain" is not advancing novel doctrine. The Roman legal maxim *pacta sunt servanda* (contracts are to be kept) reflects a characteristic human attitude. In this respect, the ancient Code of Hammurabi, the celebrated Code of Justinian, and the contemporary Uniform Commercial Code are quite alike in fundamental orientation.

The economic importance of promise making and promise keeping can hardly be exaggerated. Dean Roscoe Pound put it this way:

> In a developed economic order the claim to promised advantages is one of the most important of the individual interests that press for recognition. . . . Credit is a principal form of wealth. It is a presupposition of the whole economic order that promises will be kept. Indeed, the matter goes deeper. The social order rests upon stability and predictability of conduct, of which keeping promises is a large item.[13]

With good reason, Sir Frederick Pollock, the English legal historian, could insist: "Enforcement of good faith in matters of bargain and promise is among the most important functions of legal justice. It might not be too much to say that, next after keeping the peace and securing property against violence and fraud so that business may be possible, it is the most important. . . ."[14]

In a book with the provocative title *The Promises Men Live By*, economist Harry Scherman makes this bold assertion: "I do not think there is any single fact more important for men to recognize, with all its implications, than this simple one—*that their individual well-being, as well as the well-being of the whole society is determined by the volume of exchanges going on in the whole society.*"[15]

The facilitation of economic exchange is a basic policy of commercial law in general and contract law in particular. By encouraging a high volume of private exchanges and the economic growth that results therefrom, the law contributes to both the welfare of the individual participants and the nation as a whole. If legal impediments to voluntary exchange are kept to a minimum, the law plays a market-supporting role by providing a general framework within which private planners can rationally allocate resources. This, it can be demonstrated, is an essential ingredient of a dynamic economic order.

One cannot gainsay (1) the importance of freedom of contract to a market economy and the superiority of a market economy and (2) the superiority of such a system to the relatively unproductive command economies, which are, happily, in decline throughout the world today. But there are more than economic advantages; there are obvious political advantages as well.

As Milton Friedman, among others, reminds us, economic freedom is an indispensable means toward the achievement of political freedom.[16] He insists that historical evidence speaks with a single voice on the relation between political freedom and a free market. He writes: "I know of no example in time or place of a society that has been marked by a large measure of political freedom, and that has not always used something comparable to a free market to organize the bulk of economic activity."[17]

Private contract is a powerful tool for diffusing power in a society, for dividing decision making and opportunities between the state, on the one hand, and private persons, on the other.[18] In a sense, contracting parties who have a binding contract serve as lawmakers. By entering into a binding contract, they make law for themselves.[19] They incur obligations that are enforceable by public authority, the courts. As indicated, the amount of legal obligation of this type is staggering. Any analysis of the real government of the people must take note of this extensive network of contractual obligations.

But even as one acknowledges these enormous practical advantages, one feels the need to press beyond social considerations. The matter goes beyond both economics and politics. It touches on the very nature of a human person. In her book *The Human Condition,* Hannah Arendt relates the power to promise to the power to forgive, the one (forgiveness) providing a remedy for a painful past and the other (promise) a remedy for an uncertain future. She explains:

> The possible redemption from the predicament of irreversibility—of being unable to undo what one has done . . . is the faculty of forgiving. The remedy

for unpredictability, for the uncertainty of the future, is contained in the faculty to make and keep promises. The two faculties belong together in so far as one of them, forgiving, serves to undo the deeds of the past, whose 'sins' hang like Damocles' sword over every new generation; and the other, binding oneself through promises, serves to set up in the ocean of uncertainty, which the future is by definition, islands of security without which not even continuity, let alone durability of any kind, would be possible in the relationships between men.[20]

Only persons forgive; only persons promise. These are awesome powers, conferred by a creator who both forgives and promises and commands that we do likewise. He tells us to forgive the trespasses of others and to keep our commitments.

God's commands, the psalmist declared, are right and forever just. Hence, one does not "break" a moral law of God any more than one does a physical law, such as the law of gravity. One may, of course, ignore such a law or pretend that it does not exist. But one must then suffer the consequences of violation, as if one were to step off the roof of a skyscraper, erroneously believing that air currents would provide a safe trip to the ground. One writer sums up the objective character of these laws as follows:

> The moral laws are, just as much as the physical laws statements of how things work. If you contravene the bodily laws, you will have disease, deformity and death. If you contravene the laws by which the mind works you will be kept from discovering the truth. . . . The moral laws are just

> as objective. . . . [So] it is not simply morally wrong to go against God's laws to gain something for ourselves, it is plain foolishness: we cannot gain by going against them; because they are a statement of the way things really are, observing them goes with sanity.[21]

This adds an important dimension to ordinary actions. When we act justly, as by keeping promises made to others, we not only contribute to the common good, we help to fulfill our function as persons. We do this not in conformity to abstract rule, but in obedience to a personal God, to a "Father who art in heaven." In this way, our ordinary promise making and promise keeping are extraordinarily meaningful and profoundly personal. We strive not merely to do justice; we strive to *be* just.[22] It is significant that in Scripture the word for justice and the word for righteousness are the same word.[23]

The idea of contract as a principle of order has persisted from the dawn of human history to the present time. From Scripture, we learn that God has always dealt with people in terms of covenantal law, a law derived from both the Old Testament (or Old Covenant) and the New Testament (or New Covenant).

In light of biblical revelation, all people are bound to God in a covenantal relationship, and everyone is, invariably, either a covenant keeper or a covenant breaker. The original covenant with Adam and the renewed covenant with Noah bound everyone. Moreover, in renewing the covenant, Jesus Christ made it clear that everyone is involved. He said, as recorded in John 12:32: "And I, if I be lifted up from the earth, will draw all men to me." A leading biblical scholar, R. J. Rushdoony, comments:

By becoming the sacrifice, the priest, and the divine renewer of the covenant of God with man, Jesus would draw all men to Him, i.e., become the principle of judgment and of salvation, of curses and of blessings. The covenant and the law of the covenant, as well as the Lord of the covenant, thus judge every man.[24]

The judgment for covenant obedience and covenant disobedience comes in the form of inevitable blessings and curses. We read in Deuteronomy 30:15–19:

Here, then, I have today set before you life and prosperity, death and doom. If you obey the commandments of the Lord, your God, which I enjoin on you today, loving him, and walking in his ways, and keeping his commandments, statutes and decrees, you will live and grow numerous, and the Lord, your God, will bless you in the land you are entering to occupy. If, however, you turn away your hearts and will not listen, but are led astray and adore and serve other gods, I tell you now that you will certainly perish; you will not have a long life on the land which you are crossing the Jordan to enter and occupy. I call heaven and earth today to witness against you: I have set before you life and death, the blessing and the curse. Choose life, then, that you and your descendants may live.

According to the biblical design, everything that is comes from God's creative power, and but for his sustaining power would cease to exist. Moreover, God creates for a purpose. He has a plan for his creation. He did not make the world and then abandon or lose interest in it. This plan for the ordering of all things to the attainment of their ends is called providence. In sum, there exists a creator God whose providence extends, in the words of Scripture, "from end to end mightily and governs all things well."[25]

An integral part of God's system of governance is covenant or contract. It is not surprising that when creatures seek to displace the creator as sovereign governor, they often use the concept of contract as a technique for legitimation of governmental power and authority. Social contract theory, of whatever variety, posits as a presupposition some agreement of individuals in a state of nature that establishes binding relationships between the sovereign and the people, and among the people themselves.

Even in a secularized form, social contract can be and has been used for constructive purposes. It has been used as a means for basing governmental legitimacy on something other than force or raw power, and it reflects a desire to ground law on justice and reason rather than on the mere will of the lawmaker. But to be employed in this manner, it is essential that the theory be related to some type of natural law. That is, there must be some terms of the social contract that are permanent and not subject to modification by anyone at any time. Otherwise, those who happen to be in control of the governmental machinery can ascribe to the original contracting parties whatever they wish. The content of the agreement becomes whatever those in charge say it is. If such be the case, there can be no principled and effective resistance to totalitarian rule and imperialistic law.

One may illustrate this danger by reference to the political thought of Jean-Jacques Rousseau (1712–1778), whom many scholars hail as the "Father of the Modern

World."[26] Rousseau's classic work, *The Social Contract*, was published in 1762.

The "social contract" is a *fictitious* contract that under-girds the entire political and governmental process and is the major presupposition of his system. The clauses of the contract may be reduced to one: "the total alienation of each associate, together with all his rights, to the whole community."[27] Rousseau elaborates: "Each of us puts his person and all his power in common under the supreme direction of the general will. . . ."[28]

This association of contracting individuals is the sovereign, the absolute authority that is neither bound by nor subordinate to any other authority: "But the body politic or the sovereign, drawing its being wholly from the sanctity of the contract, can never bind itself, even to an outsider, to do anything derogatory to the original act, for instance, to alienate any part of itself, or to submit to another Sovereign. . . ."[29] (All gods are, by definition, jealous gods!) Moreover, Rousseau does not hesitate to underscore the coercive power of this sovereign. He writes:

> "In order then that the social contract may not be an empty formula, it tacitly includes the undertaking, which alone can give force to the rest, that whoever refuses to obey the general will shall be compelled to do so by the whole body. This means nothing less than that he will be forced to be free. . . ."[30]

Another important attribute of this sovereignty, "the general will" of the contracting parties, is *infallibility*. Thus, he notes, "[i]t follows from what has gone before that the general will is always right. . . ."[31] It goes without saying that this sovereignty has *total* power:

> As nature gives each man absolute power over all
> his members, the social contract gives the body
> politic absolute power over all its members also;
> and it is this power which, under the direction of
> the general will bears, as I have said, the name of
> Sovereignty. . . . The Sovereign is the sole judge of
> what is important."[32]

Despite a token reference here and there to God, there is clearly no room for God and his revealed word in Rousseau's grand scheme, which is essentially a civil religion, the same as all forms of totalitarianism, ancient and modern. Especially telling in this respect is how Rousseau seeks to put Christianity in its place: "Christianity as a religion is entirely spiritual, solely with heavenly things; the country of the Christian is not of this world. He does his duty, indeed, but does it with profound indifference to the good or ill success of his cares."[33] Thus, one may suppose, the Christian may pray and tend to his own private spiritual needs, but he may not venture to suggest that his religious principles should affect the laws of the state or any matter of public import. (For example, "I am personally opposed to abortion, but. . . .")

To his credit, Rousseau does not shrink from the logical implications of his premises:

> There is therefore a purely civil profession of faith
> of which the Sovereign should fix the articles, not
> exactly as religious dogmas, but as social sentiments
> without which a man cannot be a good citizen or a
> faithful subject. While it can compel no one to
> believe them, it can banish from the State whoever
> does not believe them—it can banish him, not for
> impiety, but as an anti-social being, incapable of

truly loving the laws and justice, and of sacrificing, at need, his life to this duty. If anyone, after publicly recognizing these dogmas, behaves as if he does not believe them, let him be punished by death: he has committed the worst of all crimes, that of lying before the law.[34]

Under the gospel according to Rousseau, God is not sovereign; men and women are. The "general will," not God's will, controls. It is not "Thy will be done," but "Our will be done."

This is the same old conflict, repeated over and over in history from the rebellion of Adam to the present. Original sin is the prototype of all humanistic challenges to God's sovereign authority. In Genesis, we see God as ruler, as one who by sovereign decree has prescribed how His creatures are to act. But the first man rebels. He would, the Bible tells us, "be like gods who know what is good and what is bad."[35] "Know" in this context means to determine for himself what is good and what is bad. Adam would make his own rules, his own laws. He denies God's ultimacy and would, in effect, become his own legislator, governor, and judge.

Private contract is a powerful mechanism of legal and social order. Promise making and promise keeping have profound implications, both for the individual and for the society of which he is a member. The idea of obligation derived from promise has deep roots, going to the very nature of our status as created by God. We are expected to make promises and to keep them.

Traditionally, our law has recognized individuals as having extensive power to stipulate the terms of an agreement. Freedom of contract has been a cherished value, with inestimable benefits to both the individual and society. But at the same time we must not assume that as individuals or as a people we are totally autonomous. Our contracting, as all things else, must be exercised in conformity to the plan of the God who is our creator, our sustainer, our savior, our ultimate lawgiver and governor, and the one with whom we hope to live in intimate union forever.

ENDNOTES

1. *Restatement of Contracts*, 2d, sec. 1 (1981).

2. 1 *Corbin on Contracts*, sec. 1. (1950).

3. See generally, E. Murphy and R. Speidel, *Studies in Contract Law*, (4th ed. 1984), pp. 331–488.

4. *Restatement of Contracts*, sec. 75 (1932).

5. E. Murphy and R. Speidel, *supra* note 3 at 428–431.

6. Ibid. pp. 445–446.

7. For a classic formulation of the doctrine, see section 90 of *The Restatement of Contracts*. This section provides as follows: "A promise which the promisor should reasonably expect to induce action or forbearance of a definite and substantial character on the part of the promisee and which does induce such action or forbearance is binding if injustice can be avoided only by enforcement of the promise."

8. *Ricketts v. Scothorn*, 57 Neb. 51, 77 N.W. 365 (1898).

9. Ibid. at Neb. at 55, N.W. at 366.

10. Ibid. Neb. at 58, N.W. at 367.

11. See generally, W. Mitchell, *An Essay on the Early History of the Law Merchant*, (1904); L. Trakman, *The Law Merchant: The Evolution of Commercial Law* (1983).

12. D. Parry, *The Sanctity of Contract*, (1959) pp. 17–18.

13. R. Pound, 3 *Jurisprudence*, (1959) pp. 162–163.

14. "Contract," vol. 7, *Encyclopedia Britannica*, 11th ed., 1910, p. 35.

15. H. Scherman, *The Promises Men Live By*, (1983) p. 393 (Italics in the original).

16. M. Friedman, *Capitalism and Freedom*, (Chicago: University of Chicago Press, 1962), p. 8.

17. Ibid. p. 9.

18. See Jones, "The Jurisprudence of Contracts," 44 *Cincinnati Law Review,* (1975) pp. 43, 50.

19. Ibid. p. 53.

20. H. Arendt, *The Human Condition,* (1958) p. 237.

21. F. Sheed, *Society and Sanity,* (1953), pp. 82–83.

22. See generally, J. Pieper, *Justice,* (1955).

23. J. McKenzie, *Dictionary of the Bible,* (1965), pp. 739–742.

24. R. Rushdoony, *The Institutes of Biblical Law* (1973), pp. 655–656. On the evening before His sacrificial death on the cross, by which he *sealed* the covenant in His own blood, Jesus refers to this covenant while instituting a sacrament by which this sacrifice will be perpetuated: "This cup is the covenant in my blood, which shall be shed for you." Luke 22:20.

25. Wisdom 8:1.

26. T. Neill, *Makers of the Modern Mind* (1949), p. 189.

27. Jean–Jacques Rousseau, In *The Great Legal Philosophers: Selected Readings in Jurisprudence,* ed. Clarence Morris (Philadelphia: University of Pennsylvania Press, 1971) p. 218.

28. Ibid.

29. Ibid. p. 219.

30. Ibid.

31. Ibid. p. 221. The "will of all" and the "general will" are not to be confused. It is obvious that within the overall system there must be an elite of some sort to declare the "general will," and there are to be no intermediate or "partial" authorities between the people and this "general will."

32. Ibid.

33. Ibid. p. 235.

34. Ibid. This celebrated oracle of Paris, who also wrote what many regard as a classic on the subject of education, chose not to raise his own children. Against the wishes of the mother, Rousseau placed their five children in a foundling home. See Neill, *Makers of the Modern Mind,* 171 n. 26.

35. Genesis 3:5.

Chapter 11

Tort Law and Natural Law

WILLIAM N. RILEY

In order for law to be just, and not just a manifestation of the raw power of the state, it must be rooted in the natural law. The same principle holds true for all of the various types of laws that attempt to be responsive to the complexities of contemporary life. This essay will examine the interaction of one area of law, torts, with the natural law. The law of torts deals with the nonvolitional and volitional infliction of injury to either a person or a property right.[1] The remedy for an injury in tort law is the payment of monetary compensation. The question is whether this current system is just under the principles of natural law, and, if it is, why? The answer to these questions is found in the interaction between the concepts of the good of harmony among individuals in the community and the duty of an individual at fault to make restitution to the injured party for the wrong committed. Both of these ideas are linked by the fundamental concept of natural law, which is integral human fulfillment.

St. Thomas Aquinas stated that law is nothing other than "an ordinance of reason for the common good, made by him who has care of the community, and promulgated."[2] When St. Thomas stated that law is an "ordinance of reason," he advanced the idea that the common good of the community is rationally discernible to the human mind. The mind can discern what brings about the common good because it is part of a definable intellectual reality—the natural law. St. Thomas also conceived the common good of the community as a universal principle of morality because the term "good," even in its utilitarian sense, has moral significance due to its inherent desirability. The definition of law as an ordinance of reason is thus linked by St. Thomas with the moral principle of the common good. For St. Thomas, law, the common good, and morality are all part of the natural law.

The common good is an aggregate of the individual goods of each member of the community. In order for the state's laws to be in accord with promoting the common good, the laws must be based on promoting and protecting the individual good. What, though, constitutes the individual good? It would seem logical that the individual good is realized in some form of personal fulfillment. The real question becomes how is human nature fulfilled, and what acts are ordered to personal fulfillment? The Scholastic natural law argument was that certain acts are in accord with, or opposed to, human nature. Acts that are not in accord with human nature would not lead to fulfillment of the individual under the theory and ought not to be chosen. In order for a person to act in a rational way, the Scholastics concluded, he ought to make choices in accordance with human nature. Choices made in accordance with human nature under the theory are moral; acts not in accord are immoral. Operative in the theory is the use of the term "is," as relating to human nature, and "ought" as relating to actions in accordance with that nature. To mix "is" and "ought" is logically impermissible. It is logically erroneous to proceed from "is" to "ought" since "ought" does not follow "is." If in dealing with human nature there is a preclusion from going from "is" to "ought," then we are also prevented from going from "is" to "is" in the field of morality. Human nature, as it is, does not provide intelligible norms as a basis for freely choosing what one ought to do. We cannot move from "is" to "is" because the natural law deals with what ought to be and not with what is. Germain Grisez, professor of Christian ethics at Mount Saint Mary's College, advocates moving from "ought" to "ought." His theory proposes that instead of looking at human nature as it is, the focus should be directed to what a human being's end ought to be, what Grisez terms "integral human fulfillment." The theory proposed by Grisez provides a methodology for determining if acts are what they ought to be, thus moving the individual toward the good of integral human fulfillment. With that foundation it is possible to make a determination of what laws are necessary to promote or protect the individual good, thus bringing about the promotion and protection of the common good.

Integral human fulfillment is concerned with human goods. The good in human goods can be defined as the fullness of being. There has been a good deal of debate through the centuries as to what will bring about fullness of being. Grisez presents integral human fulfillment as being constituted by seven incommensurable human goods. In and of themselves, the goods of integral human fulfillment are not moral principles since "they do not directly tell one which choices to make and which to avoid."[3] Rather, as already mentioned, they are goods to which all humans strive. The goods of integral human fulfillment are based on the dual aspect of the human person: the existential and the substantive. If an individual's life includes a profound share of these goods, the person will lead a fulfilling life.

The existential goods have as a common element an idea of harmony with oneself, including harmony among all the aspects of the person. The first is the harmony an individual has of inner peace (the good of integrity), and the second concerns the congruity between the way an individual really is and the way he is perceived by others (the good of authenticity). There is also harmony among persons (the good of friendship or justice) and harmony between a person and God (the good of religion). Harmony does not just transpire; it must be brought into being. Individuals must engage in some form of activity, the result of which is harmony. This is most clearly illustrated in the case of friendship. If two people are prevented from ever talking to each other, seeing each other, or engaging in any other form of activity, they will never become friends. These activities are substantive goods, the substance through which the existential goods come into being. There is the good that corresponds to the fact that the human person is an animal (the good of life and health). There is a good that corresponds to the fact that the human person is rational (the good of truth and appreciation of beauty). Finally there is the good that conforms to the fact that the human person is a rational animal (the good of play and skilled performance). All of the goods are coequal. Both the existential and substantive goods are aspects of the human person and do not possess reality apart from the person. The goods in Grisez's theory are reflexive "since they are both reasons for choosing and are in part defined in terms of choosing."[4]

What is immorality, and how does it relate to this theory? Immorality is anything that keeps the human person from reaching integral human fulfillment. When a person acts morally, that person acts in the way he ought to act, and a person ought to act in the manner by which he will reach integral human fulfillment. As stated before, the seven goods of human fulfillment are not principles of morality, but personal principles that human nature strives to obtain. Morality is deduced from St. Thomas's first principle of reason and what Grisez terms the first principle of morality, as well as what he has articulated as the eight modes of responsibility.

The first principle of reason is that "[t]he good is to be done and pursued; the bad is to be avoided."[5] This is a directive for action and not a description of good and evil. Grisez points out that

> when choices are made, the goodness of good is never directly challenged. In making life and death decisions, for instance, one assumes that life as such is good and death bad; choices to let die or even to kill are instead made on other grounds, such as the limitation of suffering or the justice of punishing criminals. Evidently, then, there is a need for moral norms which will guide choices toward overall fulfillment in terms of human goods.[6]

The first principle of morality, which is designed to guide choices toward fulfillment in the human goods, is formulated by Grisez as follows: "In voluntarily acting for human goods and avoiding what is opposed to them, one ought to choose and otherwise will those and only those possibilities whose willing is compatible with a will toward integral human fulfillment."[7] The first principle of morality is involved when a choice must be made, yet freedom is maintained in that a person can act against its dictates. Alone, the first principle of morality is too broad to provide precise answers to specific moral questions. What Grisez calls the eight modes of responsibility stand as a *via media* between the first principle of morality and the direct choices that confront the individual. Each of the eight modes of responsibility excludes certain unreasonable acts of volition that would be contrary to the attainment of integral human fulfillment.

The first mode of responsibility can be characterized by the statement "One should not be deterred by the felt inertia from acting for intelligible goods."[8] This mode essentially dictates that laziness, depression, or lack of enthusiasm should not prevent the individual from pursuing the goods that will lead to integral human fulfillment. A distinction must be made between slothful inaction and an action not undertaken because it would be too taxing or because a person needed rest. Inaction undertaken for reasons of this nature does not violate the first mode of responsibility.[9]

The second mode of responsibility is that "one should not be pressed by enthusiasm or impatience to act individualistically for intelligible goods."[10] The individual violates this mode when he acts on nonrational grounds and fails to consider or dismisses the communitarian aspect of his acts. "Unnecessary individualism is not consistent with a will toward integral human fulfillment, which requires a fellowship of persons sharing in goods."[11] It is important to always keep in mind that integral human fulfillment is not found in Social Darwinism, but in the realization of all the human goods in the totality of the human community.[12]

The third mode deals with action motivated by desire, impulse, or habit. "One should not choose to satisfy an emotional desire except as part of one's pursuit and/or attainment of an intelligible good other than the satisfaction of desire itself."[13] The end or goal of a choice that violates this mode is not an intelligible good but the satisfaction of an emotional desire; at the very least, the choice uselessly expends time and energy that should be directed to the attainment of human goods. As Grisez states:

> Violators [of this mode] are not in control of their own lives but are slaves to nonrational motives. Self-control includes at least some aspects of many traditionally recognized virtues, such as temperance, modesty, chastity, and simplicity of life. . . . The opposed vice includes at least certain aspects of lustfulness, gluttony, greed, jealousy, envy, short-sightedness, impetuosity, and so on.[14]

When actions are undertaken based on a choice motivated by a desire to fulfill some emotional satisfaction, the will is directed against integral human fulfillment.[15]

Moreover, choices based on emotion violate the fourth mode of responsibility. The directive of this mode is that "[o]ne should not choose to act out of an emotional aversion except as part of one's avoidance of some intelligible evil [which is the privation of good] other than the inner tension experienced in enduring that aversion."[16] In this mode the individual's choice yields to an emotional repugnance not founded upon an intelligible evil. This situation is distinct from the morally acceptable practice of spontaneously avoiding that which rationally should be avoided. Violation of this mode occurs when an individual abandons the duties of his vocational state solely because of adverse feelings. An example of a violation of this mode would be a doctor who refuses to treat an injured person because of a personal dislike.[17]

The fifth mode of responsibility deals with universality in the treatment of individuals. Grisez elucidates the principle that "[o]ne should not, in response to different feelings toward different persons, willingly proceed with a preference for anyone unless the preference is required by intelligible goods themselves."[18] In violating this mode, choices made are not in totality based on the achievement of human goods, but are instead motivated by the feelings of partiality, which is advantageous to one or more but acts to the detriment of the community. Grisez states:

> Although partiality is often expressed as selfishness, simple egoism is only one form. Possibly more common, and certainly as unreasonable, is allowing one's choices to be shaped by personal likes and dislikes, jealous love of one's own family, group prejudices, culturally established patterns of bias, and so on.[19]

This fifth mode's dictate of impartiality does not include the denial of special commitments that one owes to one's family or other individuals.[20]

In the sixth mode of responsibility, the triumph of form over substance is considered. This mode states that "[o]ne should not choose on the basis of emotions which bear upon empirical aspects of intelligible goods (or bads) in a way that interferes with a more perfect sharing in the good or avoidance of the bad."[21] Stated differently, individuals should not allow emotional choices to limit their participation in intelligible goods or the converse. Choices violating this mode are acts of self-deception with deleterious ramifications on the individual's concept of the intelligible goods. It is also immoral because people who allow their choices to be framed by such emotions fail to move toward integral human fulfillment. People who make such choices limit their participation in this portion of reality to mere appearance.[22]

The seventh mode of responsibility concerns the malignant volitional destruction of an intelligible human good. Grisez relates that "[o]ne should not be moved by hostility to freely accept or choose the destruction, damaging, or impeding of any intelligible human good."[23] When an individual acts on negative feelings, he embarks on a course contrary to human fulfillment by irrationally seeking to reduce human fulfillment. Two acts that are similar yet distinct need to be considered. If an action is motivated by a hatred for evil, and the act and the reason for the act are to protect a good or limit an evil, then the act is morally permissible. The other permissible case is the release of hostile feelings through means that are not destructive of human goods.[24]

The eighth mode excludes balancing among the various intelligible goods. "One should not be moved by a stronger desire for one instance of an intelligible good to act for it by choosing to destroy, damage, or impede some other instance of an intelligible good."[25] This mode is the refutation of the phrase "the end justifies the means." The violation of the eighth mode occurs when a choice is made to act against an intelligible human good in order to prevent an evil or to secure some other human good. The impetus behind the choice is the strength of the various desires present to the individual. "Thus one subordinates some possible elements of human fulfillment to others, even though there is no reasonable basis for doing so. In placing a nonrational limit on fulfillment, one proceeds in a way not consistent with a will toward integral human fulfillment."[26] The eighth mode should not be confused with a permissible choice for a human good the execution of which will incidentally result in a human evil, even though the probability of the evil was foreseen. It is also acceptable to subordinate freely nonhuman goods to human goods.[27]

The desire for integral human fulfillment is inherent in each individual, but it is not actuated by egoism; it is, rather, realized in the community. Integral human fulfillment, the first principle of reason, the first principle of morality, and the modes of responsibility are accessible to the human intellect through the faculty of reason because they are universal truths of human nature. When considered in totality, they are self-evident truths. In Grisez's thought, these principles constitute what has been classically referred to as natural law.

Two human goods form the basis of the natural law as it is manifested through tort law. The first is the existential good of harmony among persons. The second is the substantive good of life and health of the individual human being. When an individual through his actions harms another, the existential good of harmony and the substantive good of the injured person's life and health are compromised. The first principle of reason, when applied to this situation, indicates that the good is to be done by the negligent individual toward the one who has been harmed. The negligent individual, in order to comply with the first principle of morality, must base his action with regard to the injured person on a choice to advance the injured person's integral human fulfillment. The eight modes of responsibility do not have a direct bearing on the application of natural law to the foundational principles of tort law, but constitute natural law precepts of morality which should govern (1) the underlying foundation of how the negligent person treats the injured individual and (2) the morality of the act which caused the injury.

How then does a negligent individual go about undoing the injury he has done? As stated above, two human goods are affected when an individual is negligently injured. The wrongdoer must do something based on the first principles of reason and morality to help the injured individual recover the human goods that have been damaged or lost.

Grisez states: "Making restitution can promote many goods, but it always contributes to that justice which is a mode of harmony among persons and the foundation of friendship and genuine community."[28] When an individual is negligently injured there is a breakdown in the good of harmony among individuals. The injured individual will, more than likely, be angered that through the negligence of another he has suffered some harm to the good of bodily integrity. Restitution, then, is not only an attempt to repair that harmony which should exist between the parties, but also an attempt to mitigate or overcome the deprivation that the injured person has suffered. Grisez makes the following provisional definition of restitution:

> One party owes another restitution whenever, under all circumstances, the first party ought to try to mitigate or overcome some harm or deprivation being suffered by the second for this reason: that the first party either was involved in the coming about of that harm or is in possession of something which the second should have.[29]

Restitution is concerned with rectifying the injustice that exists between two parties. The goal of restitution is not to affect a conversion or change of heart in the negligent party, but to rectify the injustice that has been suffered by the injured party. There exists a conceptual difference between sorrow, contrition, or repentance that the negligent party should feel and volitionally act on under the modes of responsibility and the duty in justice to rectify the injustice committed. An example of this would be the following: Ed becomes intoxicated, attempts to drive home, runs into Mark, and in that collision injures Mark. Ed will need to rectify the wrong he has committed by making restitution to Mark for the injuries Mark has suffered. Separate from the duty in justice to make restitution, Ed should be personally sorry for his action and avoid the same course of conduct in the future. When Ed makes restitution, his action will contribute to the interpersonal harmony that is the foundation of human community. Grisez states:

> If one of two parties involved in an actually or potentially unjust state of affairs should do something to rectify or prevent the injustice, doing it eliminates a likely source of conflict from their relationship. For those who should rectify or prevent an injustice but fail to do so cannot have good will toward those who suffer it, and the latter also have a motive for bad will toward the former."[30]

The failure to make restitution thus undermines the good of harmony between individuals and weakens the bonds of harmony that should exist in the community.

How is restitution to be made? If a child is killed by a negligent driver of an automobile, how is restitution to be made to the parents? The child cannot be restored to life by the negligent party. Is restitution in this case impossible? The duty of restitution is to do what is just at the present moment, not to change what occurred when the original injustice transpired.

An individual who has been negligently injured will suffer a number of harms that arise from the injury. There may be hospital and doctor bills, the loss of pay or the opportunity for income, pain and suffering, and the possibility of permanent disability. Restitution should be made for these and other injuries the injured party may suffer as a consequence of the negligent actor's action. What norms should be applied in determining the just restitution for a particular situation? Grisez states:

> It is impossible to articulate an adequate set of specific norms for making restitution. Various norms of morality, law, and custom can be helpful, but they always admit of exceptions, and sometimes fall short of requiring what really would be fair. Hence to determine what restitution should be made, the Golden Rule must be directly applied."[31]

The Golden Rule is, of course, that one should do unto others as one would have them do unto oneself.

Grisez, in discussing the application of the Golden Rule to the concept of restitution, has developed a number of questions that should be considered in deciding the justness of the restitution. The first is a consideration of what the exact harm or loss is that the injured party suffered. In making the determination, the law should consider the consequential damages that flow from the original injury. Grisez also points out that in evaluating the injury and its consequences, "past, present, and future harm or loss should be considered distinctly, since past harm may call for compensation, present harm effective remedy, and future harm preventive measures."[32]

The next question is what can be done to compensate for the injury, remedy it, or prevent further loss or harm? In most cases, the positive law will only be able to mandate the payment of money damages for the past, present, and future harm. The payment of money damages is the only appropriate method of restitution in injury situations. In our society, the payment of money damages allows for the payment of past, present, and future medical care, along with the return of any lost earnings, both past and future, and compensation for the injured person's pain, suffering, and any future disability.[33]

The third question to be asked is, in making the restitution, does making the restitution itself violate any
moral norms? Fairness can require that a negligent party
be made to suffer more in making the restitution than the
injured party suffered from the injury. However, this cannot be carried to extremes and a tempered sense of justice, actuated by the Golden Rule, must be utilized to
make a determination of whether the restitution is
morally permissible.[34]

Grisez's fourth question that must be asked is how
exactly is the wrongdoer responsible for the loss? So far
this paper has merely discussed individuals whose conduct was negligent. The current tort law divides actions
into mere negligence, strict liability, and actions that are
deemed to be wanton and willful. The question of restitution in part depends on how the wrongdoing agent
was responsible for the injury. If an individual, while driving, is momentarily distracted and because of that dis-
traction fails to see a stop sign and causes a collision, then
that individual has been negligent but does not manifest
a bad will. If a baker uses metal wires to affix flowers
made of icing to a cake, and someone swallows a wire
and is injured, the baker will be held to be strictly liable.
If a car manufacturer markets a vehicle that it knows to be
defective and fails to recall that model because of the cost
of doing so, then that company has engaged in wanton
and willful wrongdoing and should be subject to punitive damages. The punitive damages serve the public
interest in punishing the willful wrongdoer, creating an
example, and further compensating the injured party by
way of restitution. The more wanton and willful the act,
the greater the restitution should be.[35]

The fifth and sixth questions are essentially demonstrated by cases of multiple parties at fault. The duty to make restitution should be dependent on the negligent wrongdoers' respective responsibility for the injury. In Indiana, the law used to be that defendants were held to be jointly and severally liable. Under that doctrine, a judgment against all of the defendants could be applied totally against any individual defendant. The justness of that doctrine is immediately suspect, and one can see that the point of just restitution is not served by it. Justice is a reciprocal venture, and it violates the natural law for one wrongdoer out of many to bear an unjust share of the restitution. In the same vein, an additional matter to consider is the respective ability of the wrongdoer to make restitution. If a pharmaceutical company manufactures a defective drug and the requested restitution would drive the company out of business, thus depriving the country of needed medicine and workers of jobs, then a serious question must be raised about the justness of the requested restitution, in light of the Golden Rule.[36]

Even after examining these questions there may remain lingering doubts about what fair restitution would be. In civil tort law, the trial is the forum in which the question of doubt as to negligence or the amount of restitution owed is resolved. In a civil matter, the plaintiff must prove his case as to liability and damages by a preponderance of the evidence, i.e., he must show that more likely than not the defendant is liable. If a juror believes that the plaintiff has met that burden with regard to liability, then he must put aside any lingering doubts and decide that case for the plaintiff. If, however, the juror thinks that the doubts weigh more heavily than the proof offered by the plaintiff, then a decision for the defendant is in order. The same process must be worked through with regard to the amount of restitution, if the jury should determine the negligence of the wrongdoer.

What monetary amount is just award or settlement restitution for the injury? As has already been mentioned, certain elements such as medical bills and lost wages are easy enough to calculate, but what about pain and suffering and the loss of enjoyment of life? Individuals have some idea of what they will pay for a pleasurable experience such as eating out or going to a movie. A lawyer in settlement, or a judge or juror as the finder of fact, must make a determination of how much an individual should be compensated for a painful experience. Often trial lawyers will liken the suffering of pain to the person's job and suggest that the amount of compensation should be based on the minimum wage. Another approach is to liken what a person will spend for a pleasurable experience and then multiply that by the number of hours the person has been in pain. What one should see from this is that the natural law does not dictate what the amount of restitution should be. Certainly, grossly insufficient or excessive amounts will be violative of at least the good of harmony among persons. Determinations of this sort, by the responsible party, must be guided by the modes of responsibility in order to arrive at a just amount for restitution.

What obligations, if any, are owed by the injured person to the negligent wrongdoer? Grisez posits that injured persons should not take advantage of the individuals who owe them restitution. He states:

> If the law provides well for those who deserve resti-
> tution in cases of a certain kind, injured parties
> whose cases fall into that category very often see
> that as an opportunity to obtain a large award,
> whether or not that is fair. This is especially so if the
> restitution would be paid by an insurance com-
> pany. Plainly, however, injured parties should make
> a careful judgment as to what is fair and seek no
> more; and exaggerating the injury or otherwise
> lying to obtain more than is fair clearly is an addi-
> tional, grave injustice.[37]

What role does the injured person's lawyer have to
play with regard to the negligent wrongdoer? Grisez's
statement should not be read as an indictment of the
adversarial system. Because of the very nature of the system, it will be necessary in pretrial settlement negotia-
tions for the lawyer to engage in a certain amount of
posturing and marketplace haggling. The more crucial
question becomes the responsibility of the lawyer to disclose negative facts about the case to the opposite side.
Such disclosures are not required unless the party has
availed itself of the proper discovery process to obtain
this information. The wholesale revelation of negative
facts about a client's case, disclosed without the necessity
of formal discovery, undermines the adversarial process
and renders a disservice to the attorney's client. The disservice is important because of the fact that the reciprocal
revelation of negative facts by the other side is highly
unlikely and the revealing attorney is essentially doing
the other attorney's work.

The next question is what happens if the opposing
counsel fails, through his own oversight or negligence, to

discover the compromising information? The attorney whose client is somehow compromised must not allow the client to commit perjury, neither should the attorney make a deliberate attempt to mislead the jury. If the matter is being resolved by settlement, the attorney should not deliberately mislead the other party, but he is not bound to disabuse the other side of an erroneous opinion.

Grisez also touches briefly on the principles of the efficacy of out-of-court settlements. He states:

> Rejecting an offer of restitution which one realizes is fair and using legal process to seek more is an abuse of these processes and a further injustice. Indeed, suing is wrong not only when the plaintiff seeks excessive restitution, but when other factors render the lawsuit unjust: a fair settlement could be reached out of court, the burdens of the legal process on the defendant will be unfairly great, the plaintiff seeks restitution only as revenge, and so forth.[38]

These factors should be considered by the practicing attorney when advising his client as to the course that should be taken. However, the ultimate control of the litigation resides with the client, and the lawyer functions for the most part as that person's representative in the legal system. It is not the lawyer's place to pass a moral judgment on the underlying motives of his client. The client, the party who is owed restitution, must resolve his motivations for the suit in the forum of his own conscience. The party who has been wronged through an injury should also attempt to be merciful, although the positive law cannot enact any canon to enforce that dictate of morality, which is a corollary of the Golden Rule.

The natural law in its essence is discernible by what brings about integral human fulfillment. The substantive and existential goods, the first principles of reason and morality, and the modes of responsibility provide an accurate and objective guide to the ordering of human actions toward integral fulfillment. Law is only just insofar as it comports with these principles of the natural law. The tort law serves the purpose of maintaining harmony among the individuals in the community and providing restitution for the injuries a party has suffered at the hands of another.

ENDNOTES

1. This paper will deal exclusively with injuries to person.

2. Thomas Aquinas *Summa Theologiae*, q. 90, a. 4 (Dominican Fathers' ed.)

3. Germain Grisez, *The Way of the Lord Jesus, Vol. 1, Christian Moral Principles* (Quincy Ill.: Franciscan Press, 1983), 118.

4. *Ibid.*, 124.

5. Aquinas, *Summa*, q. 94, 2, at 1009 n. 2.

6. Grisez, *Christian Moral Principles*, 183 n. 4.

7. Ibid., 184.

8. Ibid., 265.

9. Ibid., 206. Here is an example of the violation of this mode: Simply out of laziness, a man sleeps past the time when he had decided to get up and so fails to do something he had judged as worth doing. Again: A woman in authority realizes that a particular situation requires attention but somehow just doesn't get around to dealing with it. The virtuous disposition corresponding to this mode has various aspects and is usually named in reference to some particular sphere of action. Various aspects are referred to by certain words like "ambitious," "energetic," "diligent," "industrious," and "enthusiastic." Words that name the opposed vice include "lazy," "sluggish," "lackadaisical," "slothful," and "dilatory."

10. Ibid.

11. Ibid., 207.

12. Ibid., 207. Examples are often found in the tendency of a community's more active members to appropriate functions to themselves instead of foster-

ing wider, active participation, because the latter is more trouble and leads to uneven performance. Again: A person with many interests easily becomes over committed; this will lead to mediocre performance and to conflicts of responsibilities that eventually will affect others adversely.

13. Ibid., 208.

14. Ibid., 209.

15. Ibid. If a person chooses to engage in some sort of sexual behavior merely to experience pleasure and still desire, this mode is violated. But it is not violated when a married couple spontaneously take pleasure in marital intercourse. If they do not hesitate and deliberate, it is because there is no reason why they should not engage in intercourse. In their situation, it has an inherent intelligible significance, for it expresses and celebrates the larger, intelligible good to which they are committed—namely, their marriage itself as a special sort of friendship. Loving marital intercourse contributes to faithful communion in this relationship, which is structured in a way that integrates sexual behavior in the service of life and its transmission. This substantive good provides the vehicle for the reflexive good of marital friendship, and so it helps distinguish authentic marital friendship from its counterfeits, and love-giving marital intercourse from the use of the martial relationship for self-gratification.

16. Ibid., 210.

17. Ibid., 211. The soldier who chooses to leave his post to avoid being killed does not violate this mode of responsibility. His choice is not merely to escape fear itself. Rather he seeks to escape the fearful and intelligible evil of death. His choice can be morally wrong—for example, because the call of duty is a genuine one. Or the choice to flee can be morally right—for example, because he is ordered unreasonably to stand and fight by a leader who realizes defeat is inevitable but wants his army to fight to the death.

18. Ibid., 211.

19. Ibid., 212.

20. Ibid. Here are some violations. Somebody accepts favors but always finds excuses when asked to do them. People resent gossip about themselves and their loved ones, but gossip freely about others. Professional people give better treatment to more respectable and congenial clients than to others with similar needs and claims to their service. Lawmakers favor powerful interest groups that support them, rather than working for laws and policies that they think would be best for the people as a whole.

21. Ibid., 214.

22. Ibid. Here are some examples of violations. A sick man who could have treatment that would really cure his condition prefers less effective treatment that offers a feeling of quick relief.

23. Ibid., 215.

24. Ibid., 216. The following would be violations of the seventh mode. A nation that is losing a war launches all its nuclear weapons against its enemies to make its victory as costly as possible. Children who have been outvoted in planning a party stay away in order to detract from the joy of the event. A wife who resents her husband's infidelity has an affair to get even.

25. Ibid., 216.

26. Ibid., 216–217.

27. Ibid. This mode of responsibility is not violated by one who freely accepts death rather than leave an important duty unfulfilled. Nor is it violated by killing animals for food, since animals' lives are not instances of a human good. Nor is there a violation in setting aside the letter of legal requirements for the sake of fairness, since law is simply a means to this human good. Violations are present in the following: To obtain a grant to continue his research, a scientist falsifies data to make the project's initial results appear more promising than they are. To obtain information that will save many lives, a military commander tortures children. To bring about what he considers a necessary change in moral teaching, a theologian encourages people to do something they believe is wrong.

28. Germain Grisez, *The Way of the Lord Jesus, Vol. 2, Living a Christian Life* (Quincy, Ill.: Franciscan Press, 1983), 444.

29. Ibid., 446.

30. Ibid., 448.

31. Ibid., 453.

32. Ibid., 454.

33. Ibid.

34. Ibid., 455.

35. Ibid.

36. Ibid., 455–456.

37. Ibid., 457.

38. Ibid.

Chapter 12

Criminal Law and Natural Law

Ian A. T. McLean

But let me say this very candidly. I think it is the final arrogance to talk constantly about 'our religious tradition' in this country and equate it with the Bible. Sure, religious tradition. Whose religious tradition?

> Counsel arguing before the United States Supreme Court in Abington School District v. Schempp, 374 U.S. 203 (1963).[1]

When I began to write about natural law and criminal law, I spent some time thinking about how a natural law system of criminal justice would differ from our present secular system. What kind of sentences would offenders receive under a natural law system? Would *Miranda* warnings still be given to persons in custody? What evidence would a natural law court accept, and would it weigh that evidence under the presumption of innocence or some other rule of proof? Which acts, now legal, would be forbidden? The more I thought about these questions, the more I realized their irrelevance. We do not have a legal code based on natural law because our culture is implacably hostile to the whole idea. No one of consequence seriously believes that the task of a legislator or judge is to frame rules of conduct that conform to some immutable moral pattern that is independent of human consent. After all, morality cannot be legislated. Our freedom to do, say, and live according to our consciences demands that each of us be deprived of the power to impose our views on one another. Instead, our laws must rest on common decency enlightened by common sense, and the price of our liberty is eternal vigilance against "isms," which claim some divine right to dictate the outlines of our lives. Every child knows as much, and there is no point in framing natural laws that contradict these cherished first principles. But when we think about what exactly is involved in having any system of criminal justice and try to explain why this system should be allowed to operate, we see that our current "first principles" are wrong, dangerous, and valuable only because they prolong the day when we will confront the grim fact that our laws have no foundation save popular enthusiasm and the power of the state, and that by chasing religion out of the public square, away from the seat of government, we have turned our legislatures and courtrooms into empty houses ready for the approach of devils.

There have been many attempts to distinguish "criminal" from other areas of law. All of them contain elements of the truth, and yet none of them fully appreciates the uniqueness of criminal law. Some say that criminal law is unique because it protects a society's "core" values. But is this always so? The law of contracts deals with one of the most fundamental values in life, the value of a promise, but prosecutors and police do not enforce contracts. Others say that criminal law is unique because it is the exclusive province of state action. But the state acts exclusively for itself in a host of legal contexts such as the construction of public roads. I think we can distinguish criminal law from other kinds of law by paying attention to the role of "violence," by which I mean the deprivation of liberty or bodily integrity by the use of forceful means to which consent is irrelevant.

Criminal law is unique because it prefers, in first resort, violence as a response to activity that deviates from a rule. People who refuse to perform their contracts have problems with the law, but they are not subjected to violence. But the individual who commits a crime is immediately subjected to violence. He is deprived of his liberty by arrest and his subsequent movements are closely controlled. He may be forced to stand in a lineup for identification. His house and other property can be searched, by violent and destructive means when necessary. He may even be compelled to provide parts of his body, such as breath, blood, urine, skin, or hair samples, for examination by state scientists and physicians. If he is judged guilty of the crime he will be subjected to the violence of imprisonment, death, or allegedly "remedial" measures required by the authorities. This distinguishing feature of criminal law is not erased by false distinctions between "old, punitive" and "modern, treatment-based" systems of criminal

justice. What we do to criminals is violence regardless of
whether we confine them in maximum-security prisons or
treat them in secure mental institutions.

The use of criminal law depends on whether the behavior in question is seen as a serious threat to the social order.
The threats posed by murderers, rapists, and robbers are
beyond the need for comment now. But consider the case
of a man who refuses to pay his bills. He is served with a
civil complaint for the amount of the bill. He ignores the
complaint, and one day the sheriff comes and tells him
that unless he pays the judgment that has been entered
against him, the sheriff will have to sell his house. The
man can refuse to accept either alternative, but eventually
the sheriff will violently force the man to leave his house.
This violence will not be inflicted because the man broke
his contract, but because the man has directly threatened
the social order by refusing to obey the decrees of an
important social institution, the court. He has repudiated
the state's authority, and it will be the state in its own
right, not those with whom he entered into the contract,
that will return violence against him. The same pattern
applies to a woman who has refused to pay her child support; if she is jailed, it is because she has willfully repudiated the court's authority to arrange individual affairs
according to the law and not because she has failed to pay
the sums required. In both cases, the repudiation of social
authority triggers the use of laws we call "criminal"; and,
surely enough, both the contract-breaking man and the
recalcitrant woman will be provided with the range of
protection common to criminal cases such as the right to
an attorney, etc. Criminal laws are used when society
esteems a pattern of human conduct so highly that a break

with the pattern cannot be accepted and must be met with an immediate and forceful response.

Of course, a society can declare any activity threatening enough to warrant the operation of criminal laws. Society has changed its mind frequently in this respect. The possession of bourbon was once seen as a threat justifying violence, and now is not. Fornication by teenagers was not seen as such a threat, and now has been prosecuted in at least one jurisdiction. Regardless of the particular choices a society makes, the fact remains that criminal laws are created and enforced to protect values held dear by society:

> It comes down to this. There are certain forms of conduct which at any given place and epoch are commonly accepted under the combined influence of reason, practice, and tradition as moral or immoral. . . . Law accepts as the pattern of its justice the morality of the community whose conduct it assumes to regulate.[2]

Law cannot make an individual personally and sincerely believe an act is wrong or right, and if this is what we mean by "morality," then trying to legislate morality would be a fool's errand. Modern culture, which sees morality only as a contemplative and private part of life, without any significant public dimension, has done a lot to foster this very idea. But in spite of this culture, we persist in punishing acts without regard to how personally and sincerely someone believes the act to be right. We do this because we hold to the ancient truth that morality is more than an idea contemplated with affection. Morals come fully alive precisely at that moment when we interact with the world around us, and it is in this sense that we base our laws on morals. We do not make laws with the intention of forcing men to believe that the value proclaimed by the law is right and proper, but with the intention of obliging men to respect that value with their actions. If by doing so some men come to personally believe the value is right, then we may have done added good. But law's primary purpose is to regulate social conduct, to enable men who believe in the moral value behind the law to live their belief and to guarantee those without an equal belief benefits of something beyond their comprehension.

Something interesting happens when we see criminal laws as means of expressing or securing moral values. Crimes begin to look like acts of dissent from those values. To a greater or lesser degree, all men think about the results of their actions. This is a basic human attribute. You don't need a Ph.D. in philosophy to think that if you rob a bank you'll be trying to create a world where your own property is not safe, where credit is more expensive, and where people are punished for working hard and saving their money. You don't need training in metaphysics to think that if you rob a bank you'll get something you have a right to, the money's insured, and only the pigs who own the bank will get hurt. But you have to think about robbing the bank before you decide to go through with it or not. And all your thoughts on the matter will revolve around a central moral principle, set out in law, that people shouldn't rob banks. If you decide to rob the bank, your decision constitutes a dissent from this moral idea. The kind of dissent that surrounds criminal behavior is more often a shallow, repugnant, or unintelligible set of excuses than an educated and articulate moral position. But no matter how elegant or crude the form of dissent, it amounts to claiming that the moral idea contained in the law is flawed and can be disregarded. Consider this passage from St. Augustine's *City of God*:

> Justice being taken away . . . what are kingdoms but great robberies?. . . The [robber] band itself is made up of men; it is ruled by the authority of a prince, is knit together by the pact of the confederacy; the booty is divided by the law agreed on. If...this evil increases to such a degree that it holds places, fixes abodes, takes possession of cities, and subdues peoples, it assumes the more plainly the name of a kingdom, because the reality is now manifestly conferred on it, not by the removal of covetousness, but by the addition of impunity. Indeed, that was an apt and true reply which was given to Alexander the Great by a pirate who had been seized. For when the king had asked the man what he meant by keeping hostile possession of the sea, he answered with bold pride, "What you mean by seizing the whole earth; but because I do it with a petty ship, I am called a robber, while you do it with a great fleet and are styled emperor."[3]

Society must be perpetually ready to answer these *tu quoque* accusations, to explain why the values protected by the law are superior to different values that may be held by individuals. This explanation must claim a vision of the common good so powerful that it can reject arguments advanced to justify disobedience, even when those arguments go beyond special pleading to frame a competing vision of the common good. No legal order can survive if it fails to provide, or if it contradicts, this explanation.

Explanations of justice behind the law do more than legitimate law enforcement. If laws reflect strongly held beliefs about social justice they will be more widely obeyed and a better guarantee of social peace. No state will ever be powerful enough to force everyone to obey the law: even George Orwell's unrestrained vision of a total state contained opportunities for "crime." Widespread obedience to the moral norms embodied by the law cannot come solely from an estimate of the state's ability to identify and arrest lawbreakers. Ultimately, the best guarantee that your neighbor won't murder you comes from his vision of what it means to be truly human. Of course, it is not enough that I and my neighbor have our own moral views. For a society to exist, our ideas of moral action must be similar, if not identical, on a host of questions ranging from proper use of our own land to respect for each other's children. If our sharing of these moral patterns is to be worthy of our trust and reliance they will be set out in laws, creating a kind of collective security agreement in which our proclaimed values are enforced by neutral parties without regard to our momentary lapses of will or belief. Laws can also do much to encourage fidelity to these underlying moral beliefs. For example, the offense of conspiracy requires two or more persons to agree to commit a crime and take a substantial step toward fulfilling their pact. The law also contains a defense called "abandonment," which applies to a conspirator who abandons the enterprise without regard to other factors and before the crime becomes inevitable.[4] A conspirator who changes his mind and decides to obey the law is rewarded by a defense to the charges that may be brought against him. Laws that mirror shared moral beliefs raise the relations of men from the uncertain promises of the moment to the continuity and strength of a society.

These characteristics of law are especially interesting in light of our collective phobia about religious influence. If the laws are to apply to everyone, the moral values upheld by the laws must be seen as universal. If the state is to act immediately when a crime is committed, the moral values protected by the law must be so indisputably consistent with society's vision of the common good that any and all claims or arguments advanced with the purpose of justifying or excusing disobedience can be immediately rejected. If the laws are to be enforced with violence or the threat of violence, the moral vision they uphold must be superior to individual consent. The Constitution of Indiana says that the criminal law "shall be founded on the principles of reformation, and not of vindictive justice."[5] It is impossible to justify "reforming" criminals unless the laws they have broken uphold moral principles that inform their humanity better than their own individual beliefs about their actions. The explanation, the moral norm, may change over time and with debate, but the result will always be a vision of the common good so powerful, intimate, and universally applicable that it overrides particular individual choices and directs action in the most important areas of individual and communal life.

The Protestant theologian Paul Tillich told us that we can identify "God" in terms of our ultimate concern, of what we take seriously without reservation. His thoughts are similar to those of Martin Luther, who wrote:

> What is it to have a god? Answer: A god is that to
> which we look for all good and in which we find
> refuge in every time of need. To have a god is noth-
> ing else than to trust and believe him with our
> whole heart. As I have often said, the trust and faith
> of the heart alone make both God and an idol.[6]

Unless we are thoroughly modern, we do not think laws
are the source of all good, nor do we try to find refuge in
them in every time of need. But regardless of how modern we are, we must admit that our laws and statutes do
express ideas and values that are of ultimate concern to
us, in which we trust and believe wholeheartedly. We
expect men and women to die upholding the laws that
proclaim these values and beliefs. We expect men and
women to forego their own desires and conform to the
principles contained in the laws. The values in the laws
will be religious, the laws will have a religious sanction,
and they will make ultimate demands on our lives and
the lives or our neighbors. We cannot say our religious
beliefs are one thing and our laws are another. Our laws
come from beliefs of religious dimension, and we must
therefore take our religion very seriously.

Modern culture spends a great deal of time and energy
denying this. Its perspective on the relationship, or lack
thereof, between religion and laws comes largely from
humanist thinking. Note the following discussion of the
basis of criminal laws by the humanist Barbara Wootton:

> Here as elsewhere the Humanist attitude implies
> on the one hand a distinctive set of values; and on
> the other hand a characteristic reliance upon the
> methods of scientific investigation. Humanism is
> thus, on both counts, at variance with traditional

attitudes. Traditionally in the Western Christian world the whole field of social pathology has long been permeated by religious ideas—by concepts of taboo, sin, punishment and atonement set in the supernatural framework of the Christian dogmas; whereas the Humanist's standards are earthly, in a broad sense utilitarian, and, where possible, scientific. In determining the foundations of morality and the ultimate objectives of social pathology, the Humanist is concerned with man's happiness and welfare in this life alone, and with the development of each and every individual's maximum potentiality for the good life conceived in these terms. All arguments that are derived from religious dogmas, or that rest solely upon appeals to the will of God, pass the Humanist completely by. Admittedly such phrases as 'potentiality for the good life' are far from being precise terms . . . but for practical purposes it is clear enough what they mean. Indeed, in the present state of the world, even if we did not go beyond the purely negative definition that the Humanist is against hunger, poverty, ignorance, cruelty and bloodshed, we should have a sufficient basis for social policy. . . . So much for values.[7]

What stands out in this passage is a patent attempt to have it both ways, to condemn religious dogmas and revelation as improper grounds for public policy while at the same time proclaiming "distinctive values" such as being "against . . . cruelty and bloodshed" which transcend any individual's opinion under all circumstances and justify enforcement of the laws. It matters little whether a life sentence for murder rests on "Thou shalt not kill" or some "distinctive" belief that cruelty and bloodshed are wrong. Whenever a commitment to a moral principle acquires sufficient power to justify violence against deviance, it has necessarily acquired an ultimate, religious character. We cannot profit by the fruitless modern pretense that the question is whether the laws will serve God. The question is, was, and always will be: *Which god will the laws serve?*

The natural law is one answer to this debate. Briefly stated, and without going into the arguments between natural law theorists, it is the proposition that the God identified in the Old and New Testaments created everything, including man, with an ideal nature, and that man, by proper use of his own reasoning ability and truth revealed by God, can know his own nature and arrive at certain knowledge about the moral quality of his actions. Thus, for example, men can examine their natures and know that murder is contrary to their own ideal natures and the good of the community. In addition to this natural faculty of reason, God has provided us with revelation of truth for several reasons:

> [B]ecause, on account of the uncertainty of human judgment, especially on contingent and particular matters, different people form different judgments on human acts; whence also different and contrary laws result. In order, therefore, that man may know without any doubt what he ought to do and what he ought to avoid, it was necessary for man to be directed in his proper acts by a law given by God, for it is certain that such a law cannot err. . . .

> [B]ecause man can make laws in those matters of which he is competent to judge. But man is not competent to judge of interior movements, that are

hidden, but only of exterior acts which appear; and yet for the perfection of virtue it is necessary for man to conduct himself aright in both kinds of acts. Consequently, human law could not sufficiently curb and direct interior acts; and it was necessary for this purpose that a Divine law should supervene.[8]

Revelation about the wrongness of murder was given because human reason, though capable of reaching that conclusion, is capable of reaching different conclusions about the wrongness of murder as a whole or the wrongness of murder in particular circumstances. Revelation of divine law was also given because many things bearing on man's relationship with God, such as his individual moral culpability or interior attitudes toward worship, are not within the competence of man's governments. In all cases, however, man's use of reason within the framework of revelation to make laws for the common good is a reflection of God's perfect justice.

I hope by now that the relevance of this concept of law to a system of criminal justice is obvious. In fact, if natural law theory did not exist, secular thinkers would have to invent it. And in a way, they have. Look again at Wootton's description of the basis of true "humanist" criminal laws. She posits values that transcend the individual, values that are known by the light of reason applied to the human condition. What she and her fellow humanists do not have is a largely coherent philosophical system composed with 2,000 years of experience with the ends of man, the justice of social action, and the proper limits of government. Nor do they have a compelling justification for accepting the conclusions of "scientific" reason applied to the laws. Nor do they have the theoretical means to control their own government and prevent it from turning against "the potentiality for the good life." But more of this later. It is enough if you are convinced that some tradition of religious dimension is a necessary underpinning to any legal system and that the natural law can fulfill this need.

A criminal law system based on natural law would look remarkably like our present system. There would be laws against murder, rape, robbery, theft, arson and many of the other offenses that currently characterize our criminal law. Since the accused as a person has a dignity and value that the state cannot remove, the procedural protections we take to preserve the rights of the accused would be present. For example, the privilege against self-incrimination was created in our law as a deterrent to extorting confessions from the accused. As the danger of coerced confessions is no less present in a natural law system than a secular system, the inadmissibility of statements compelled from the accused should continue. Juries, in which the collective experience and wisdom of persons who are not agents of the state is used to determine guilt or innocence, could (and should) remain as the means for resolving criminal prosecutions. After all, it is worth noting that all these features of our criminal justice system were instituted in legal systems that were expressly Christian. I do not want to pretend that serious differences would not exist; the illegality of abortion is but one of the changes we would experience in a system based on natural law. But I think it should be stressed that many of the features we think are uniquely modern are quite compatible with (and arose within) natural law theory. Rather than set out an entirely revamped criminal code, I would like to look at one or two pressing modern legal issues and suggest how they might be resolved in a natural law system.

Laws regarding human sexuality and marriage would be noticeably affected by the acceptance of natural law. We moderns believe that our sexual experiences and unions are the inviolate provinces of individual choice. The Supreme Court has gone so far as to enunciate a new sphere of rights to intimate and personal decision making which includes, but is not limited to, the right to abort a child. What other intimate and personal decisions may be made? Homosexual-rights activists have asserted an intimate and personal right to enter into the legal state of marriage. A legal system that is solely concerned with "man's happiness and welfare in this life alone, and with the development of each and every individual's maximum potentiality for the good life conceived in these terms" would have a difficult time denying this right. At least one state has already recognized it. Humanists would approve:

> In sexual as in all other matters the Humanist thinks only in terms of the happiness and welfare of all persons who are or may be affected in a concrete case. . . . At some points, it is true, the Christian Churches have come to terms with contemporary developments . . . prominent churchmen, again both Catholic and Protestant alike . . . have accepted the view that, though sinful, homosexuality need not also be criminal. Plainly, what is actually happening in the world is the result of accommodation of religious to evolving humanistic ideas and not *vice versa*.[9]

The natural law is not as accommodating as these promi-
nent churchmen and insists that lovemaking occur only
within a marriage between one man and one woman that
is properly directed toward the human ends of children,
the comforts of family life, and conformity to God's creation of men and women for each other. Laws against
homosexuality, bigamy, and other sexual behavior that
does not conform to this pattern have more right reason
than the modern world might be willing to admit.

Suppose we agree with the Supreme Court's new
gospel that there is a right enshrined in the Constitution
to make intimate personal and sexual decisions. Surely
marriage is such a decision, and so this right of autonomy
would extend to marriage laws. On what basis could we
preserve laws against simultaneous marriage? We could
not, so long as the prevailing notion of immediate happiness, informed but not dictated by hunting and pecking
through statistical surveys, decided the issue. If I were a
stereotypical lawyer, I would gleefully contemplate our
new divorce laws. Think of the fees I could charge litigat-
ing cases such as these: Can Wife #2 claim visitation privileges with the children of Husband and Wife #4 on the
grounds that an emotional bond had arisen within the
context of the progressive family? How is Husband #3's
pension to be divided between himself and the two other
husbands who want to remain married to Wife? If Wife
#1, who was barren, prevailed on Wife #2 to have
Husband's child, are both Husband and Wife #1 to pay
child support when Wife #2 wants out of the marriage?
Perhaps at this point modern legislators would be scram-
bling to find statistics proving that such arrangements are
harmful to children and recommending remedial laws,

but the damage would be done. And even if we found statistics to justify our sentiment that this kind of domestic chaos harmed children, haven't we already recognized a fundamental right to polygamy? How can a right be fundamental, but incapable of exercise? Life without the natural law is not as free and easy as one might think, and will likely be a good deal more miserable.

I think the use of the death penalty would be very different under a natural law system. When I earlier discussed violence as an inseparable element of criminal law, I did not address the idea of proportionality. It was my intention to stress the seriousness of the criminal law and the resulting requirement for a serious justification for that law. But a requirement of proportionality exists in the natural law's treatment of war. The violence of the criminal law is somewhat like an armed conflict, although I use that phrase very cautiously, since we moderns are accustomed to thinking only of total conflicts in which any violence is acceptable if it eradicates an opponent. Natural law tells us that violence to protect an ideal of social justice must be proportionate to the good sought and must use the least destructive means of achieving that good. Our current laws inflict the death penalty with little regard to these requirements and do not conform to the natural law. Although the death of a murder victim can wryly be called a prolonged violation of his fundamental right to life, the first criterion does not allow us to put murders to death. What do we seek by punishing a murderer? We seek the good of society and of the murderer; we should not be deterred by natural and understandable feelings of disgust or dissatisfaction that occur whenever a murderer is not repaid in kind for his deed. The good of society is protection from the offender's proven capacity for murder. Both death and life in prison serve this need, but should death be a preferred option in all cases?

Augustine tells us that "God does not desire the death of a sinner, but that he be converted and live." Christ himself told us that God does not want the expiation of sins by the shedding of blood, but by repentance. The murderer's life has a value from God himself, and we should not tread lightly on this value by preferring death for all who commit murder. We may inflict that penalty only on those whom Aquinas referred to as "pestiferous men," men whose exterior acts have demonstrated that no one can remain safe so long as they live. Indiana law, like that of most states, makes some attempts to identify such individuals. For example, the death penalty may be sought when

> [t]he victim of the murder was a corrections employee, probation officer, parole officer, community corrections worker, home detention officer, fireman, judge, or law enforcement officer, and either: (A) the victim was acting in the course of duty; or (B) the murder was motivated by an act the victim performed while acting in the course of duty.[10]

But these laws also permit the death penalty in cases where no rational person would deny that life imprisonment would serve just as well, such as when the murder was committed by someone on probation for a felony or by discharging a firearm from a vehicle. These laws must change, and with them the current "lottery system" by which sentimental factors, such as the reluctance of society to execute women, or the prosecution's ability to demonize a defendant, play an important role in deciding who lives and who dies.

Lastly, I would like to address the repeated claims that systems of law based on religious traditions will always be used to compel total obedience to a single and identical pattern of human virtue. Some might think this a curious fear in a legal system like ours, which chastely and purely disavows any connection to religion yet requires hundreds of people to undergo "sensitivity training" about racial and sexual issues on pain of imprisonment for contempt of court. Some might think it odd that the same legal system, vigilant to prevent something like the Index from having the force of law, would yet accept reading *The Shotgun News* as a grounds for a search warrant. But it is a persistent concern, always raised in opposition to a Christian view of law, and should be addressed. Recall St. Thomas's statement, that divine law is revealed:

> because man can make laws in those matters of which he is competent to judge. But man is not competent to judge of interior movements, that are hidden, but only of exterior acts which appear; and yet for the perfection of virtue it is necessary for man to conduct himself aright in both kinds of acts. Consequently, human law could not sufficiently curb and direct interior acts; and it was necessary for this purpose that a Divine law should supervene.[11]

St. Thomas is saying that human law has limits that prevent it from compelling men to live as saints in all things. The law exists for the common good and "does not forbid all vicious acts . . . as neither does it prescribe all acts of virtue."[12] St. Thomas goes on to issue a wise warning that rebellion or unrest may occur if the state requires men to participate in acts of virtue they do not understand or that are beyond their abilities. The common good is not served by using the limited resources of the state to demand perfect virtue in all things by all men; the state only has enough power to demand some virtue in few things. Moreover, there are many matters in which God's will for individuals might be different regarding the same subject. He might, for example, desire one married couple to have a two-career family and desire that another have only one partner working outside the home. It would be futile for the natural law, bound as it is to the concept of human limits, to pretend that the state was created to enforce all these particular and individual elements of God's plan for the salvation of each human being.

Since the natural law does not sanction codifying saint-hood or covert surveillance of citizens to ensure their attendance at divine service, the temptation arises to dismiss natural law as either unexceptional or dangerous. After all, the aims and methods of natural law do not seem too different from the aims and methods of any other set of modern moral principles such as Humanist Manifesto II or the Universal Declaration of Human Rights. Indeed, conventional thinking has it that natural law differs from those sources of moral and social principle only in its greater potential for abuse. By imbuing the state with divine authority, natural law allegedly stifles constructive social change by transforming dissidence into heresy. The modern paradigm claims superiority in this regard because, in recognizing law as a thing subject only to human will, it also recognizes the possibility of human error and the need to restrain the state from asserting divine rights over the minds and lives of men. The natural law is also criticized because it is an integral part of a religious tradition—Christianity—that encourages its adherents to arrange their lives around a single, divinely ordained pattern. Whether or not this pattern and the means by which it may be achieved are misunderstood by crude critics or crude practitioners, it is predicted that natural law will put the state in service of this pattern in all its myriad variations and details and sanction untold intrusions into individual freedom. And since it is supposedly well known that, for the true Christian, "[t]he bearing of a particular form of conduct on earthly happiness and well being [is] not given even a passing thought," and all "[q]uestions of right and wrong [are] determined solely as regards their effect upon salvation in the world beyond life,"[13] these intrusions are likely to make us unhappy as well as unfree.

This view results from the myopia alluded to elsewhere in this essay. Critics of theologically derived legal systems are exquisitely alert to the dangers of such systems, but are either unable or unwilling to understand that the same dangers characterize *any system of law:* one accepts the danger by accepting law itself. A most curious bias, one might even say bigotry, assumes that when people believe their institutions are sanctioned and directed by a divine rule they always act against the interests of humanity in general.[14] Examples from history are routinely used (and even abused) to "prove" this assumption, while examples of secular society creating even far more terrible disasters while professing many of the ideals of the Humanist Manifesto, Humanist Manifesto II, and Universal Declaration of Human Rights, are ignored or twisted from the point.[15] We waste time debating whether Christianity is "guilty" of the Inquisition, or if Secular Humanism is "responsible" for the Holocaust. We must reject the false paradigm of "religion and persecution" versus "irreligion and freedom." We must realize that civilization requires law, law requires moral justification, this justification will be religious in scope, *and that all these things threaten man in the same way that his medicines, technology, art, or education pose threats.*

The dominant American legal paradigm is in broad outlines secular and positivist. It speaks and acts as though "moral values derive their source from human experience[:] Ethics is *autonomous* and *situational*, needing no theological or ideological sanction."[16] Moral principles enforced by law are simply chosen by the community from an infinite range of possibilities through the application of supposedly scientific standards to selected data. Note this exchange between counsel and Justice Thurgood Marshall during the oral arguments in *Roe v. Wade:*

> **Counsel:** We say there is life from the moment of impregnation.
>
> **Justice Marshall:** And do you have any scientific data to support that? . . . . I want you to give me a medical, recognizable medical writing of any kind that says that at the time of conception that the fetus is a person.[17]

What has been said of modern man is equally well said of our legal system:

> [Modern man has] been taught . . . to stand against any external and corporate authority, except it be

mediated to him by democratic processes; to stand against any law in whose making he had no voice; to stand finally against any society which asserts itself to be an independent community of thought, superior to the consensus created by the common mind of secular democratic society, and empowered to pass judgment, in the name of higher criteria, on this common mind and on the consensus it assembles.[18]

Modern legal orders, including our own, find the source of law in human will alone:

If, however, it is recognized that only relative values are accessible to human knowledge and human will, then it is justifiable to enforce a social order against reluctant individuals only if this order is in harmony with the greatest possible number of equal individuals, that is to say, with the will of the majority. It may be that the opinion of the minority, and not the opinion of the majority, is correct. Solely because of this possibility, which only philosophical relativism can admit—that what is right today may be wrong tomorrow—the minority must have a chance to express freely their opinion and must have full opportunity of becoming the majority.[19]

Once a legal order adopts these principles, it claims all of life as a fit subject for government. Under God, the law derives from metaphysics; without him, the law is metaphysics.

The immediate threat here is not that the state will coerce teenagers to become drug addicts or require us to worship images of Baal. But the absence of a transcendent justification that is beyond the control, but not the reach, of man creates a vacuum in which the state is inevitably transformed into a thing of godlike dimensions.[20] In this state man will not only lack protection, he will lack even the language to articulate his need for protection:

> Some doubts have been expressed as to the source of the immunity of a sovereign power from suit . . . but the answer has been public property since before the day of Hobbes. A sovereign is exempt from suit, not because of any formal conception or obsolete theory, but on the logical and practical ground that *there can be no legal right as against the authority that makes the law on which the right depends. . . .*[21] (emphasis added)

One of the greatest slanders leveled at natural law is the accusation that by tying the enforcement of secular law with the church, it preached a divine right of kings to do all their power permits. The "divine right of kings" was advanced as an *alternative* to natural law. Far from being a logical outgrowth of natural law, the divine right of kings represents the first stirring of the modern idea that individual, nation, and state are one, and that the state, which is a collective that represents all persons, has total authority to define the good of each individual. All that remained necessary for the rise of modern totalitarian power was the separation of the state's power from a preexisting theory of divinely ordained law. Once that was done, the state became free to exercise the moral abilities previously attributed to God alone.

A state that claims total moral authority over the individual is the inevitable result of modern thinking. But the power modern law gives the state does not fully persuade us against the modern legal paradigm. It can be asked whether this degree of power and the potential for its abuse are not necessary risks of human society. If the aims of the state are the purposes of man, and if man is capable of bad purposes (which is just as true under natural law as any other paradigm), perhaps the only task is to recognize our potential for evil and do our best to ensure that our laws are beneficial. If this is so, then natural law is not a unique legal theory that deserves special consideration among, or even preference over, other legal theories.

But the matter is not so easily dealt with for several reasons. The first reason, original sin, will be dealt with briefly, since the person under modern tutelage does not believe in it, and his unbelief requires a work of missionary zeal, which is beyond my humble capacity. Man is not now in his original, intended condition. This defect results from the sinful act of the first human couple who disobeyed God's plan for mankind and thus marred the condition of mankind. No individual living today is morally culpable for this choice; we are akin to children infected with AIDS in the womb. Just as the consequences of the disease will mar the baby, so original sin renders us wounded in our natures and is causally connected with the "overwhelming misery which oppresses men and their inclination toward evil and death."[22] Persons in such a condition are incapable of using an all-powerful state wisely for any significant length of time without Christ's grace, which alleviates and cures the conditions caused by original sin. Power does not corrupt, nor does absolute power corrupt absolutely. It is man himself who is corrupt, and his corruption makes him unfit to possess any degree of unrestrained power.

Modern man cannot appreciate this fact and insists that he can create a society of justice, harmony, and peace by his own unaided efforts. Because he is oppressed by overwhelming misery and inclined to evil and death, he routinely fails, and fails spectacularly.

While the abuse of power in the name of truth is a threat common to both natural and modern legal theories, the jurisdiction claimed by the modern state exceeds that of any state organized under natural law. A state organized under natural law has ends already articulated by a power higher than itself. In achieving these ends, the state, inasmuch as it is composed of men, confronts a range of means that may be forbidden or permitted. This concept puts the ends and means of government beyond the control, although not the reach, of man and introduces concrete and inherent limits on state power, recognized by no less a modern than Rousseau:

> . . . Jesus came to establish a spiritual kingdom on earth, which, by separating the theological from the political system, made the State no longer one, and caused those intestine dissensions which have never ceased to agitate the Christian peoples. . . . [T]he consequence resulting from this double power has been a perpetual conflict for jurisdiction which has made any system of good polity impossible in Christian States; and men could never inform themselves whether it was the master or the priest they were bound to obey.[23]

Though he denies the merits of Rousseau's judgment, the Christian would otherwise agree with all Rousseau says. This division and resulting tension, insofar as it is acted upon with prudence, is part of God's plan for human society. When men question what belongs to Caesar and what belongs to God, they participate in a constant tension between the moral criteria of human life and the function of government. The natural law guarantees this tension by depriving man and the state of absolute power over each other, thereby making both vulnerable to government. A state in this legal frame lacks the ontology of totalitarianism. It loses its legitimacy whenever it attempts to redefine its own ends and whenever it permits its citizens to redefine those ends. This balance is not perfect, but it works. A natural law state cannot plausibly exercise total power over man and is therefore superior in theory to the state created by modern legal thinking.

Lastly, we can ask what remedy is available when the state acts contrary to man. Modern legal systems have many answers, all of which come down to politely asking the state to change its mind. These remedies are available in the natural law as well. But the natural law goes further than modern legal theory:

> Armed *resistance* to oppression by political authority is not legitimate, unless all the following conditions are met: 1) there is certain, grave, and prolonged violation of fundamental rights; 2) all other means of redress have been exhausted; 3) such resistance will not provoke worse disorders; 4) there is well-founded hope of success; and 5) it is impossible reasonably to foresee any better solution.[24] (emphasis in original)

The modern theory of the state cannot envision a legal right to resist the state: *"There can be no legal right as against the authority that makes the law on which the right depends."*[25]

In modern thinking, resistance to the state is impossible because as Thomas Hobbes said, "Temporal and spiritual government are but words brought into the world to make men see double and mistake their lawful sovereign." A modern man who opposes the state is a traitor to his own concept of human government. Even if it were possible for a population indoctrinated in the modern legal tradition to conceive of requiring the state to undergo reformation on other than its own terms, such a people would most likely lack the will to carry out such reform. A law that can govern the state and expose it to punishment must enable men to believe they are better off suffering in defense of it than living in deviation from it. It is no accident that the civil rights movement in the United States was explicitly Christian in the Protestant tradition, and no coincidence that the death knell of Communism was sounded by a Catholic workers' association. The natural law provides men with the moral justification for replacing a corrupt state, and this is a better guarantee of justice under law than anything that relies on the good intentions of kings and presidents.

It can be no secret that I profoundly desire the United States to recognize the natural law as the legal theory that both gave rise to and justifies our Constitution and legal system. But the kind of reforms I would like to see cannot come from law. As I have tried to point out, law derives from moral culture. If our laws are corrupt, it is because our culture is corrupt; and our culture thrives only because we nourish it. The reform of man cannot be imposed by law. In this, I think Christians have already learned from our wars of religion what the modern world has—hopefully—

relearned from its own twentieth-century massacres. Perhaps now we can begin to seriously talk about ourselves and our society by focusing first on our humanity under God, and then on how the state can aid us in achieving it. Whenever I watch what passes for this discourse in the media I grow pessimistic, until I realize what television announcers and newspaper editors never say, that we can do all things through Christ, who strengthens us.[26]

ENDNOTES

1. Peter Irons & Stephanie Guitton, eds., *May It Please the Court* (New York: The New Press, 1993), 67.

2. Benjamin N. Cardozo, *The Paradoxes of Legal Science* (New York: Columbia University Press, 1928; reprint, Birmingham: *Legal Classics Library* 1982), 37.

3. St. Augustine, *City of God*, trans. Marcus Dodds (New York: Random House, 1950), 112–13.

4. *Babin v. State*, 609 N.E. 2d 3, 5 (Ind. App. 1993).

5. Indiana Constitution, art. 1, § 18.

6. Martin Luther, "Large Catechism," in *The Book of Concord*, trans. & ed. Theodore G. Tappert (Philadelphia: Fortress Press, 1959), 365.

7. Barbara Wootton, "Humanism and Social Pathology," in *The Humanist Frame*, ed. by Julian Huxley (New York: Harper & Brothers Publishers, 1961), 348.

8. St. Thomas Aquinas, *Summa Theologiae*, 1–2, q. 91, art. 4.

9. B. Wootton, "Humanism and Social Pathology," 349–50.

10. Indiana Code Sec. 35-50-2-9(6) (19).

11. Aquinas, *Summa Theologiae*, 1–2 q. 91, art. 4.

12. Aquinas, *Summa Theologiae*, 1–2, q. 96, art. 3

13. Harry Elmer Barnes, *An Intellectual and Cultural History of the Western World*, vol. 2, (New York: Dover books, 1965), 817.

14. Pope Leo XIII wrote well about this bigotry: "[A] hackneyed reproach of old date is leveled against her, that the Church is opposed to the rightful aims of the civil government, and is wholly unable to afford help in spreading that welfare and progress which justly and naturally are sought after by every well-regulated State. From the very beginning Christians were harassed by slanderous accusations of this nature, and on that account were held up to

hatred and execration, for being (so they were called) enemies of the empire."
Immortale Dei, November 1, 1885.

15. For example, Paul Kurtz claims that the oppressive history of the Soviet regime did not result from unchecked secularism, but from its refusal to separate church and state. See P. Kurtz, *In Defense of Secular Humanism* (Buffalo, New York: Prometheus Books, 1983). I agree with Kurtz's implication that the Soviet regime was trying to enforce a religious basis of human life. I disagree with his assumption that such evils disappear once a regime reviles the idea of absolute truth. Any government of which Kurtz would approve would still justify coercion against the individual by moral claims superior to him, regardless of whether it also "eschews all dogma." Kurtz, Hans Kelsen, and other secular humanists do not want to alter the power of these claims, only their content. A morally relativistic regime will not appear so to anyone it arrests and incarcerates: What do we gain if we reject truth as a basis for taking absolute actions against individuals? All we "gain" is the freedom of the community to act in absolute ways against individuals on any basis the community prefers. This may be exciting to adherents of a new moral vision but it cannot provide, as it claims, the infallible cure for despotism.

16. *Humanist Manifestos I and II,* ed. Paul Kurtz (Buffalo, New York: Prometheus Books, 1973).

17. Irons and Guitton, *May It Please the Court,* 348, 352.

18. John Courtney Murray, "The Freedom of Man in the Freedom of the Church," 1 (fall 1957), 134–145.

19. Hans Kelsen, "Absolutism and Relativism in Philosophy and Politics," 42 *American Political Science Review* (1948), 906, 913–14.

20. The conception of the modern state is in fact godlike. Compare Rousseau's description of the civil state given in the *Encyclopédie,* under the article "Economie politique," with the description of God's church found in the New Testament:

> According to Rousseau, "The body politic, taken in itself, may be likened to a living body with organs, like that of a man. The sovereign power represents the head . . . the citizens are the body and limbs, by which the machine moves. . . . The body politic is, then, a moral being with a will, and this General Will which tends ever towards the preservation and well-being of the whole and the parts, which is the source of laws."

In 1 Corinthians 12: 12–31, St. Paul wrote:

> "[T]he body is a unit, although it is made up of many parts; and though all its parts are many, they form one body. So it is with Christ. For we were all baptized by one Spirit into one body. . . .

> Now the body is not made up of one part but of many. If the foot should say, 'Because I am not a hand, I do not belong to the body,' it would not for that reason cease to be part of the body. . . . God has arranged the parts in the body, every one of them, just as he wanted them to be. If they were all one part, where would the body be? As it is, there are many parts, but one body."

Rousseau's expropriation of St. Paul demonstrates the modern state's tendency to replace God as the source of human meaning. This is not progress, but regression to the primitive state in which men imagined that their rulers were divine.

21. *Kawananakoa v. Polyblank*, 205 U.S. 349, 353 (1907) (Holmes, J., writing for the majority).

22. *Catechism of the Catholic Church*, Paragraph 403.

23. Jean-Jacques Rousseau, *The Social Contract*, trans. Charles Frankel (New York: Hafner Publishing Co., 1947), Book IV, Chapter 8.

24. *Catechism of the Catholic Church*, Paragraph 2243. It is the absence of the second criteria that renders those who kill abortionists subject to punishment. Other means of redress, such as a constitutional amendment overruling *Roe v. Wade*, alteration of the composition of the Court, etc. have not been exhausted.

25. *Kawananakoa*, 205 U.S. at 353 (emphasis added).

26. Phillipians 4:13.

Part IV

Prospects for the Twenty-First Century

Chapter 13

Natural Law in the Twenty-First Century

CHARLES E. RICE

Dr. Arthur Caplan, University of Minnesota ethicist, has stated that if Leonardo da Vinci suddenly appeared in the United States, he would "show him a reproductive clinic. I'd tell him, 'We make babies in this dish and give them to other women to give birth.' And that would be more surprising [to Leonardo] than seeing an airplane or even the space shuttle."[1]

The new reproductive technology would indeed be a surprise not only to Leonardo, but also to a Rip Van Winkle type who had dozed off for only a few decades. They would be impressed that researchers at George Washington University have cloned human embryos, splitting embryos into identical twins or triplets. Since embryos can be frozen for later use, it might soon be possible for parents to have a child and then, years later, use a cloned, frozen embryo to give birth to an identical twin, possibly as an organ donor for the older child. Or parents could keep such an embryo as a backup in case their first child died, so they could create an "identical" replacement.[2]

Leonardo and Rip would surely write home also about the disclosure by British researchers of their technique to retrieve eggs (i.e., ova) from aborted female babies, fertilize them by in vitro fertilization, and implant them in the wombs of infertile women. This technique, of course, treats the unborn child—the mother—not as a human being but as an object, a repository of component parts. "This consumerist approach to the creation of life," said Member of Parliament David Alton, "puts it on a par with an American fast-food outlet." The London Sunday Express warned of "fetus farming," in which women would "conceive babies, have abortions and sell their fetuses for cash."[3]

More surprising to Leonardo and Rip than the new technology, however, might be our failure to subject these and other technological developments to critical moral analysis in the light of hard facts. For example, the new method of making the aborted child herself a mother proves, beyond misunderstanding even by academics, what we already knew, that every abortion, at whatever stage of gestation, kills a living—and necessarily innocent—human being. How can an unborn child be the mother of a human being if she is not one herself? "If a fetus can be a mother," asked columnist Alan Keyes, "how can we deny that it is a human being? Every time scientists develop a child using an egg taken from an aborted female fetus, they will be proving beyond doubt that they have violated the most basic human right of its mother."[4]

However, the abundant documentation that abortion is murder makes not the slightest dent in the general public's acceptance of at least some abortion. Surgical abortions in the United States kill about 1.6 million unborn children every year. Uncounted millions more are killed by early abortion techniques, including the intrauterine device, most birth-control pills, Norplant, and other techniques that enjoy an immunity conferred by their protective labeling as contraceptives. And the euthanasia juggernaut, which John Cardinal O'Connor predicted "will dwarf the abortion phenomenon in magnitude, in numbers, in horror," has not even shifted yet into high gear.[5]

Clearly, something is amiss in our perception of the relation between law and morality. Other essays in this collection, by Edward J. Murphy, Ian McLean, and William Riley, have dealt with natural law and contracts, criminal law and torts. Another essay, by Janet Smith, explored the implications for law and society of Pope Paul VI's 1968 encyclical, *Humane Vitae*, with respect to life and family issues. In all these areas, one can perceive a tendency to exalt the positive law enacted by legislators or courts and to minimize the role of the reasonable person in determining not only what is moral but also what should be legal. As Alasdair MacIntyre put it in his essay in this collection:

> In the United States today, we inhabit a society in which a system of positive law with two salient characteristics has been developed. At a variety of points, it invades the lives of plain persons, and its tangled complexities are such that it leaves those plain persons no alternative but to put themselves into the

hands of lawyers. It is notorious that ours has
become a society of incessant litigation, in which
plain persons can all too rarely hope to resolve matters of dispute by appeal among themselves to evident and agreed moral principles—for the loss of an
adequate understanding of the natural law has
resulted in a widespread belief that there are no such
principles—but instead must resort to courts and
therefore to lawyers. Of course, in any society, there
is some need for positive law and for litigation as a
last resort. But it is an index of great moral deprivation when litigation so often becomes the first resort.
Perhaps it has done so because the dominant culture
of North American modernity is inimical to any adequate conception of the natural law.[6]

How did this happen, that our "dominant culture" is
"inimical to any adequate conception of the natural law"?
To understand, we have to go back a few years. We
should first recall the classic phrase of Francis Canavan,
S.J., of Fordham University, who described the present
stage of American culture as "the fag-end of the
Enlightenment."[7]

"The fundamental dogma of the Enlightenment," in
the words of Joseph Cardinal Ratzinger, "is that man
must overcome the prejudices inherited from tradition;
he must have the boldness to free himself from every
authority in order to think on his own, using nothing but
his own reason."[8]

Three aspects of Enlightenment thought are pertinent
here:

1. *Secularism.* The Enlightenment rejected not only
the Church but all revealed religion as irrelevant to society and the state. For the past three centuries, Western

philosophers have sought to organize society as if God did not exist. Those efforts have achieved striking success in recent decades. "Only in the past two generations, in my lifetime," wrote Harold Berman, "has the public philosophy of America shifted radically from a religious to a secular theory of law, from a moral to a political or instrumental theory, and from a historical to a pragmatic theory."[9] If there is no God and therefore no ultimate lawgiver higher than the state, then there is no basis for affirming a transcendent dignity of the human person against the state. And there are no limits to what the state—and science under its patronage—can do to manipulate human beings.

2. *Relativism.* The Enlightenment denied the capacity of reason to know objective moral truth. In recent decades, the dominant American culture has denied as well the very possibility of such truth. As recently as four decades ago, public debate was premised on an assumed objective morality. The occasional "mercy killing" cases, for example, where a physician or a spouse would end the life of a suffering patient, were discussed in terms of whether such an act was "right or wrong." Opinions differed as to what was right in a given case, but it was generally assumed that the act was one or the other, right or wrong. Today, as Allan Bloom noted in the introduction to *The Closing of the American Mind*,

> [r]elativism is . . . the only virtue . . . which all primary education for more than fifty years has dedicated itself to inculcating. Openness . . . is the great insight of our times. The true believer is the real danger. The study of history and of culture teaches that all the world was mad in the past; men always

thought they were right, and that led to wars, persecutions, slavery, xenophobia, racism, and chauvinism. The point is not to correct the mistakes and really be right; rather it is not to think you are right at all. The students, of course, cannot defend their opinion. It is something with which they have been indoctrinated. The best they can do is point out all the opinions and cultures there are and have been. What right, they ask, do I or anyone else have to say one is better than the others?[10]

This denial of objective moral reality permeates our culture. "Post-modernists," said a recent *New York Times* analysis,

now place quotation marks around words like "reality," insisting that the old notion of objective knowledge has become obsolete. Multiculturalists argue for new curriculums not on the basis of factual accuracy, but on the basis of "self-esteem." And politicians and their spin doctors use pseudo-events and photo-ops to market virtual-reality versions of themselves to the public. Throughout our culture, the old notions of "truth" and "knowledge" are in danger of being replaced by the new ones of "opinion," "perception" and "credibility."[11]

Relativism leads to legal positivism: Since no one can know what is right or wrong, the resolution of such questions must be left up to the political process. Whatever that process turns out must be accepted as valid law, whether Auschwitz or legalized abortion. Thus, Justice Oliver Wendell Holmes defined truth as "the majority vote of the nation that could lick all others," and said "the sacredness of human life is a purely municipal ideal of no validity outside the jurisdiction."[12]

A utilitarian, positivistic philosophy dominates the American legal profession. "[P]erhaps the most consistent expression of analytical positivism in legal theory" is Hans Kelsen's "pure theory of law." Legal positivism "contemplates the form of law rather than its moral or social contents, . . . it confines itself to the investigation of the law as it is, without regard to its justness or unjustness, and . . . it endeavors to free legal theory completely from all qualification or value judgments of a political, social, or economic nature."[13] Legal positivism offers no rationale for arguing that a law can be void for injustice rather than merely unwise or unconstitutional. "[J]ustice," according to Kelsen, "is not ascertainable by rational knowledge at all. . . . From the standpoint of rational knowledge there are only interests and conflicts of interests. . . . Justice is an irrational ideal."[14] Kelsen asserted that with respect to

> [T]he norms of morals . . . all the individual norms can be derived from the basic norm by an operation of thought, namely, by deduction from universal to particular. With legal norms the case is different. These are not valid by virtue of their content. Any content whatsoever can be legal; there is no human behavior which could not function as the content of a legal norm. A norm becomes a legal norm only because it has been constituted in a particular fashion born of a definite procedure and a definite rule. . . . The individual norms of the legal system are not to be derived from the basic norm by a process of logical deduction. They must

be constituted by an act of will, not derived by an act of thought.[15]

For the legal positivist, therefore, as Kelsen put it, "any kind of content might be law. . . . The validity of a legal norm may not be denied for being (in its content) in conflict . . . with that of another norm which does not belong to the legal order whose basic norm is the reason for the validity of the norm in question."[16]

3. *Individualism.* The third contribution of the Enlightenment to our current malaise is its emphasis on an exaggerated autonomy of the individual. Alasdair MacIntyre, in his essay, emphasized that

> human beings are essentially sociable, that I achieve whatever I achieve as an individual by being and acting as an individual who is bound to others through a variety of familial, social, and political relationships expressed in joint activity aimed at achieving our common good. My good therefore is the good of someone who is a part of an ordered set of social wholes. My own good can only be achieved in and through the achievement of the common good. . . .[17]

Where Aristotle, Aquinas, and others such as MacIntyre affirmed that man is social by nature, Enlightenment thinkers postulated a mythical "state of nature" populated by autonomous individuals who were not social but "sociable." Those individuals formed the state according to the social contract. The purpose, according to Thomas Hobbes, was to achieve security; according to John Locke, it was for the protection of rights; for Jean-Jacques Rousseau, it was to implement the "general will." The origin of the state was therefore not in nature and the divine plan but in the social contract, with the authority of the state conferred not by God but by man. "The Declaration of the Rights of Man at the end of the eighteenth century," wrote Hannah Arendt, "was a turning point in history. It meant nothing more nor less than that from then on Man, and not God's command or the customs of history, should be the source of law."[18] Of course, if man rather than God is the source of rights, man can take them away.

The autonomous individual of the Enlightenment was bound to others only to the extent that he consented to be so bound. Even the mother would have no intrinsic relation to the child in her womb. This is the origin of "pro-choice." The utilitarian positivism of the Enlightenment can offer no basis, other than the aesthetic or pragmatic, for restricting that right to choose, including the choice to kill through abortion, euthanasia, or new reproductive technologies. Nor can it offer any remedy for the decline of the family, which is seen in Enlightenment terms as a utilitarian association of individuals rather than as a society in itself.

The moral collapse of American culture, under the influence of secularism, relativism, and individualism, has accelerated over the past three decades. *The Index of Cultural Indicators,* devised by former Secretary of Education William J. Bennett, tabulates statistical indicators of America's cultural collapse from 1960 to 1990. During that period, Bennett writes,

> there has been a 560 percent increase in violent crime; more than a 400 percent increase in illegitimate births; a quadrupling in divorce rates; a

> tripling of the percentage of children living in single-parent homes; more than a 200 percent increase in the teenage suicide rate; and a drop of almost 80 points in SAT scores. . . . The social regression of the last 30 years is due in large part to the enfeebled state of our social institutions and their failure to carry out a critical and time-honored task: the moral education of the young.[19]

We have to ask, however, a further question: What happened in the early 1960s to precipitate this decline? We can point to two developments at that time that reflected the growing cultural dominance of secularism, relativism, and individualism. First, the Supreme Court decreed, in *Torasco v. Watkins* (1961), *Engel v. Vitale* (1962), and *School District of Abington Township v. Schempp* (1963), that the federal and state governments must suspend judgment on the question of whether God exists. But this suspension of judgment is a false neutrality and results in a governmental preference of agnostic secular humanism. Several generations of public school children have seen the state, in the persons of its agents, the teachers, suspend judgment on the existence of God. In effect, they have never seen the state acknowledge that in fact there is a moral standard of right and wrong higher than the state. When school courses deal with questions of family life, abortion, homosexual activity, etc., they must do so nonjudgmentally, without affirming any moral position as correct. But this suspension of judgment is itself the adoption of a religious position, that the answers to such questions are relative and that those questions can properly be considered without affirming the controlling character of God's law.

This implied establishment of secularism requires that the right to life of the unborn child and others must be evaluated in secular, utilitarian terms. Similarly, any legislative treatment of homosexual activity, pornography, condom distribution in schools, etc., cannot be based on the moral law, let alone the Ten Commandments. The result is a jurisprudential Gresham's Law, with bad laws and policies increasingly driving out the good, to the point that the state comes to subsidize fornication and other conduct that, only a few years ago, it had seen itself obliged to discourage.

Every society has to have a god, an ultimate moral authority. If the real God is displaced, another will take his place. Today, the replacement god is the autonomous individual who makes himself the defining authority; ultimately, of course, such authority will be assumed by the state.

The second occurrence in the early 1960s that reflects this deification of the autonomous individual was the approval of the contraceptive pill by the Food and Drug Administration in 1960. American law and culture thereafter adopted an important tenet of the secularist religion, that there is no inherent connection between the unitive and procreative aspects of sex, so that the individual is wholly autonomous in determining whether sex will have any relation to procreation. We tend to forget that the treatment of recreational sex as an end in itself is a fairly recent development. It was not until 1930, with the Anglican Lambeth Conference, that any Christian denomination ever said that contraception could ever be objectively right. When a committee of the Federal Council of Churches followed Lambeth by endorsing "careful and restrained" use of contraceptives, a *Washington Post* editorial responded:

> It is impossible to reconcile the doctrine of the divine institution of marriage with any modernistic plan for the mechanical regulation or suppression of human birth. The church must either reject the plain teachings of the Bible or reject schemes for the "scientific" production of human souls. Carried to its logical conclusion, the committee's report if carried into effect would sound the death-knell of marriage as a holy institution, by establishing degrading practices which would encourage indiscriminate immorality. The suggestion that the use of legalized contraceptives would be 'careful and restrained' is preposterous.[20]

The legitimacy of contraception has become an assumption not only of the general culture but of government policy as well. The nearly universal acceptance of contraception has shifted the public debate on various issues toward conclusions preordained by the acceptance of contraceptive premises and hostile to traditional Christian belief. Thus, homosexual activity, an obvious separation of the unitive and procreative aspects of sex, is widely regarded as a civil right, subject to restriction only on nonmoral grounds such as the need to prevent disease. Numerous cities have adopted "domestic partnership" ordinances to confer on homosexual, as well as heterosexual, unions some of the legal characteristics of marriage. Abortion, too, is treated as a right that takes precedence over any claims for the unborn child, who is defined as a nonperson. If there is no inherent relation between sex and life, if no one can know what is right or wrong, and if God is excluded, it is difficult to see how the result could be otherwise. If man makes himself the arbiter of when life begins, he will predictably make himself, as in abortion and euthanasia, the arbiter of when it shall end. Similarly, in the natural order of things, one reason why sex is reserved for marriage and why marriage is permanent is that sex has something to do with babies and it is good for children to be raised by their own parents who stay married to each other. But if it is entirely man's choice as to whether sex will have anything to do with procreation, why should sex be reserved for marriage and why should marriage be permanent?

The dominance from the early 1960s of official secularism and the relativist, individualist contraceptive ethic goes far to explain the cultural decline documented by William Bennett, as well as the liberation of science from objective moral standards.

A coherent alternative to the law and culture of the Enlightenment must be based on the natural law. The idea of natural law is neither a merely sectarian Catholic teaching nor even a Christian invention. Aristotle affirmed the existence of "natural justice,"[21] and Cicero said that "right is based, not upon men's opinions, but upon Nature."[22]

Everything is governed by a natural law according to its own nature. Thus, a rock will sink and wood will burn. The natural moral law governs human conduct. It can be known certainly by reason. The first principle of the natural law is self-evident, that, in Thomas Aquinas's words, "good is to be done and pursued, and evil is to be avoided."[23] The good is that which is in accord with the nature of the subject, whether a car or a man. The natural law is the story of how things work according to their nature. It is good to feed gasoline to a car and not good to feed it to a man. It is not good, i.e., it is evil, for a man to steal, since theft is contrary to the natural human inclination to live in community. As Robert P. George said in his essay, we make the natural law "effective" through our own choices. However, "[t]he principles of natural law possess and retain their normative and prescriptive force independently of anyone's decision to adopt or refuse to adopt them in making the practical choices to which they apply."[24]

St. Thomas described the function of the natural law as "the light of natural reason, whereby we discern what is good and evil."[25] However, to declare that an action such as theft, abortion, etc., is objectively wrong is not to judge the subjective culpability of the person who does it. To be morally culpable, one must know it is wrong and yet choose to do it. We generally have neither the right nor the capacity to judge the subjective culpability of anyone. Nevertheless, as Pope John Paul II has said, "Moral truth is objective, and a properly formed conscience can perceive it."[26] In his essay, Alasdair MacIntyre described the "Thomistic understanding of natural law" as "the only account of natural law which . . . justifies plain persons in regarding themselves as already having within themselves the resources afforded by a knowledge of fundamental law, resources by means of which they can judge the claims to jurisdiction over them of any system of positive law."[27]

Thomas Aquinas, however, is not the only expositor of natural law. Therefore, the question arises: Whose natural

law are you going to apply? Proponents of natural law in
the context of American constitutionalism have never
recovered from Supreme Court Justice James Iredell's
dictum in support of his rejection of natural law as a basis
for invalidating state legislation: "The ideas of natural
justice are regulated by no fixed standard: the ablest and
the purest men have differed upon the subject."[28] Those
who advance secular arguments for natural law tend to
go down for the count when hit by the retort, "Whose
natural law?" If Iredell is right, and if the meaning of the
natural law is ultimately determined by consensus, it is
relatively useless as a higher standard for law and a guide
for human conduct. Suppose you think abortion or military service or whatever, is wrong. Who are you to say?
Even if we recognize that there is a natural law, how do
we know for sure what it means?

The first step in solving this problem is to recall that
every law must have a lawgiver. The natural law of your
Chevrolet is built into it by its manufacturer, General
Motors. So, too, the natural law that governs human conduct is built into us by our Manufacturer. The natural law
is a rule of reason, promulgated by God in man's nature,
whereby man can discern how he should act so as to
achieve his end of salvation.

Reason can attain to the truth in moral matters. But if
reason were our only guide we would find ourselves in
confusion. Our intellects are weakened by original sin,
and sincere advocates can be found on both sides of most
moral issues. Aristotle, who was a fair student himself,
sanctioned infanticide. Some Christians in the last century upheld the morality of slavery. Today, people differ
on the morality of abortion. They cannot all be right. As

St. Thomas tells us, "If . . . we consider one action in the moral order, it is impossible for it to be morally both good and evil."[29] But how are we to know what the natural law requires? Although the natural law can be known by reason without the aid of explicit supernatural revelation, St. Thomas states:

> Besides the natural and the human law it was necessary for the directing of human conduct to have a Divine law. And this for four reasons.
>
> *First* . . . since man is ordained to an end of eternal happiness which is inproportionate to man's natural faculty . . . therefore it was necessary that, besides the natural and the human law, man should be directed to his end by a law given by God.
>
> *Secondly*, because, on account of the uncertainty of human judgment, especially on contingent and particular matters, different people form different judgments on human acts; whence also different and contrary laws result. In order, therefore, that man may know without any doubt what he ought to do and what he ought to avoid, it was necessary for man to be directed in his proper acts by a law given by God, for it is certain that such a law cannot err.
>
> *Thirdly*, because man can make laws in those matters of which he is competent to judge. But man is not competent to judge of interior movements, that are hidden, but only of exterior acts which appear: and yet for the perfection of virtue it is necessary for man to conduct himself aright in both kinds of acts. Consequently human law could not sufficiently curb and direct interior acts; and it was nec-

essary for this purpose that a Divine law should supervene.

> *Fourthly,* because . . . human law cannot punish or forbid all evil deeds: since while aiming at doing away with all evils, it would do away with many good things, and would hinder the advance of the common good, which is necessary for human intercourse. In order therefore, that no evil might remain unforbidden and unpunished, it was necessary for the Divine law to supervene, whereby all sins are forbidden.[30]

Probably the most important document issued in this century on the integration of the natural law and the Divine Law is the encyclical *Veritatis Splendor (The Splendor of Truth),* issued by Pope John Paul II on August 6, 1993, the Feast of the Transfiguration of Christ.[31] In *Veritatis,* John Paul affirms the existence of objective moral norms that bind without exception. He also affirms that to live morally requires our own transformation in Christ. However, *Veritatis* is not a sectarian directive. Rather, it raises transcendent issues of universal concern. "I have been a Protestant minister for nearly half a century," wrote Rev. Harvey N. Chinn, of the California Council on Alcohol Problems, in *The Sacramento Bee,*

> but I consider *The Splendor of Truth* to be a brilliant, compelling analysis of the world's current moral dilemma. . . . *Splendor of Truth* is biblical. By actual count I found 315 direct quotations from the Bible. The document is about moral authority. It possesses an intrinsic authority of its own. *Splendor of Truth* is about values—those objective, immutable, eternal standards of right and wrong that are built

into the very structure of the universe. It is a witness that above and beyond our pretenses and intellectual sophistication there shines a moral north star that never changes. . . . The encyclical's first paragraph begins with creation: humans are "created in the image and likeness of God" which means that we are capable of understanding the truths of God. "Truth enlightens man's intelligence and shapes his freedom." In contrast, humanity today has lost its way by "giving himself over to relativism and skepticism". . . . God's unchanging absolutes include respect for life, "from the moment of conception through natural death," absolute truth and honesty in all relationships, family loyalty, personal dignity, concern for others, temperance, and justice. These are more than agreed-upon social mores; they are revealed truths from the Creator. . . . In knowing the truth, we find freedom. . . . Social progress and personal freedom are impossible apart from the authority of divine moral precepts. Christ is the ultimate standard of morality. I am a better Protestant for having studied this magnificent Catholic document. The world needs to learn from this wise man, who speaks with clarity, understanding, compassion, and authority. His words reflect the "splendor of truth" and provide renewed hope for a confused world."[32]

In *Veritatis Splendor,* John Paul II insists that freedom must be grounded in truth. He directly confronts the basic errors of the Enlightenment. Against secularism, he insists that morality must not be separated from faith:

The attempt to set freedom in opposition to truth, and indeed to separate them radically, is the consequence, manifestation and consummation of *another more serious and destructive dichotomy, that which separates faith from morality.* This separation represents one of the most acute pastoral concerns of the Church amid today's growing secularism, wherein many, indeed too many, people think and live "as if God did not exist.". . . It is urgent then that Christians should rediscover *the newness of the faith and its power to judge* a prevalent and all-intrusive culture. (No. 88; emphasis in original)

John Paul, we must remember, is not expounding a set of abstract principles:

[T]he Christian faith . . . is not simply a set of propositions to be accepted with intellectual assent. Rather, faith is a lived knowledge of Christ, a living remembrance of his commandments, and *a truth to be lived out.* . . . Faith also possesses a moral content. . . . Through the moral life, faith becomes 'confession' not only before God but also before men; it becomes witness. (No. 89)

In the first chapter of *Veritatis,* John Paul says,

[f]ollowing Christ is . . . the essential and primordial foundation of Christian morality. . . . To imitate the Son, the image of the invisible God . . . means to imitate the Father. (No. 19)

For three centuries the Enlightenment project has attempted to construct a morality without faith and a society without God. John Paul reminds us that such a project is doomed to ultimate failure.

Against relativism, John Paul insists on the reality of objective moral norms. The twentieth century has produced more declarations of human rights than any century. Yet it has also produced the greatest violations of those rights. *Veritatis* explains why. The denial of objective truth ultimately reduces law to a function of raw, totalitarian power:

> Totalitarianism arises out of a denial of truth in the objective sense. If there is no transcendent truth, in obedience to which man achieves his full identity, then there is no sure principle for guaranteeing just relations between people. Their self-interest as a class, group or nation would inevitably set them in opposition to one another. If one does not acknowledge transcendent truth, then the force of power takes over, and each person tends to make full use of the means at his disposal in order to impose his own interests or his own opinion, with no regard for the rights of others. . . . [T]he root of modern totalitarianism is . . . the denial of the transcendent dignity of the human person who, as the visible image of the invisible God, is therefore by his very nature the subject of rights which no one may violate—no individual, group, class, nation or state. Not even the majority of a social body may violate these rights, by going against the minority, by isolating, oppressing, or exploiting it, or by attempting to annihilate it. (No. 99)

As John Paul puts it, recognition of objective moral norms is essential for freedom and "genuine democracy":

> [T]here can be no freedom apart from or in opposi-
> tion to the truth. . . . [O]nly by obedience to universal
> moral norms does man find full confirmation of his
> personal uniqueness and the possibility of authentic
> moral growth. For this very reason . . . [t]hese norms
> in fact represent the . . . foundation . . . of genuine
> democracy, which can . . . develop only on the basis
> of the equality of all its members, who possess com-
> mon rights and duties. When it is a matter of the
> moral norms prohibiting intrinsic evil, there are no
> privileges or exceptions for anyone. It makes no dif-
> ference whether one is the master of the world or the
> "poorest of the poor" on the face of the earth. Before
> the demands of morality, we are all absolutely equal.
> (No. 96)

If we do not affirm objective norms that always prohibit certain conduct, how can we define any moral limits to what the state can do? The Pope sees this point as
relevant to the nations that composed the former Soviet
Union. He sees a "grave" danger in those nations of *an
alliance between democracy and ethical relativism,* which
would remove any sure moral reference point from political and social life, and on a deeper level make the
acknowledgment of truth impossible. Indeed, "if there is
no ultimate truth to guide and direct political activity,
then ideas and convictions can easily be manipulated for
reasons of power. As history demonstrates, a democracy
without values easily turns into open or thinly disguised
totalitarianism." (No. 101)

American universities have an abundant supply of
professors who are absolutely sure that they cannot be
sure of anything. Such an attitude has historical prece-
dent. "Pilate's question: 'What is truth?'" said John Paul,

reflects the distressing perplexity of a man who often no longer knows *who he is, when he comes and where he is going.* Hence we not infrequently witness the fearful plunging of the human person into situations of gradual self-destruction. According to some, it appears that one no longer need acknowledge the enduring absoluteness of any moral value. All around us we encounter contempt for human life after conception and before birth; the ongoing violation of basic rights of the person; the unjust destruction of goods minimally necessary for a human life. (No. 84)

Against the autonomous individualism of the Enlightenment, John Paul prompts us to reflect that freedom without truth inevitably degenerates into a self-centered and nihilistic individualism. The answer to this separation of freedom and truth is the person of Christ. "Christ reveals, first and foremost, that the frank and open acceptance of truth is the condition for authentic freedom: 'You will know the truth and the truth will set you free.' (Jn 8:32)" (No. 87). Moreover, it is "in the Crucified Christ" that we find

the answer to the question troubling so many people today: how can obedience to universal and unchanging moral norms respect the uniqueness and individuality of the person, and not represent a threat to his freedom and dignity? . . . *The Crucified Christ reveals the authentic meaning of freedom; he lives it fully in the total gift of himself* and calls his disciples to share in his freedom. (No. 85)

"I'm aboard, pull up the gangplank" would be a fitting motto for the jurisprudence of the autonomous, alienated individual of the Enlightenment. In response, as John Paul puts it, the crucified Christ reveals to us "the full meaning of freedom: the gift of self in service to God and one's brethren." (No. 87)

The considerations offered in *Veritatis* are relevant to the technological marvels that would have so greatly surprised a visiting Leonardo da Vinci. If there is no God and no objective knowable standard of right and wrong, and if man (including, of course, both sexes in the term), is the autonomous arbiter of whether, when, and how human life should begin, without restriction by a higher moral law, how can one object except on aesthetic or pragmatic grounds to various practices that would treat the human person as an object? Why not quick-freeze a cloned embryo for later use in case his brother needs a spare part or total replacement? Why not raid the unborn female child for her ova so as to make her a mother? Never mind how you tell the resulting child that he is the product of a salvage expedition on the body of his dead mother, who herself was never born because she was killed before birth by the child's grandmother. The farming of the unborn body for eggs is useful; it enables a new life to come into the world; and it does no harm to the unborn mother who had just been killed anyway.

Veritatis Splendor offers a radical solution in that it goes to the root of the secular, relativistic individualism that defines this pagan culture. *Veritatis* affirms that "there exist acts which *per se* and in themselves, independently of circumstances, are always seriously wrong by reason of their object." (No. 80) *Veritatis*, however, is not a catalogue of condemnations. It does mention various actions that are "intrinsically evil" (See No. 80), but it is essentially an invitation to reflect on the principles and realities of God and human nature.

Veritatis Splendor ought to prompt us all, regardless of creed, to reflect on who and what we are, why we are here, and what are the limits on the actions of ourselves and of the state. In the third chapter of *Veritatis*, as described by Cardinal Ratzinger,

> [t]he Pope shows here that "at the heart of the issue of culture we find the moral sense"; in the face of social and economic injustices and political corruption, he speaks of "the acute sense of the need for a radical personal and social renewal," which alone is "capable of ensuring justice solidarity, honesty and openness" (No. 98). The text reveals the intellectual foundation of totalitarianism to consist in "the denial of truth in the objective sense" (No. 99), and indicates the way to overcoming it."[33]

The failure of the Enlightenment, in its effort to achieve freedom apart from the truth of Christ is so clear that a radical reorientation is required. The words of John Paul II, as Rev. Chinn put it, "provide renewed hope for a confused world." Some describe our time as a "post-Christian" era. But *Veritatis Splendor* indicates instead that this is a "pre-Christian" era. This important document points the way to the future, which must be built on the recovery of truth, including the natural law, which is an aspect of that truth. It should call us to study and prayer.

ENDNOTES

1. Gina Kolata, "Reproductive Revolution is Jolting Old Views," *New York Times*, 11 January 1994, sec. A, 1.

2. Ibid. See also Gina Kolata, "Scientist Clones Human Embryos and Creates an Ethical Challenge," *New York Times,* 24 October 1993, sec. A, 1.

3. William Tuohy, "Use of Fetus Eggs for Fertility Sparks Furor," *Los Angeles Times,* 3 January 1994, sec. A, 1.

4. Alan Keyes, "Children Born of the Dead," *Washington Times,* 5 January 1994, sec. A, 16.

5. John Cardinal O'Connor, "A Cardinal's Chilling Warning," *New Covenant,* May 1989, 23–24.

6. Alasdair MacIntyre, "Theories of Natural Law in the Culture of Advanced Modernity," *supra* 113.

7. Francis Canavan, S. J., "Commentary," *Catholic Eye,* 10 December 1987, 2.

8. Joseph Cardinal Ratzinger, "The Problem of Threats to Human Life," *L'Obsservatore Romano,* 8 April 1991, English edition, 2, 36.

9. Harold Berman, "The Crisis of Legal Education in America," 26 *Boston College Law Review,* 347, 348 (1985).

10. Allan Bloom, *The Closing of the American Mind* (New York: Simon & Schuster, 1987), 25–26.

11. Michiko Kakutani, "Opinion vs. Reality in an Age of Pundits," *New York Times,* 28 January 1994, sec. B, p.1.

12. Oliver Wendell Holmes, "Natural Law," 32 *Harvard Law Review,* 40 (1918); Holmes to Pollock, Washington, D.C., February 1, 1920, *Holmes-Pollock Letters,* vol. 2, ed. Mark DeWolfe Howe (Cambridge: Harvard University Press, 1944), 36.

13. Edgar Bodenheimer, *Jurisprudence* (New York: McGraw-Hill, 1940), 285.

14. Hans Kelsen, "The Pure Theory of Law," 50 *Law Quarterly Review* 474, 482 (1934).

15. Idem, 51 *Law Quarterly Review* 517 (1934) Kelsen's article was in two parts.

16. Hans Kelsen, *Pure Theory of Law,* trans. M. Knight (Berkeley: University of California Press, 1967), 198. See Charles E. Rice, "Some Reasons for a Restoration of Natural Law Jurisprudence," 24 *Wake Forest Law Review,* 539, 541–42 (1989).

17. *supra* MacIntyre, p. 108.

18. Hannah Arendt, *The Origins of Totalitarianism* (New York: Harcourt, Brace and World, 1966), 290.

19. William J. Bennett, *The Index of Cultural Indicators* (Washington D.C.: Heritage Foundation, March 1993), i, iii.

20. Editorial, *Washington Post,* 22 March 1931.

21. Aristotle, *Nicomachean Ethics,* ed. T. Irwin (Indianapolis, Indiana: Hackett Publishing Company, 1985), Book V, ch. 7, sec. 5.74.

22. Cicero, *Laws*, in *The Great Legal Philosophers*, ed. C. Morris (Philadelphia: Univeristy of Pennsylvania Press, 1959), 44.

23. Thomas Aquinas, *Summa Theologiae*, 1–2, q. 94, a. 2.

24. Robert P. George, "Natural Law and Positive Law," *supra* 157.

25. *Summa Theologiae*, 1–2, q. 91, a. 1.

26. "Address to Youths Gathered at a Prayer Vigil," *New York Times*, 15 August 1993, sec. 1, p. 12.

27. MacIntyre, *supra* 113.

28. *Calder v. Bull*, 3 Dall. 386, 399 (1798).

29. *Summa Theologiae*, 2, q. 20, a. 6.

30. *Summa Theologiae*, 1–2, q. 91, a. 4 (Emphasis added).

31. 23 *Origins* 297 (1993).

32. Harvey N. Chinn, "Protestant Cheers Pope's Message," *The Sacramento Bee*, 15 January, 1994, p. 10.

33. Joseph Cardinal Ratzinger, "Veritatis Splendor: A Presentation," in *Position Paper* 241 (Dublin: Four Courts Press, January 1994), 6, 9.

Notes on Contributors

Virgina Black is associate professor of philosophy at Pace University. Her specialty is legal and political philosophy. Founder and editor of *Vera Lex*, journal of the Natural Law Society, which she established in Basel, Switzerland in 1979, Professor Black also serves as associate editor of natural law studies for the Value Inquiry Book Series. Professor Black has written 40 scholarly articles and made numerous presentations on various aspects of law and politics; her articles "Natural Law" and "Dignity" appear in *The Philosophy of Law: An Encyclopedia* (Garland, 1999).

J. Rufus Fears is professor of classics at the University of Oklahoma, where he holds the G. T. and Libby Blankenship Chair in the History of Liberty. He is Director of the Center for the History of Liberty. Professor Fears received his Ph. D. from Harvard University and has been a fellow of the American Academy in Rome, a Guggenheim fellow, and twice a fellow of the Alexander von Humboldt Foundation. The author of one book, three monographs, three volumes of edited works, and over 70 articles and reviews on Greek and Roman history and the classical tradition, Fears has won awards for undergraduate teaching fourteen times. In 1996 and again in 1999, Professor Fears was named the University of Oklahoma Professor of the Year.

Timothy Fuller earned his B. A. from Kenyon College and his Ph.D. in political science from Johns Hopkins University. He is Dean of the College and Dean of Faculty at Colorado College. His academic specialty is political philosophy, particularly British political thought from the seventeenth to the twentieth centuries. In addition to editing the *International Hobbes Association* newsletter, Professor Fuller edits a multivolume collection of the writings of Michael Oakeshott for Yale University Press. Four volumes have appeared to date. He has been awarded fellowships from the National Endowment for the Humanities and the Colorado Endowment for the Humanities.

Robert P. George is Cyrus Hall McCormick Professor of Jurisprudence at Princeton University. A graduate of Swarthmore College and Harvard Law School, he also holds a doctorate in the philosophy of law from Oxford University. Professor George is the author of *Making Men Moral: Civil Liberties and Public Morality* (1993) and *In Defense of Natural Law* (1999) and is the editor of three volumes in legal philosophy, all published by Oxford University Press. He is the recipient of an American Bar Association Silver Gavel Award (1991), the Federalist Society's Paul Bator Award (1994), and Wabash College's Peck Medal (1999). Professor George recently completed a six-year term as a presidential appointee to the United States Commission on Civil Rights. He is a former Judicial Fellow at the Supreme Court of the United States, where he received the 1990 Justice Tom C. Clark Award.

Russell Hittinger holds the Chair of Catholic Studies at the University of Tulsa, where he is also a research professor in the School of Law. He specializes in issues of theology and law. His books and articles have been published by Oxford University Press, the University of Notre Dame Press, the *Review of Metaphysics*, the *Review of Politics*, and the *International Philosophical Quarterly*, as well as by several law journals. He is on the editorial boards of *First Things* and the *American Journal of Jurisprudence*.

The Rev. John Jenkins, C. S.C., is an associate professor in the department of philosophy at the University of Notre Dame. He received a Licentiate in Sacred Theology from the Jesuit School of Theology at Berkeley and a D. Phil. in philosophy from Oxford University. He is the author of *Knowledge and Faith in Thomas Aquinas* (Cambridge University Press, 1997). His articles have appeared in *The Journal of Philosophy, Medieval Philosophy and Theology,* and the *Journal of Religious Ethics.*

Ralph McInerny, Michael P. Grace Professor of Medieval Studies and Director of the Jacques Maritain Center at the University of Notre Dame, earned his Ph.D. at Laval University. He is the author of *The Logic of Analogy* (1961), *Thomism in an Age of Renewal* (1966), *St. Thomas Aquinas* (1977), *Ethica Thomistica* (1982), *A First Glance at St. Thomas Aquinas: A Handbook for Peeping Thomists* (1990), *Boethius and Aquinas* (1990), *Aquinas on Human Action* (1992), *The Question of Christian Ethics* (1993), and *Aquinas Against the Averroists* (1993). Professor McInerny is a fellow of the

Pontifical Academy of St. Thomas Aquinas and past president of the Fellowship of Catholic Scholars, the American Metaphysical Society, and the American Catholic Philosophical Association. In 1999–2000 Professor McInerny delivered the Gifford Lectures at the University of Glasgow.

Alasdair MacIntyre is Arts and Sciences Professor of Philosophy at Duke University. His latest book is *Dependent Rational Animals: Why Human Beings Need the Virtues* (1999).

Edward B. McLean holds the Eugene N. and Martin C. Beesley Chair in Political Science at Wabash College. He served nineteen years as deputy prosecutor in Montgomery County, Indiana. He received his J.D. and Ph.D. from Indiana University. Professor McLean has published *The Legal Thought of Roscoe Pound* and has edited *Derailing the Constitution: The Undermining of American Federalism* (ISI Books) and *An Uncertain Legacy: Essays on the Pursuit of Liberty* (ISI Books).

Ian A. T. McLean was clerk for the late Judge Clarkson S. Fisher of the U.S. District Court of New Jersey and for Pasco Bowman of the U.S. Court of Appeals for the 8th Circuit. McLean also has served as a deputy attorney general representing the state of Indiana in criminal cases before the Indiana Courts of Appeal and the Indiana Supreme Court. He has served as chief deputy prosecutor in Union County, Indiana and deputy prosecutor for

Montgomery County, Indiana. McLean currently practices criminal and civil law in Crawfordsville, Indiana. The views expressed in his essay are entirely his own and should not be attributed to any previous employer.

Edward J. Murphy was professor of law at the University of Notre Dame Law School from 1957 until his death in 1994. He earned his college and law degrees from the University of Illinois and practiced law for six years before joining the Notre Dame faculty. Professor Murphy, one of the leading authorities on contract law, was also a leading proponent of a jurisprudence based on natural law.

Charles E. Rice, professor of law at the University of Notre Dame Law School, specializes in jurisprudence and constitutional law. From 1970 to 1998, he served as coeditor of the *American Journal of Jurisprudence.* He is the author, among other books, of *50 Questions on the Natural Law: What It Is and Why We Need It. His* latest book is *The Winning Side: The Coming Demise of the Culture of Death.*

William N. Riley is a senior partner with Young, Riley & Dudley in Indianapolis, Indiana. Focusing on personal injury, products liability, medical malpractice, toxic torts, premises liability, and class actions, Mr. Riley also has served as a continuing education faculty lecturer for the National Business Institute, Inc. He is a member of the Association of Trial Lawyers of America and a sustaining member of the Indiana Trial Lawyers Association.

Janet E. Smith is an associate professor in the philosophy department of the University of Dallas. She is the author of *Humanae Vitae—A Generation Later* and the editor of *Why Humanae Vitae was Right—A Reader*. She has published and spoken widely on virtue ethics, natural law ethics, and bioethics. Professor Smith is working on a study of Aquinas as a commentator on Aristotle's theory of ethics.

Index